D1558911

Could You Not Watch with Me One Hour?

FLORIAN RACINE

Could You Not Watch with Me One Hour?

~

*How to Cultivate a Deeper
Relationship with the Lord through
Eucharistic Adoration*

TRANSLATED BY
C. A. THOMPSON-BRIGGS

IGNATIUS PRESS   SAN FRANCISCO

Original French edition:
Adorer sans se lasser
© 2011 by Éditions de l'Emmanuel, Paris

Front cover photograph by AgnusImages.com

Cover design by Davin Carlson

© 2014 by Ignatius Press, San Francisco
All rights reserved
ISBN 978-1-58617-777-5
Library of Congress Control Number 2014908820
Printed in the United States of America ⊚

CONTENTS

Outline of the Itinerary (52 weeks)

II. THE FATHER
Through the Son, Ascending to the Father and
Letting Oneself Be Transformed by His Love
(*ten stages*)

*He Is the Good Shepherd Who Leads Me to the Father
(allowing oneself to love)* (*five stages*)

*Spiritual Warfare (from sensible graces to the adoration of the Father
"in spirit and truth")* (*five stages*)

8

Can You Not Watch with Me One Hour?

III. THE SPIRIT

Animated by the Spirit,
Engaging in the Church's Mission
(*fourteen stages*)

In the School of Mary, Eucharistic and Missionary Woman
(*three stages*)

56789012345

The Living Water that Flows from the Pierced Heart (*three stages*)

"All Things New" (*three stages*)

The Five Graces of Adoration and Mission (*five stages*)

FOREWORD

Since the Second Vatican Council, Eucharistic adoration has been experiencing a true renewal, and this movement, encouraged by the successors of Peter, only continues to grow. The Council recalled the centrality of the Eucharist, "the fount and apex of the whole Christian life" (LG 11), "the source and the apex of the whole work of preaching the Gospel" (PO 5). And, the more we enter into the Eucharistic mystery, the more we are drawn into the Blessed Sacrament, which we desire to contemplate in order to live from it better. Eucharistic adoration cannot be separated from the Eucharistic celebration, as the ritual *Holy Communion Outside Mass* (1983) recalls: "When the faithful adore Christ present in the sacrament, they should remember that this presence derives from the sacrifice and is directed toward both sacramental and spiritual communion" (no. 80).[1] Indeed, practicing Eucharistic adoration leads to living the celebration of the Mass more intensely and bears evident fruit: "In consequence, the devotion which leads the faithful to visit the Blessed Sacrament draws them into an ever deeper participation in the Paschal Mystery. It leads them to respond gratefully to the gift of Him who through His humanity constantly pours divine life into the members of His body" (ibid.). Father Florian Racine has gathered and quoted some testimonies of the fruits of Eucharistic adoration; I am thinking in particular of that of Mother Teresa, who saw a positive change in her community starting from the moment the Sisters began adoring the Blessed Sacrament exposed to their gaze. This book expresses the strong conviction of the fruitfulness of adoration of the Blessed Sacrament.

When practiced superficially, Eucharistic adoration is perceived as a custom that provokes the enthusiasm of pious and sensitive souls

---

[1] Quoting the Sacred Congregation of Rites, *Eucharisticum Mysterium: Instruction on Eucharistic Worship* (1967), no. 50; trans. from the *Adoremus Bulletin*.

or the annoyance of those who fear a "reification" of the Eucharist. The former are seeking a perceptible experience of the living Jesus, a heart-to-heart that can wind up being very self-centered; the latter hold that keeping oneself on one's knees before a monstrance stems from narrow-minded devotion.

In this book Father Florian Racine offers us a formation in Eucharistic adoration that will enable practicing it in all its depth and with a missionary perspective. This program seeks to confirm believers in the validity of Eucharistic adoration, just as it seeks to open a journey of faith—of growth and perseverance in faith—to adorers, so that they become worshippers in spirit and truth: "But the hour is coming, and now is, when the true worshipers will worship the Father in spirit and truth, for such the Father seeks to worship him" (Jn 4:23). If God is present everywhere, he has made himself particularly close to mankind in Jesus his Son. The redemptive Incarnation of his Son is the means chosen by God for reconciling mankind and all creation with himself; the death and Resurrection of Christ are the only path to the Father; the memorial of the Passover of Christ is therefore at the heart of our relationship with God. In the Blessed Sacrament, the delivered and resurrected Jesus is really present and acting; he draws all mankind into his filial relationship with the Father, through the power of the Holy Spirit. Thus, it is logical that, in accordance with the plan of God, believers put the Eucharist at the heart of their life and take time to adore Jesus in this Sacrament. The adorer wants to abide within the dynamic of the Eucharist, just as he wishes also that the Eucharist might transform all his life.

"The Teacher is here and is calling for you" (Jn 11:28). Tied to the celebration of the Eucharist, well-practiced adoration of the Blessed Sacrament unites the believer to Jesus and through him to the Father, builds up the Church, supports her mission in the world, and elevates and transforms creation.

Like every form of prayer, Eucharistic adoration has its stages. Our pilgrimage of faith begins with welcoming the gift of God; the spiritual life experiences, at first, some of the personal love that God bears for us: the coming of Christ before us and into our life; sensible graces can thus be frequent. This first step gives way to a deeper and less sensible path of faith, which through trials and consolations decenters us from ourselves in order to center us on God. Through Jesus, with him and in him, in the Holy Spirit, we are turned toward the Father; we seek to enter into his sight and to do his will. Then, at the inspiration of the Holy Spirit, we are commissioned. Adoration and Eucharistic life transform believers into the image of Christ by incorporating them into his ecclesial Body and makes of their person an offering to the glory of God for the salvation of the world.

Thus the author of this book invites us on an itinerary, a journey of faith, in fifty-two stages, as many as the weeks in a year; starting with the Word of God, he shows us how it is made present in the Eucharist and invites us to mature in faith and let ourselves be transformed for a greater communion with Christ and a better collaboration with God's plan in the world. The Word of God sheds light on the Eucharistic mystery and receives a greater light from it. Father Florian Racine turns to the experience of Saint Peter Julian Eymard, who said about the reading of the Word of God during adoration: "If you read the Gospel, bring it to the Eucharist and, from the Eucharist, into yourself. You then have a much greater power. The Gospel becomes clear, and you have before your eyes and in reality the continuation of what you are reading."[2]

The fifty-two stages are grouped into three phases corresponding to the three theological virtues: "I adore the Son", "I adore the Father through the Son", "I adore the Father through the Son, in the Spirit." These phases lead to a development within the spiritual life toward a life given over to God, commissioned by him at the inspiration of the Spirit, in the school of Mary.

I hope that this book enlightens and nourishes the adorers of the Father, that is to say, all believers, and that it encourages them to put out into the deep, under the guidance of Christ and at the inspiration of the Holy Spirit, for the glory of God and the salvation of the world.

+ Guy de Kerimel
Bishop of Grenoble-Vienne

---

[2] *Adorer en esprit et en vérité* (Paris: Éditions F.-X. de Guibert, 2009), 186.

The School of
Adoration

STAGE I

Introduction to the Itinerary

In his last encyclical, Pope John Paul II wrote:

> The mystery of the Eucharist—sacrifice, presence, banquet—*does not allow for reduction or exploitation*; it must be experienced and lived in its integrity, both in its celebration and in the intimate converse with Jesus which takes place after receiving communion or in a prayerful moment of Eucharistic adoration apart from Mass. These are times when the Church is firmly built up and it becomes clear what she truly is: one, holy, catholic and apostolic; the people, temple and family of God; the body and bride of Christ, enlivened by the Holy Spirit; the universal sacrament of salvation and a hierarchically structured communion. . . . The treasure of the Eucharist, which the Lord places before us, impels us towards the goal of full sharing with all our brothers and sisters to whom we are joined by our common Baptism.[1]

Holy	*Holy*	*Adoration of the*
Sacrifice	*Communion*	*Blessed Sacrament*

• What are the three dimensions of the Eucharistic mystery?

• What is the meaning of the two terms "mystery" and "treasure" that John Paul II uses for the Eucharist?

• "The Eucharist builds up the Church and the Church makes the Eucharist." What are the names given to the Church?

• "The treasure of the Eucharist . . . impels us towards [its] full sharing." Just what is this?

Here, the term "mystery" designates an effective action and presence of God in the Church, for the life of the world and the sanctification of souls. The "mystery" exceeds the intellect without, however, contradicting it. Jesus is really present in the Eucharist. All the sacraments

---

[1] John Paul II, Encyclical Letter *Ecclesia de Eucharistia* (2003), no. 61.

15

are acts of Christ through which he gives us his grace. But, in the Eucharist, he is there himself, permanent, living, and acting, hidden under the appearances of the sacred Host. The itinerary will present the divine life of Jesus in the Blessed Sacrament, what he does there and what he expects of us. The word "treasure" reminds us that the Eucharist is our greatest treasure. Saint Augustine, in speaking of God, wrote about the Eucharist:

> All-powerful that he is, he could make nothing greater; all-wise that he is, he could find nothing more admirable; all-wealthy that he is, he could not make a more precious present.

In other words, God cannot give us a greater gift than that of the Eucharist. In his omnipotence, he cannot bear greater witness to his love. He has nothing greater to offer. Saint Peter Julian Eymard said: "Happy the soul that knows how to find Jesus in the Eucharist and, in the Eucharist, all things."[2] Through the Eucharist, we enter into the great movement of love: "From the heights of the Trinity, the incarnate Word descends to man in the Eucharist in order that, through Communion, man may ascend to his final end, the most-lovable Trinity."[3]

Eucharistic grace "impels us towards . . . the full sharing" of this treasure. In the context of the encyclical, the concern is the communal celebration of the Eucharist between all Christians who have received the same baptism. To arrive at this goal, we must work toward the reestablishment of full ecclesial communion. But we can understand it more broadly: we cannot keep this treasure for ourselves: on the one hand, it has to be announced to all, and, on the other, it has to drive us to give ourselves to others as Christ handed himself over for us. *Evangelization* and *charity*, these are the two dimensions of the Church's mission.

Through different stages founded on biblical texts, the itinerary will present what the Eucharist is, what is fulfilled in the Holy Mass, what Communion and adoration are, and why and how to adore, for "true worshipers will worship the Father in spirit and truth, for such the

---

[2] Saint Peter Julian Eymard, *Adorer en esprit et en vérité* (Paris: Éditions F.-X. de Guibert, 2009), 26.

[3] Bernadot, *De l'Eucharistie à la Trinité* (Paris: Éditions du Cerf, 1920), 15.

Father seeks to worship him" (Jn 4:23). Through illustrations, Magisterial texts, and quotations from the saints, the adorer will discover how to enter into the following movement: in adoring the Son, to be driven toward the Father to receive the Holy Spirit and thus become a missionary, by announcing this treasure and by sharing the charity that flows from it. And all this in the Church, who gives us the Eucharist and who lives from the Eucharist. The itinerary will also stress the spiritual attitudes required for entering into adoration "in spirit and truth" as well as the practical means for remaining faithful to prayer, despite inevitable times of dryness and purification. The adorer will learn to draw from this "spring of water welling up to eternal life" (Jn 4:14), which comes from the Eucharistic Heart of Jesus.

The itinerary consists of fifty-two stages, one per week during a full year. Each stage can be made during or after the weekly hour of adoration, with the aid of the Bible. It is a self-taught course, a school of adoration offered to every believer. Those responsible for adoration in a parish will be able to have successive evaluations with the adorers of their staffs in order to clarify certain points or respond to their potential questions. Here is the outline of the itinerary offered:

- *Introduction* (*one stage:* the three dimensions of the Eucharist)

Part I (The Son): The Lord Comes to Me, He Calls Me, I Respond to Him (*twenty-seven stages*):

- *God Comes to Meet Me* (*seven stages:* the burning bush; the tent of meeting; God alone shall you worship, "choose life"; God frees me from idols; Elijah meets God on Mount Horeb; the calling of Samuel; the Incarnation, and the birth of Jesus at Bethlehem).

- *I Respond, by Faith, to His Love* (*seven stages:* everlasting love and the parable of the hidden treasure; "Come to me", the Eucharist is the invention of love; the anointing at Bethany; Martha and Mary and the great commandment of love; the hemorrhaging woman and the act of faith; modes of Christ's presence and extensions of the Incarnation; the shock of the bodily presence of the Resurrected One).

- *The Signs of the Covenant* (*thirteen stages:* covenants in the Bible; the memorial; the Holy Sacrifice of the Mass; the Paschal Lamb;

divine mercy; parable of the marriage feast [baptism and confession]; marriage in the Bible; the Eucharist makes the Church [incorporation into the Church]; the suffering servant and kenosis; "I am the living bread"—John 6 parts 1 and 2; Isaac's blessing and transubstantiation; the tree of life recovered).

Part II (The Father): Through the Son, Ascending to the Father and Letting Oneself Be Transformed by His Love (*ten stages*):

- *He Is the Good Shepherd Who Leads Me to the Father (allowing oneself to love)* (*five stages:* Cain's and Abel's offerings and the offering of oneself; "the Lord is my shepherd", the evangelization of my being; "the clay in the potter's hands"; "Not what I will, but what you will"; "Abba, Father", adoration: remedy for pride and despair).

- *Spiritual Warfare (from sensible graces to the adoration of the Father "in spirit and truth")* (*five stages:* "Be still, and know that I am God"; Jacob's struggle and spiritual advice; the trial of the wilderness [adoration in battle, recollection, contemplation]; Moses fights against the Amalekites, and the paralytic: the power of intercession; "a prophet is without honor in his own country").

Part III (The Spirit): Animated by the Spirit, Engaging in the Church's Mission (*fourteen stages*):

- *In the School of Mary, Eucharistic and Missionary Woman* (*three stages:* the Mass and the Annunciation; the Magnificat, Mary ark of the New Covenant; Jacob's ladder and the angels, Our Lady of Fatima).

- *The Living Water that Flows from the Pierced Heart* (*three stages:* Our Lady of Lourdes; the water gushing from Christ's side; the Mass and the disciples at Emmaus).

- *"All Things New"* (*three stages:* the sorrowful Hearts of Jesus and Mary, Our Lady of the Blessed Sacrament; Mary gives birth to a people of adorers; the Lamb shall be its Light).

- *The Five Graces of Adoration and Mission* (*five stages:* the Transfiguration and mission; "Abide in my love" [the grace of transformation]; vocations [graces of reparation and salvation]; the reign of the Eucharist in the soul [grace of sanctification]; the Samaritan Woman [grace of restoration]).

I. THE SON

The Lord Comes to Me,
He Calls Me, I Respond to Him

God Comes to Meet Me

STAGE 2

The Burning Bush: Moses
Adores God and Receives a Mission

Now Moses was keeping the flock of his father-on-law, Jethro, the priest of Midian; and he led his flock to the west side of the wilderness, and came to Horeb, the mountain of God. And the angel of the LORD appeared to him in a flame of fire out of the midst of a bush; and he looked, and behold, the bush was burning, yet it was not consumed. And Moses said, "I will turn aside and see this great sight, why the bush is not burnt." When the LORD saw that he turned aside to see, God called to him out of the bush, "Moses, Moses!" And he said, "Here am I." Then he said, "Do not come near; put off your shoes from your feet, for the place on which you are standing is holy ground." And he said, "I am the God of your father, the God of Abraham, the God of Isaac, and the God of Jacob." And Moses hid his face, for he was afraid to look at God.

Then the LORD said, "I have seen the affliction of my people who are in Egypt, and have heard their cry because of their taskmasters; I know their sufferings, and I have come down to deliver them out of the hand of the Egyptians, and to bring them up out of that land to a good and broad land, a land flowing with milk and honey, to the place of the Canaanites, the Hittites, the Amorites, the Perizzites, the Hivites, and the Jebusites. And now, behold, the cry of the sons of Israel has come to me, and I have seen the oppression with which the Egyptians oppress them. Come, I will send you to Pharaoh that you may bring forth my people, the sons of Israel, out of Egypt." But Moses said to God, "Who am I that I should go to Pharaoh, and bring the sons of Israel out of Egypt?" He said, "But I will be with you; and this shall be the sign for you, that I have sent you: when you have brought forth the people out of Egypt, you shall serve God upon this mountain."

> Then Moses said to God, "If I come to the sons of Israel and say to them, 'The God of your fathers has sent me to you,' and they ask me, 'What is his name?' what shall I say to them?" God said to Moses, "I AM WHO . . . AM." (Ex 3:1–14)

In the Bible, it is always God who comes to meet man. It is he who, in love, takes the initiative for the encounter. He expects only our response. Here, "the angel of the LORD" represents God himself who visits his people. He chooses the form of a burning bush. For some Church Fathers, the burning bush prefigures the wonderful mystery of the *Incarnation*, in which the divine nature unites itself to the human nature without destroying it ("with neither confusion, nor separation") in the person of the Son. Present in the Blessed Sacrament, Emmanuel, the God who visits his people, is truly the burning bush. This fire also evokes the infinite love of Christ, which purifies, transforms, and heals. God calls Moses by his name. He invites him to a personal encounter, a relation of love, a heart-to-heart.

How does Moses behave before God? For what reason? The position of the body is fundamental in prayer before the Blessed Sacrament. By taking up a position that is too comfortable for the body (sitting, even slouching on one's kneeler or chair), the heart loses some of its vigor and strength. The soul grows lukewarm and finds itself in a state of slumber, unable really to pray. It is by putting one's body at prayer that one puts one's heart at prayer. To adore the Lord with all one's heart, with all one's soul, and with all one's strength (cf. Deut 6:4) is to adore the Lord with one's entire person, thus also with one's body. In the following passage from Revelation, John sees how God is adored in heaven. "To cast one's crown before the throne" signifies the adoration of one who offers his person, with all he has and all he is, before the divine majesty:

> The twenty-four elders fall down before him who is seated on the throne and worship him who lives for ever and ever; they cast their crowns before the throne, singing, "Worthy are you, our Lord and God, to receive glory and honor and power, for you created all things, and by your will they existed and were created." (Rev 4:10–11)

The Latin etymology of the word "adoration" is *ad os*, or "toward the mouth", which refers to the kiss and, by extension, to love. To adore is to give back one's life to the Lord; it is to embrace him, because he loves us as we are. In adoration, we dare to approach him with the reverence of our body, the light of our faith, and the love of our heart. Since love always tends to humble itself and since the Lord makes himself so small in the sacred Host, the adorer is invited to humble himself before the divine majesty. Some bow profoundly, as Moses must have done before the burning bush. One of the remedies for tepidness and spiritual dryness in prayer is the quality of the bodily position.

Some practical advice: begin adoration kneeling, if possible by prostrating upon the floor for a few moments. Remain in this kneeling position (perhaps using a prie-dieu). If the position becomes painful, sit down! Do not hesitate to get back on your knees from time to time to get your heart back to adoration if distractions distance you from prayer. End adoration in the position that you took at the beginning.

God gives his name to Moses. How is the name of God to be understood? This name is mysterious, unpronounceable. We cannot name that which exceeds us, that which we cannot grasp or understand. In the Bible, one's name signifies one's mission. It characterizes the person. Here the name "I am who am" recalls that God alone exists in himself and that God needs nothing and no one in order to exist. To the contrary, God, the source of being, of every being, keeps all that lives in existence. From the sacred Host, the Lord Jesus supports the universe. How can we not marvel before the Host, which contains in its entirety what the universe cannot contain! If the earth revolves around the sun, the cosmos revolves around the Host! To approach it in faith is to hold oneself in the heart of the world. The Host is our heaven on earth. It is God who gives himself, our Alpha and our Omega, our beginning and our end. It is the resurrected Body of Christ, Savior of the world.

From this encounter with God, Moses will receive a mission. What precisely is this mission? What is the mission that God gives us, following our encounter with Jesus, present in the sacred Host?

I warmly encourage the faithful to adore Christ, present in the Blessed Sacrament of the altar, letting him heal our consciences and purify us, enlighten us and unite us. In their encounter with him, Christians will find strength for their spiritual life and their mission in the world. In fact, in communing heart to heart with the divine Teacher, they will discover the Father's infinite love and will be true worshipers in spirit and in truth. Their faith in him will be revitalized; they will enter into God's mystery and be profoundly transformed by Christ. In their trials and in joys, they will conform their life to the mystery of our Saviour's Cross and Resurrection. . . . Every day they will become more and more sons and daughters in the Son. Then, love will be spread through them in human hearts, in order to build up the Body of Christ which is the Church to establish a society of justice, peace and brotherhood. They will be intercessors for all humanity, because every soul which is lifted up to God also lifts up the world and mysteriously contributes to the salvation freely offered by our Father in heaven.[1]

~

[1] John Paul II, "His Heart, the Most Outstanding Sign of Love", Message of John Paul II to Archbishop Louis-Marie Billé on the One Hundredth Anniversary of the Consecration of the Human Race to the Divine Heart of Jesus (June 4, 1999), in *L'Osservatore romano*, no. 29 (July 21, 1999), 6.

STAGE 3

The Tent of Meeting and the Pillar of Fire: Speaking with Jesus as a Friend

And the LORD went before them by day in a pillar of cloud to lead them along the way, and by night in a pillar of fire to give them light, that they might travel by day and by night; the pillar of cloud by day and the pillar of fire by night did not depart from before the people. (Ex 13:21–22)

Now Moses used to take the tent and pitch it outside the camp, far off from the camp; and he called it the tent of meeting. And every one who sought the LORD would go out to the tent of meeting, which was outside the camp. Whenever Moses went out to the tent, all the people rose up, and every man stood at his tent door, and looked after Moses, until he had gone into the tent. When Moses entered the tent, the pillar of cloud would descend and stand at the door of the tent, and the LORD would speak with Moses. And when all the people saw the pillar of cloud standing at the door of the tent, all the people would rise up and worship, every man at his tent door. Thus the LORD used to speak to Moses face to face, as a man speaks to his friend. When Moses turned again into the camp, his servant Joshua the son of Nun, a young man, did not depart from the tent. (Ex 33: 7–11)

During the crossing of the desert, God protected and accompanied his people. In what manner did God accompany them? God did not address himself directly to the Israelites; rather, he spoke to them through Moses. Moses interceded for them. He met personally with God in the tent of meeting, presenting the requests of the people. What sort of relation was there between God and Moses within this tent of meeting?

We all know that the more we love someone, the more we want to be with this person. Parents' joy is to be with their children; grandparents' to be with their grandchildren; two young people who love each other want to marry in order to spend their life together. It is the same for the most beautiful mystery of our Catholic faith: the Real Presence of Jesus in the Blessed Sacrament. He remains with us day and night in the tabernacle, because he loves us so much that he never wants to leave us. He says: "I am with you always" (Mt 28:20), "for where your treasure is, there will your heart be also" (Lk 12:34). In other words, we are his treasure. Thus Jesus is here in person with his Heart burning with infinite love for us in the Blessed Sacrament.

The Curé of Ars often pointed to the tabernacle, saying: "Jesus is really there, and if you knew how much he loves you, you would be the happiest person in the world." More than anything on earth, God wants us to be happy and to come near to him, because true happiness is knowing true love:

> a love that never changes . . .
>
> a love that has neither limits nor conditions . . .
>
> a love that is always there . . .
>
> this love awaits us in the Blessed Sacrament.

Pope John Paul II says: "Jesus waits for us in this sacrament of love",[1] where he repeats his eternal call: "Could you not watch with me one hour?" (Mt 26:40).

And Jesus wishes all the world to know that an hour of adoration is easy to do, because Jesus is truly the easiest person in the world to meet and to love. You can help yourself with a prayer book, meditate on sacred writings, pray the rosary—thus loving Jesus with the very Heart of Mary. You can also simply speak to Jesus as to a friend, in silence. It may happen that you are so tired that you do not wish to do anything but sit down and rest while feeling the sweet peace that comes from the simple fact of being in the presence of him whom you love most, Jesus in the Blessed Sacrament, who says: "Cast all your

---

[1] John Paul II, Apostolic Letter *Dominicae Cenae* (1980), no. 3.

anxieties on [God], for he cares about you" (1 Pet 5:7); "My peace I give to you" (Jn 14:27).

Saint Thérèse of Lisieux wrote: "O darling, think, then, that Jesus is there in the Tabernacle expressly for *you*, for *you alone*; He is burning with the desire to enter your heart";[2] "the nature of love is to humble oneself";[3] "In order that Love be fully satisfied, it is necessary that It lower Itself to nothingness and transform this nothingness into *fire*."[4]

Spiritual advice: "Consider your allotted hour of adoration as an hour of paradise; go there as one goes to heaven, to the divine banquet, and this hour will be desired, greeted with happiness. Sweetly keep alive the desire for it in your heart. Tell yourself: in four hours, in two hours, in one hour, I will go to our Lord's audience of grace and love; he invited me, he awaits me, he desires me."[5]

No longer do I call you servants, for the servant does not know what his master is doing; but I have called you friends, for all that I have heard from my Father I have made known to you. (Jn 15:15)

Just as a lighthouse illuminates the night, guiding boats safely to port, so a chapel of perpetual adoration spreads the Light of Christ upon the parishioners, the city, and the whole world, guiding them on the path of sanctity and abundantly pouring forth the divine mercy upon all.

∼

---

[2] Saint Thérèse of Lisieux, letter to Marie Guérin (LT 92; May 30, 1889), *General Correspondence*, vol. 1, *1877–1890*, trans. John Clarke, O.C.D. (Washington, D.C.: ICS Publications, Institute of Carmelite Studies, 1982), 568.

[3] Saint Thérèse of Lisieux, *Story of a Soul*, trans. John Clarke, O.C.D., 2nd ed. (Washington, D.C.: ICS Publications, Institute of Carmelite Studies, 1976), 14.

[4] Ibid., 195.

[5] Saint Peter Julian Eymard, *Adorer en esprit et en vérité* (Paris: Éditions F.-X. de Guibert, 2009), 22.

STAGE 4

"God Alone Shall You Worship"
"Choose Life"

Here is the beginning of the Ten Commandments:

"I am the LORD your God, who brought you out of the land of Egypt, out of the house of bondage.

"You shall have no other gods before me.

"You shall not make for yourself a graven image, or any likeness of anything that is in heaven above, or that is on the earth beneath, or that is in the water under the earth; you shall not bow down to them or serve them; for I the LORD your God am a jealous God . . . showing merciful love to thousands of those who love me and keep my commandments." (Deut 5:6–10)

"Hear, O Israel: The LORD our God is one LORD; and you shall love the LORD your God with all your heart, and with all your soul, and with all your might. And these words which I command you this day shall be upon your heart." (Deut 6:4–6)

"Behold, I set before you this day a blessing and a curse: the blessing, if you obey the commandments of the LORD your God, which I command you this day, and the curse, if you do not obey the commandments of the LORD your God, but turn aside from the way which I command you this day, to go after other gods which you have not known." (Deut 11:26–28)

The first, great commandment of God to the people of Israel is given in Deuteronomy 6:4. What is it? Hearing the Word of God is a question of life or death for Israel. The people, moreover, have experience of this in the desert. Without God, the desert remains a place of desolation and death. But through the hearing of the Word, the desert becomes the privileged place of encounter with the Lord. God offers his people ten words of life to help them pass from slavery to freedom. God does not give the Ten Commandments to hold sway over his people, which would amount to a new form of slavery and submission (cf. Deut 5). To the contrary, God gives ten words of life, to free his people from idols and teach them to love in truth.

In Deuteronomy 11:26–28, God confronts man with his own freedom and responsibility. God shows two paths: one brings happiness, and one leads to unhappiness. The path of happiness consists in faithfulness to God and to his words of life (the Commandments). He who chooses it receives the bounty of divine blessing. But man can misuse his freedom and follow the opposite path, a path without God. On this path, God cannot give his blessing. To reject the Lord is to cut oneself off from his blessings. The Deuteronomist even speaks of a curse: apart from God, nothing good can come. How does Jesus recall this in John 15:5?

In the text of Paul VI below, what is the "living heart of our churches"? How does the pope qualify adoration? What should our response to this presence be?

> The unique and indivisible existence of the Lord glorious in heaven is not multiplied, but is rendered present by the sacrament in the many places on earth where Mass is celebrated. And this existence remains present, after the sacrifice, in the Blessed Sacrament, which is, in the tabernacle, the living heart of each of our churches. And it is our very sweet duty to honor and adore in the blessed Host which our eyes see, the Incarnate Word whom they cannot see, and who, without leaving heaven, is made present before us.[1]

When speaking of Eucharistic adoration, it is common to remark that it prolongs what is celebrated at Mass. This is true. Nevertheless, let us not forget that in the Bible God invites his people to adoration long before having instituted the Holy Mass. To adore God alone, this is the first commandment. This goes back even to creation. Adoring God is a "very sweet duty".[2] A "duty" because every man must recognize in God his creator and the source of his being. It is a duty of

[1] Paul VI, Apostolic Letter *Solemni hac liturgia* (1968), no. 26.
[2] Ibid.

divine justice to adore our creator, our savior, him in whom every man finds his existence. We cannot speak of social justice if it is not founded on divine justice, that is, on the adoration of the one God. Adoring is thus a duty, but Paul VI adds an adjective: "sweet". In what way is our adoration "sweet"?

Adoration is awestruck submission before the majesty of God. Thanks to revelation, the Christian knows that his adoration must pass through Jesus to return to God: "I am the way, and the truth, and the life; no one comes to the Father, but by me" (Jn 14:6). Jesus' whole life was a life of adoration of the Father. Jesus leaves his great adoration of the Father in the tabernacle. He wants to bring the whole Church there. In adoring the Eucharist, we enter into Jesus' adoration of his Father.

The book of Revelation centers on the adoration of God and of the Lamb. In its sacrificial presence, "the Lamb" signifies Jesus, who completely hands himself over to save us and who alone deserves the honor, glory, and praise of each man.

> I saw another angel flying in mid-heaven, with an eternal gospel to proclaim to those who dwell on earth, to every nation and tribe and tongue and people; and he said with a loud voice, "Fear God and give him glory, for the hour of his judgment has come; and worship him who made heaven and earth, the sea and the fountains of water." (Rev 14:6–7)

In this passage, the angel is the messenger. That he is flying in heaven shows that his message is above all others. It is an "eternal gospel". He invites mankind to the adoration of God. Adoration is the first and most fundamental act of every man. In adoring, man discovers the Father, welcomes the Son, and lets himself be filled by the Spirit who gives life.

"Judgment" (cf. Rev 14:7) in the Bible should neither scare us nor give rise to a servile fear. God judges by revealing himself and in revealing to all his light and truth. God judges by showing himself as he is: a God who is all love. But also, a God jealous for the love of his children. For our salvation is too precious to the Father for him to endure seeing us turn away from him and attach ourselves to what is passing, what cannot fulfill. God wants all our heart. He wants to fill it with his charity in giving it the capacity to love our neighbor, even the least lovable.

Today in Rome, a monument is dedicated to Victor Emmanuel. In tribute to his efforts for the unification of Italy, two soldiers make up an honor guard day and night before a large statue. Many other countries do the same to commemorate their hero. Should we not give as much honor to the "King of kings and Lord of lords" (Rev 19:16); not to a statue but to the living God, present in the Blessed Sacrament? For Scripture says: "Worthy is the Lamb who was slain, to receive . . . honor and glory and blessing" (Rev 5:12) "day and night within his temple" (Rev 7:15), for "by your blood you ransomed men for God" (Rev 5:9). And the book of Revelation reminds us that when we proclaim Jesus King by giving him the glory that belongs to his name, he takes possession of his kingdom.

It is God's love for man that created the world. It will be man's love for the Son of God in the Blessed Sacrament that will recreate the world and bring the advent of "a new heaven and a new earth" (Rev 21:1). For Jesus said to Saint Margaret Mary: "I thirst, and with a thirst so ardent to be loved by men in the Blessed Sacrament that this thirst consumes me, and I find no one who, in accordance with my desire, strives to quench it, by giving some return to my love",[3] but "I will reign by the all-powerfulness of my Heart, and you will see the magnificence of my love."[4]

~

[3] Saint Margaret Mary, *Vie et œuvres de sainte Marguerite-Marie Alacoque*, letter 133, to the Reverend Father Croiset (Paris: Éditions Saint Paul, 1990), 2:487.
[4] Ibid., letter 97, to the Mother Superior of Saumise, end of February 1689, 2:328.

God Comes to Meet Me

STAGE 5

God Frees Me from Idols

In the Bible, the word "idol" means "breath". An idol is a passing breath of air. Ephemeral, an idol claims to fill the heart but shows itself to be powerless. It is only an illusion, a mirage. All that we love before God or more than God, these are our idols. In themselves, they may be worthy of esteem and love. But they cannot assume more importance than God. For all idols will pass, but God, his Word, his Love, will remain eternally:

> "Do not think that I have come to abolish the law and the prophets; I have come not to abolish them but to fulfil them. For truly, I say to you, till heaven and earth pass away, not an iota, not a dot, will pass from the law until all is accomplished." (Mt 5:17–18)

Going through the beginning of the book of Ecclesiastes (cf. chapters 1–3), name some of the vanities or idols listed by Qoheleth: "Vanity of vanities! All is vanity" (Eccles 1:2).

Note how the author ends his meditation: "All has been heard. Fear God, and keep his commandments; for this is the whole duty of man" (Eccles 12:13). Fear, in the Bible, is the attitude that pushes us to seek God and to receive his will. God loves us. He shows us what leads to happiness through his commandments, his words of love. To fear God is to respond to his invitation of love by following his ways. By listening to the Word of God and by putting it into practice, man discovers a path of unhoped-for freedom and happiness. In opposition to idols that pass away and only give the impression of happiness, God, his Word, his Love, will never pass away. Saint Augustine said: "You have made us for yourself, and our heart is restless until it rests in you."[1]

[1] Saint Augustine, *Confessions*, trans. Henry Chadwick, Oxford World Classics (Oxford and New York: Oxford Univ. Press, 2009), 3.

Let us return to the book of Exodus. When God had finished speaking with Moses on Mount Sinai, he gave him the two tables of the Covenant, tables of stone, written with the finger of God:

> When the people saw that Moses delayed to come down from the mountain, the people gathered themselves together to Aaron, and said to him, "Up, make us gods, who shall go before us; as for Moses, the man who brought us up out of the land of Egypt, we do not know what has become of him." And Aaron said to them, "Take off the rings of gold which are in the ears of your wives, your sons, and your daughters, and bring them to me." So all the people took off the rings of gold which were in their ears, and brought them to Aaron. And he received the gold at their hand, and fashioned it with a graving tool, and made a molten calf; and they said, "These are your gods, O Israel, who brought you up out of the land of Egypt!" When Aaron saw this, he built an altar before it; and Aaron made proclamation and said, "Tomorrow shall be a feast to the LORD." And they rose up early the next day, and offered burnt offerings and brought peace offerings; and the people sat down to eat and drink, and rose up to play. And the LORD said to Moses, "Go down; for your people, whom you brought up out of the land of Egypt, have corrupted themselves; they have turned aside quickly out of the way which I commanded them; they have made for themselves a molten calf, and have worshiped it and sacrificed to it, and said, 'These are your gods, O Israel, who brought you up out of the land of Egypt!'" (Ex 32:1–8)

The people of Israel crossed the desert, passing from slavery to freedom. To what form of slavery where they submitted in Egypt? To what new form of slavery did they submit themselves by worshipping a golden calf? Worship of the one God frees man from every alienation that closes him in upon himself.

Let us not forget that the first request that God, from the burning bush, made to Pharaoh through the intermediary of Moses was: "Let us go a three days' journey into the wilderness, that we may sacrifice to the LORD our God" (Ex 3:18). Even before bringing up the physical liberation from the slavery imposed by the Egyptians, God wanted to free his people from a much more tragic slavery: that which consists in adoring false gods. Since Egypt worshipped certain animals (the ram, the calf, the bull), ranking them as divine, God asked his people to go out into the desert a three days' journey, far from the sight of the Egyptians, to sacrifice these animals. For the chosen people, this gesture meant a radical rejection of the worship of these animals. Since Pharaoh refused this request of Moses, God would bring his people out of the oppression of Egypt through the ten terrible plagues. For decades afterward, in the context of his divine education, God requested that his people sacrifice these animals, considered divinities by the surrounding peoples, so that there was never a risk that they be worshipped anew. Thus their heart was free for the adoration of the one God.

For a moment, let us ask the Spirit to show us the idols in our life. Afterward, let us receive Benedict XVI's invitation to adore the Eucharist so as to be delivered from these idols and enter into the true freedom of the children of God:

We cannot forget the beginning of the "Decalogue", the Ten Commandments, where it is written: "I am the Lord your God, who brought you out of the land of Egypt, out of the house of bondage. You shall have no other gods before me" (Ex 20:2–3). Here we find the meaning of the third constitutive element of *Corpus Christi:* kneeling in adoration before the Lord. Adoring the God of Jesus Christ, who out of love made himself bread broken, is the most effective and radical remedy against the idolatry of the past and of the present. Kneeling before the Eucharist is a profession of freedom: those who bow to Jesus cannot and must not prostrate themselves before any earthly authority, however powerful. We Christians kneel only before God or before the Most Blessed Sacrament because we know and believe that the one true God is present in it, the God who created the world and so loved it that he gave his Only Begotten Son (cf. Jn 3:16). We prostrate ourselves before a God who first bent over man like the Good Samaritan to assist him and restore his life, and who knelt before us to wash our dirty feet. Adoring the Body of Christ means believing that there, in that piece of Bread, Christ is really there, and gives true sense to life, to the immense universe as to the smallest creature, to the whole of human history as to the most brief existence. Adoration is prayer that prolongs the celebration and Eucharistic communion and in which the soul continues to be nourished: it is nourished with love, truth, peace; it is nourished with hope, because the One before whom we prostrate ourselves does not judge us, does not crush us but liberates and transforms us.[2]

In the following passage, God addresses himself to one of the Churches founded by John. The sharp two-edged sword is the living Word of God. It wishes to free us from our idols, which make us slaves. Here God reproaches his people for having a divided heart and for receiving the foreign teachings of false gods. Every sin leads us astray from true love and enslaves us. The Word of God reveals to man his own identity and how to become free. In his eagerness for the salvation of every man, God comes to free us and make us his children.

"And to the angel of the Church in Pergamum write: 'The words of him who has the sharp two-edged sword. I know where you dwell, where Satan's throne is; you hold fast my name and you did not deny my faith even in the days of Antipas my witness, my faithful one, who was killed among you, where Satan dwells. But I have a few things against you: you have some there who hold the teaching of Balaam, who taught Balak to put a stumbling block before the sons of Israel, that they might eat food sacrificed to idols and practice immorality. So you also have some who hold the teaching of the Nicolaitans. Repent then. If not, I will come to you soon and war against them with the sword of my mouth. He who has an ear, let him hear what the Spirit says to the churches. To him who conquers I will give some of the hidden manna.'" (Rev 2:12–17)

~

STAGE 6

Elijah Meets God on Mount Horeb
Prayer—Adoration

[Elijah] walked . . . forty days and forty nights to Horeb the mount
of God. And there he came to a cave, and lodged there; and behold,
the word of the LORD came to him, and he said to him, "What are you
doing here, Elijah?" He said, "I have been very jealous for the LORD,
the God of hosts; for the sons of Israel have forsaken your covenant,
thrown down your altars, and slain your prophets with the sword;
and I, even I only, am left; and they seek my life, to take it away."
And he said, "Go forth, and stand upon the mount before the LORD."
And behold, the LORD passed by, and a great and strong wind tore
the mountains, and broke in pieces the rocks before the LORD, but
the LORD was not in the wind; and after the wind an earthquake, but
the LORD was not in the earthquake; and after the earthquake a fire,
but the LORD was not in the fire; and after the fire a still small voice.
And when Elijah heard it, he wrapped his face in his mantle and went
out and stood at the entrance of the cave. And behold, there came a
voice to him, and said, "What are you doing here, Elijah?" He said,
"I have been very jealous for the LORD, the God of hosts; for the sons
of Israel have forsaken your covenant, thrown down your altars, and
slain your prophets with the sword; and I, even I only, am left; and
they seek my life, to take it away." And the LORD said to him, "Go,
return on your way to the wilderness of Damascus; and when you
arrive, you shall anoint Hazael to be king over Syria." (1 Kings 19:
8–15)

The prophet Elijah is the last remaining defender of the one God, of the
God of Abraham, Isaac, and Jacob. He proclaims this God who brought
his people out of Pharaoh's slavery, this God who spoke to Moses in
the desert and who fed his people manna so that they might come to

the Promised Land. Elijah becomes the guardian of the Covenant, of faithfulness to God, of adoration of the one God, and of the purity of the faith. Why does Elijah choose mount Horeb (cf. Ex 3; *Stage 2*)? God shows himself to Moses in a burning bush. How does he show himself to Elijah?

This unassuming encounter with God reconfirms Elijah in his vocation. Let us note well the contrast between the sweetness of the divine encounter and the radical nature of the prophet Elijah's mission! What is this mission? Let us beseech God to show us what he expects of us after the sweet encounter with Jesus in the Blessed Sacrament.

God acts, not by noise, thunder, strikes of lightning, exterior power, but in the silence of the heart. He seeks, not fusion, but intimacy. Adoration is a "face-to-face" that leads to a "heart-to-heart". Here are the definitions of Carmelite prayer and of Eucharistic adoration:

> Contemplative prayer . . . in my opinion is nothing else than a close sharing between friends; it means taking time frequently to be alone with him who we know loves us. (Saint Teresa of Avila)[1]

> The object of Eucharistic adoration is the Divine Person of our Lord Jesus Christ present in the Most Blessed Sacrament. He is living; he wants us to speak to him; he will speak to us. And this conversation, which develops between the soul and our Lord, is true Eucharistic meditation; this is adoration. (Saint Peter Julian Eymard)[2]

Prayer is the "heart-to-heart" with Jesus. Adoration is the "face-to-face" that leads to the "heart-to-heart". Is it an unnecessary detour or a surer path for arriving at the same goal? Here are some reflections to help us understand better these two intimately related forms of prayer that the Church has never placed in opposition:

> In Saint Teresa of Avila's definition of prayer, each word is carefully thought out: friendship, fidelity, solitude, love of God. The mystics of Mount Carmel teach us that prayer consists in letting the Holy Spirit

---

[1] *Catechism of the Catholic Church* (hereafter abbreviated CCC), no. 2709, quoting Saint Teresa of Jesus, *The Book of Her Life*, 8, 5, in *The Collected Works of St. Teresa of Avila*, trans. K. Kavanaugh, O.C.D., and O. Rodriguez, O.C.D. (Washington, D.C.: ICS Publications, Institute of Carmelite Studies, 1976), 1:67.

[2] Saint Peter Julian Eymard, *Adorer en esprit et en vérité* (Paris: Éditions F.-X. de Guibert, 2009), 21.

overcome the spirit of the disciple in such a way that his soul becomes totally united to God. This work of the Spirit is possible only in the soul of him who surrenders and totally exposes himself to the work of grace. Adoration is not opposed to this path. Prayer itself calls us to adore the God to whom we give ourselves over like wood to fire. The Eucharist is the sublime means that God gives to man so that man may unite himself to God. The Church today heartily encourages the practice of Eucharistic adoration. It would be a shame to neglect it. To want to encounter God within us in a heart-to-heart without passing through the face-to-face of adoration requires a purification of the inner self and a solid formation, an ability to fight the passions without gloves, without which prayer runs the risk of leading us back to ourselves in an unfortunate introspection and not to God present within us. In the face-to-face of adoration, the resurrected body of Jesus purifies us, transforms us, and divinizes us. It is pointless to oppose prayer and adoration. Within the Church, they complete each other, even if, at the individual level, each man is led according to the manner and the paths pleasing to the Lord. Thus each member of the faithful responds to God according to the inspirations that the Spirit whispers in his heart.[3]

Jesus explains the importance of Eucharistic adoration to Father Courtois:

It is under the Eucharistic radiance that you enrich your soul with my presence, I was almost going to say with my perfume. . . . If I desire to be exposed to your gazes in the sacrament of my Eucharist, it is not for my sake, but for yours. I know better than anyone just how much your faith, in order to concentrate its attention, needs to be drawn to a sign that expresses a divine reality. Your adoration often needs to support the eyes of your faith through the sight of the consecrated Host. This is a concession to human weakness, but it is perfectly in accord with the laws of psychology. . . . Here, it is the law of incarnation that is in play: so long as you are on earth, you are not pure spirits or abstract intellects; your whole being, physical and moral, must work as one in expressing your love in order to intensify

[3] Father Ludovic Lécuru and Father Florian Racine, *L'adoration eucharistique* (Paris: Éditions de l'Emmanuel, 2009), 139.

this love. For certain privileged souls, it is possible to pass beyond this at least for a time, but why refuse to the masses of men of goodwill what can help them to pray better, to unite themselves better, to love better?[4]

Adoration is not prayer; it is first of all contemplation of the mystery of the Eucharistic presence of Christ. Christ present in the monstrance is of course just as present in the tabernacle, but if the Church has us adore Christ in this way, it is to help us to enter more profoundly into the Eucharistic mystery and to live more intensely from his Real Presence.[5]

Benedict XVI highlights the importance of silence for the meeting of "I" and "Thou":

In life today, often noisy and dispersive, it is more important than ever to recover the capacity for inner silence and recollection. Eucharistic adoration permits this not only centered on the "I" but more so in the company of that "You" full of love who is Jesus Christ, "the God who is near to us".[6]

Well, it is very simple! When we adore Jesus in the Host, we adore him at once substantially present in the Host and—just as really, but spiritually—present within us. Heaven is at once on the altar and in our heart. We are like one of those lovely sponges plunged into the ocean. We are in the water, but the water is also in us: "Abide in me, and I in you." We let ourselves be filled on every side by the love of our God, from outside and from within. What is our role? It too is simple. Let us remember the words of Saint John: "[Jesus] came to his own home, and his own people received him not." If the lovely sponge retracts, closes itself, it cannot absorb the water that is offered to it. . . . Let us also ask the Holy Spirit to help us open ourselves to the love offered in us and in front of us. Let us receive it, let us allow ourselves to act, let us abandon ourselves with confidence, "entirely awakened, in faith, to the creative action of God in us". Let us receive

---

[4] Father Gaston Courtois, *Quand le Seigneur parle au cœur*, 13th ed. (Paris: Éditions Medias-paul, 1993), 173.

[5] Bishop Patrick Chauvet, *Il est là! L'adoration eucharistique* (Saint-Maur: Éditions Parole et Silence, 2008), 92.

[6] Benedict XVI, Angelus, Corpus Christi, June 10, 2007.

this offered love as much as possible, so that the over-saturated sponge that we become may overflow upon others. Such is the fount of living water that the Lord promised to the Samaritan woman.[7]

Finally, the Anomoeans used to say: "We can pray very well at home; we have no need of going to the church." Saint John Chrysostom responded: "You are in great error; for while you may, it is true, pray in your dwelling, you will not, however, do it as well as in the church!"[8]

~

[7] Anne-Françoise Vater, *Initiation à la prière et à l'adoration* (Paris: Éditions de l'Emmanuel, 2011), 152.

[8] Saint John Chrysostom, homily 30, quoted in *Mois de Marie de Notre-Dame du Très Saint-Sacrement*, meditations excerpted from Saint Peter Julian Eymard (Paris: Librairie Ch. Poussielgue, 1982), 297.

STAGE 7

The Calling of Samuel

Behind the second curtain stood a tent called the Holy of Holies, having . . . the ark of the covenant covered on all sides with gold, which contained a golden urn holding the manna, and Aaron's rod that budded, and the tables of the covenant (Heb 9:3–4).

"And you shall command the sons of Israel that they bring to you pure beaten olive oil for the light, that a lamp may be set up to burn continually. In the tent of meeting, outside the veil which is before the covenant, Aaron and his sons shall tend it from evening to morning before the LORD. It shall be a statute for ever to be observed throughout their generations by the sons of Israel." (Ex 27:20–21).

Now the boy Samuel was ministering to the LORD under Eli. And the word of the LORD was rare in those days; there was no frequent vision. At that time Eli, whose eyesight had begun to grow dim, so that he could not see, was lying down in his own place; the lamp of God had not yet gone out, and Samuel was lying down within the temple of the LORD, where the ark of God was. Then the LORD called, "Samuel! Samuel!" and he said, "Here I am!" and ran to Eli, and said, "Here I am, for you called me." But he said, "I did not call; lie down again." So he went and lay down. And the LORD called again, "Samuel!" And Samuel arose and went to Eli, and said, "Here I am, for you called me." But he said, "I did not call, my son; lie down again." Now Samuel did not yet know the LORD, and the word of the LORD had not yet been revealed to him. And the LORD called Samuel again the third time. And he arose and went to Eli, and said, "Here I am, for you called me." Then Eli perceived that the LORD was calling the boy. Therefore Eli said to Samuel, "Go, lie down; and if he calls you, you shall say, 'Speak, LORD, for your servant hears.'" So Samuel went and lay down in his place. And the LORD came and stood forth, calling as at other times, "Samuel! Samuel!" And Samuel said, "Speak, for your servant hears." . . . And Samuel grew, and the LORD was with him and let none of his words fall to the ground. (1 Sam 3:1–10, 19)

Samuel was sleeping in the temple, near the ark of God. What did this ark contain? What is the origin of the candle that burns continuously before the tabernacle? "The lamp of God had not yet gone out" (1 Sam 3:3). This light was the last one shining in the temple. It prefigures the light that remains lit day and night before the tabernacle in our churches. This light not only signifies that the loving presence of Christ abides continuously in his Church, like a magnet that attracts everything to itself: "I will not leave you desolate" (Jn 14:18); "I am with you always, to the close of the age" (Mt 28:20). But this light also recalls that Jesus is our true Light in the Blessed Sacrament. He drives away the shadows of our heart and of our world.

> The presence of Jesus in the tabernacle must be a kind of *magnetic pole* attracting an ever greater number of souls enamored of him, ready to wait patiently to hear his voice and, as it were, to sense the beating of his heart.[1]

Jesus is the Bridegroom. The Church, represented by our parish community, is the Bride. The presence and thus continuous availability of Christ the Bridegroom to his Church-Bride calls for the total response of the Church-Bride to Christ the Bridegroom in the Eucharist. Through perpetual adoration, it is the whole community that returns love for love to Jesus, by showing up day and night before the Lord. Sadly, it is often the real absence of the community that responds to the Real Presence of Christ in the Eucharist.

Dina Bélanger, beatified by John Paul II in 1993, wrote in her journal: "If souls understood what treasure they possess in the divine Eucharist, it would be necessary to protect tabernacles with impregnable ramparts; because, in the delirium of a holy and devouring hunger, they would go themselves to feed on the Manna of the Seraphim. Churches, at night as in daytime, would overflow with worshipers wasting away with love for the august prisoner."[2]

---

[1] John Paul II, Apostolic Letter *Mane Nobiscum Domine* (2004), no. 18.

[2] Blessed Dina Bélanger, *Autobiographie*, ed. by the Religious of Jesus and Mary in Canada.

How does God call Samuel? And how does Samuel respond to him? God always calls by the first name. It is an invitation to live a personal, intimate relationship with our God, who alone can fill the heart. Reading this passage from John Paul II, how does God love us in the Eucharist?

> The Eucharist is the sacrament of the presence of Christ, who gives himself to us because he loves us. He loves each one of us in a unique and personal way in our practical daily lives: in our families, among our friends, at study and work, in rest and relaxation. He loves us when he fills our days with freshness, and also when, in times of suffering, he allows trials to weigh upon us: even in the most severe trials, he lets us hear his voice.
>
> Yes, dear friends, Christ loves us and he loves us for ever! He loves us even when we disappoint him, when we fail to meet his expectations for us. He never fails to embrace us in his mercy. How can we not be grateful to this God who has redeemed us, going so far as to accept the foolishness of the Cross? To God who has come to be at our side and has stayed with us to the end? . . .
>
> Dear friends, when you go back home, set the Eucharist at the center of your personal life and community life: love the Eucharist, adore the Eucharist and celebrate it, especially on Sundays, the Lord's Day. Live the Eucharist by testifying to God's love for every person.
>
> I entrust to you, dear friends, this greatest of God's gifts to us who are pilgrims on the paths of time, but who bear in our hearts a thirst for eternity. May every community always have a priest to celebrate the Eucharist! I ask the Lord therefore to raise up from among you many holy vocations to the priesthood. Today as always the Church needs those who celebrate the Eucharistic Sacrifice with a pure heart. The world must not be deprived of the gentle and liberating presence of Christ living in the Eucharist!
>
> You yourselves must be fervent witnesses to Christ's presence on the altar. Let the Eucharist mold your life and the life of the families you will form. Let it guide all life's choices. May the Eucharist, the true and living presence of the love of the Trinity, inspire in you ideals of solidarity, and may it lead you to live in communion with your brothers and sisters in every part of the world.[3]

[3] John Paul II, Homily for the Closing of World Youth Day, Tor Vergata, Rome, August 20, 2000, nos. 4, 6.

Some practical advice: let us know how to respond like Samuel: "Speak, for your servant hears." Too often, we say to the Lord, "Hear, Lord, for your servant speaks"! Through adoration, Jesus wants to de-center us from ourselves to make us open to the divine will. When we enter into the chapel of adoration, let us know how to begin with love and not with our problems:

> Begin all your periods of adoration with an act of love, and you will open your soul deliciously to his divine action. It is because you begin with yourselves that you give up on the way; or else, if you begin with some virtue other than love, you are on the wrong track. Does a child not kiss his mother before obeying her? Love is the only door to the heart.[4]

~

---

[4] Saint Peter Julian Eymard, *Adorer en esprit et en vérité* (Paris: Éditions F.-X. de Guibert, 2009), 24.

STAGE 8

The Incarnation and the
Birth of Jesus at Bethlehem

Now the birth of Jesus Christ took place in this way. When his mother Mary had been betrothed to Joseph, before they came together she was found to be with child of the Holy Spirit; and her husband Joseph, being a just man and unwilling to put her to shame, resolved to send her away quietly. But as he considered this, behold, an angel of the Lord appeared to him in a dream, saying, "Joseph, son of David, do not fear to take Mary your wife, for that which is conceived in her is of the Holy Spirit; she will bear a son, and you shall call his name Jesus, for he will save his people from their sins." All this took place to fulfil what the Lord had spoken by the prophet: "Behold, a virgin shall conceive and bear a son, and his name shall be called Emmanuel" (which means, God with us). (Mt 1:18–23)

And the Word became flesh and dwelt among us. (Jn 1:14)

Beginning with Adam, God saw that his greatness provoked resistance in man; that man felt limited in his very being and threatened in his freedom. This is why God chose a new way. He became a child. He made himself dependent and weak, in need of our love. Today, this God who has made himself a little child tells us, you can no longer be afraid of me, from now on you can only love me. In the table below, link the boxes of the different columns by connecting the bullet points.

If necessary, reread the passages of Matthew 2:1–12 and Luke 2:1–20 (see the table below).

The verse "He dwelt among us" is literally translated as "He pitched his tent among us." This expresses the permanence of Christ's presence in the midst of his people. Thus John Paul II said:

Jesus at Bethlehem		Today, Jesus in the Eucharist
	Mt 2:1–12	
Bethlehem ("House of bread")	• •	Tabernacle lamp
Manger	• •	My Savior
Poverty of the crib	• •	Adoration of Jesus in the Eucharist
The Magi render homage to the newborn	• •	My God
The star comes to rest over the place	• •	Food, living bread
Gold	• •	Church ("Body of Christ")
Frankincense	• •	My King
Myrrh	• •	Poverty of the altar
	Lk 2:1–20	
Crib, place where the newborn rests	• •	Blessed are the poor in spirit (Mt 5:3)
Wrapped in swaddling cloths	• •	Thanksgiving after Communion
Birth at Bethlehem	• •	The joy of knowing oneself to be eternally loved
The shepherds receive Good News, a great joy for all the people	• •	Announcing the love of Christ offered in the Eucharist
They made known that which had been told them	• •	My Heart, Jesus' place of rest
Praising and glorifying God	• •	Consecration at Mass
Mary kept all these things in her heart	• •	Under the appearances of bread
	Jn 1:14	
He dwelt among us	• •	Permanent presence in the Church (Tent)

The Lord Jesus has pitched His tent among us and, from this His Eucharistic dwelling, He repeats to each man and each woman, "Come to me, all you who labor and are overburdened, and I shall give you rest" (Mt 11:28).[1]

Starting with the two etymologies of the word "adoration" given by Benedict XVI, find the principal fruit adoration bears in the soul:

The Greek word is *proskynesis*. It refers to the gesture of submission, the recognition of God as our true measure, supplying the norm that we choose to follow. It means that freedom is not simply about enjoying life in total autonomy, but rather about living by the measure of truth and goodness, so that we ourselves can become true and good. This gesture is necessary even if initially our yearning for freedom makes us inclined to resist it. We can only fully accept it when we take the second step that the Last Supper proposes to us. The Latin word for adoration is *ad-oratio*—mouth to mouth contact, a kiss, an embrace, and hence, ultimately love. Submission becomes union, because he to whom we submit is Love. In this way submission acquires a meaning, because it does not impose anything on us from the outside, but liberates us deep within.[2]

The "mouth to mouth" of which the pope speaks expresses two different gestures: either the kiss between two lovers or the lifeguard's action upon a drowned person, breathing into his lungs so that he might regain his own breath. In adoration, Christ not only invites us into a real relationship of love with him; he also breathes into our heart his own breath, his Spirit, which gives vigor and strength to our interior life.

Archbishop Kébreau of Cap-Haïtien responds in an interview to the question, "What do you think of Eucharistic adoration?":

It is a time of encounter between the depths of our misery and the depths of God's love. It is there that I can know that I am loved by Christ who delivered himself for me. Everything is from him. He knows how to untie the knots that keep me in their grip. There, I

[1] John Paul II, Message for the Thirty-seventh World Day of Prayer for Vocations, May 14, 2000.
[2] Benedict XVI, homily at Marienfeld for World Youth Day in Cologne, August 21, 2005.

learn how to be silent in the deepest part of myself in order to be transformed by the Holy Spirit, real problems resolving themselves at the foot of the tabernacle. Jesus said to Angela of Foligno: "Concern yourself with me, and I will concern myself with you." Adoration nourishes faith, trains it to avoid lapsing into unbelief or superstition. It is essential among this people that believes that it is being injured. Adoration is not a pharmacy but the gratuitousness of God's gift.

A meditation on Christmas, the Incarnation, and the Eucharist by Archbishop Fulton Sheen:

If we were naturally good and naturally progressive, there would have been no need of Christ coming to earth to make men good. Those who are well have no need of a physician. If all were right with the world, God would have stayed In His Heaven. His Presence in the crib in Bethlehem is a witness not to our progress, but to our misery. . . . Just as Christmas is a season for exchanging gifts with friends, so Our Lord came to this poor earth of ours to exchange gifts. He said to us, as only a good God could say: "You give Me your humanity and I will give you My divinity; you give Me your time and I will give you My eternity; you give Me your weary body and I will give you redemption; you give Me your broken heart and I will give you love; you give Me your nothingness and I will give you My All."[3]

Humanism is impossible because it is too academic; "love of humanity" is impossible because there is no such thing as *humanity*—there are only men and women; the religion of progress is impossible because progress means nothing unless we know whither we are progressing. Philosophical systems, scientific constructions, and slogans leave the heart of man cold. Even a theory about love means little as long as it remains a theory. But let Love become personal in Some One, and then it pulls at every heartstring in the world. There is the secret of the appeal of the Incarnation. Love became incarnate and dwelt amongst us. Since that day hearts that have known what the Incarnation means can never content themselves with any system which asks us to adore the cosmos. Man never has loved, never will love, anything he cannot get his arms around—and the cosmos is too

[3] Archbishop Fulton Sheen, quoted in the Jefferson City, Mo., *Sunday News and Tribune*, December 20, 1964, p. 7.

big and bulky. *That is why the Immense God became a Babe in order that we might encircle Him in our arms.*[4]

This is why the boundless God continues to make himself small in the Eucharist. He wants to descend upon our heart and find the same love that he found at Bethlehem, from Mary, Joseph, shepherds, Magi. He comes in the sacred Host to become our center! He wants us to love him with all our feelings, our affection, our will, and our intelligence, according to his words: "You shall love the Lord your God with all your heart, and with all your soul, and with all your strength, and with all your mind" (Lk 10:27). He will make us apostles of his Love!

∼

[4] Archbishop Fulton J. Sheen, "God's Quest for Man", *The Divine Romance* (1943), as quoted on CatholicCulture.org: http://www.catholicculture.org/culture/library/view .cfm?id=3784&repos=1&subrepos=0&searchid=1274851 accessed March 6, 2014.

I Respond, by Faith, to His Love

Everlasting Love and the
Parable of the Hidden Treasure

I have loved you with an everlasting love; therefore I have continued my faithfulness to you. (Jer 31:3)

For God so loved the world that he gave his only-begotten Son, that whoever believes in him should not perish but have eternal life. (Jn 3:16)

The kingdom of heaven is like treasure hidden in a field, which a man found and covered up; then in his joy he goes and sells all that he has and buys that field. (Mt 13:44)

Again, the kingdom of heaven is like a merchant in search of fine pearls, who, on finding one pearl of great value, went and sold all that he had and bought it. (Mt 13:45–46)

How does the Lord love us? What is God's greatest gift for us (see also Ps 36:8; Ps 63:4; Rom 8:35)?

The parable of the hidden treasure can be read in two different ways, each enriching the other:

1. First, Jesus himself is our treasure. He is present in the Eucharist, our greatest treasure on earth. Here are the words of Benedict XVI, spoken after having visited the "treasury" of a magnificent German cathedral:

Eucharistic adoration is an essential way of being with the Lord. Thanks to Bishop Schraml, Altötting now has a new "treasury". Where once the treasures of the past were kept, precious historical and religious items, there is now a place for the Church's true treasure: the permanent presence of the Lord in his Sacrament. In one of his parables the Lord speaks of a treasure hidden in the field; whoever finds it sells all he has in order to buy that field, because the hidden treasure is more valuable than anything else. The hidden treasure, the good greater than any other good, is the Kingdom of God—it is Jesus himself, the Kingdom in person. In the sacred Host, he is present, the true treasure, always waiting for us. Only by adoring this presence do we learn how to receive him properly—we learn the reality of communion, we learn the Eucharistic celebration from the inside. Here I would like to quote some fine words of Saint Edith Stein, Co-Patroness of Europe, who wrote in one of her letters: "The Lord is present in the tabernacle in his divinity and his humanity. He is not there for himself, but for us: for it is his joy to be with us. He knows that we, being as we are, need to have him personally near. As a result, anyone with normal thoughts and feelings will naturally be drawn to spend time with him, whenever possible and as much as possible" (*Gesammelte Werke* VII, 136ff.). Let us love being with the Lord! There we can speak with him about everything. We can offer him our petitions, our concerns, our troubles. Our joys. Our gratitude, our disappointments, our needs and our aspirations. There we can also constantly ask him: "Lord send laborers into your harvest! Help me to be a good worker in your vineyard!"[1]

2. The parable can be read in the opposite sense: each person is Jesus' treasure. This other interpretation complements the preceding one. In this case, Jesus is the man who finds the treasure. How should we interpret "sells all that he has"? "buys that field"? Reread Revelation 5:9.

Note the "all". In his love for us, Jesus gave his body on the Cross, in order to give us his body in the holy Eucharist and unite us to himself in his eternal glory. Just as wheat is crushed and ground to become bread, so Jesus accepted to be beaten, crucified, and pierced to become, for us, "the living bread which came down from heaven" (Jn 6:50). In delivering his body on the Cross, Jesus said "I thirst." So

---

[1] Benedict XVI, homily at Marian Vespers with the Religious and Seminarians of Bavaria, Basilica of Saint Anne, Altötting, September 11, 2006.

too, in delivering himself entirely in the Eucharist, he says: "I thirst with such a terrible thirst to be loved by men in the Blessed Sacrament that this thirst consumes me."[2]

We can make the same double interpretation of these words of Jesus: "For where your treasure is, there will your heart be also" (Lk 12:34). On the one hand, the Eucharist is our treasure and must attract all the movements of our heart. On the other hand, we are his treasure. Jesus is thus here in person with his heart burning with infinite love for us in the Blessed Sacrament. What do we make of this treasure?

The value of a single hour of prayer of adoration extends far beyond our capacity to think, to imagine, or even to desire. There is a story of a married couple who inherited a house, and, in the house, there was an old painting of a flowerpot. They were on the verge of throwing it out while they were tidying up to invite over some friends. Then, one of those invited, who worked in a museum, was drawn to the old painting on the wall that the couple had forgotten to throw out. He brought the painting to the museum to have it examined. It was not a copy but an original Vincent van Gogh, worth several millions; it made the couple one of the richest in Europe.

It is impossible to imagine the value of a simple hour of adoration. Too often Christ in the Eucharist remains in the tabernacle like that old painting whose value we have forgotten. And the monstrances are left in the dusty cupboards of sacristies. Yet Pope Leo XIII remarked about the Eucharist: "In this one mystery the entire supernatural order, with all its wealth and variety of wonders, is in a manner summed up and contained."[3] Like the young couple, we will be shocked, eternally shocked, upon discovering in heaven the value of an hour of adoration! For it is measured by the degree of love that Jesus has for us in the Blessed Sacrament, which is infinite for him who says: "As the Father has loved me, so have I loved you" (Jn 15:9).

Let us end with a few comments from Blessed Charles de Foucauld: "Adoration of the Blessed Sacrament is repose, refreshment,

[2] Saint Margaret Mary, *The Letters of St. Margaret-Mary Alacoque*, letter 133, to the Reverend Father Croiset (Charlotte, N.C.: TAN Books, 1997), 234.
[3] Leo XIII, Encyclical Letter *Mirae caritatis* (1902), no. 7.

joy."[4] "Adoring the sacred Host: this ought to be the heart of every human being's life."[5] Charles, before the splendor of the Sahara, exclaims:

> Here we are at the gates of eternity. One almost believes that here, looking at these two infinities of the great sky and of the desert. You who like to see the setting of the sun, which, descending, sings eternal peace and serenity, you would like seeing the sky and the great horizons of this little Fraternity. But the best, the true infinity, the true peace is at the feet of the divine Tabernacle. There, no more in an image but in reality, is all our good, our love, our life, our all, our peace, our beatitude: there is all our heart and all our soul, our time and our eternity, our All.[6]

> From his tabernacle, Jesus will shine upon these lands and attract adorers to himself. . . . Does my presence do some good here? If it does not, the presence of the Blessed Sacrament certainly does much: Jesus cannot be in a place without shining.[7]

> I seek to do the will of Jesus from day to day and am in great interior peace. Do not worry yourself seeing me alone, without a friend, without spiritual help: I do not suffer at all from this solitude, I find it very sweet: I have the Blessed Sacrament, the best of friends, to speak to day and night.[8]

> Sacred Heart of Jesus, thank you for this first tabernacle in Tuareg country. Sacred Heart of Jesus, shine from the heart of this tabernacle upon this people who worship you without knowing you. Enlighten, lead, save these souls that you love.[9]

∽

[4] Charles de Foucauld, *Lettres de Mme de Bondy: de la Trappe à Tamanrasset* (Paris: Desclée de Brouwer, 1966), letter of January 19, 1903.

[5] Charles de Foucauld, *Correspondances lyonnaises (1904–1916)* (Paris: Karthala, 2005), letter of December 15, 1904.

[6] Charles de Foucauld, *Lettres de Mme de Bondy*, letter of January 19, 1903.

[7] Ibid., letter of November 18, 1907.

[8] Ibid., letter of December 16, 1905.

[9] Charles de Foucauld, Diary, July 8, 1903.

I Respond, by Faith, to His Love

"Come to Me"
The Eucharist Is the Invention of Love

"Come to me, all who labor and are heavy laden, and I will give you rest. Take my yoke upon you, and learn from me; for I am gentle and lowly in heart, and you will find rest for your souls." (Mt 11:28-29)

"Come away by yourselves to a lonely place, and rest a while." (Mk 6:31)

On the last day of the feast, the great day, Jesus stood up and proclaimed, "If any one thirst, let him come to me and drink. He who believes in me, as the Scripture has said, 'Out of his heart shall flow rivers of living water.'" Now this he said about the Spirit, which those who believed in him were to receive. (Jn 7:37-39)

"Follow me, and I will make you fishers of men." (Mt 4:19)

"Come and have breakfast." (Jn 21:12)

Jesus' prayer can be summed up in one noun: "Abba". His message begins with a verb: "Come." What does Jesus promise to those who approach him in the five invitations above?

Father Damien (1840-1886), apostle of the lepers went to the island of Molokai to be near those he would call his brothers. There, he encouraged them to adore the Blessed Sacrament to find strength and hope in it despite the sufferings of their disease. Before he too caught and died from leprosy, he reminded his community of brothers that Jesus in the Blessed Sacrament was his best friend. From the tabernacle, Jesus says even today:

"Cast all your anxieties on him, for he cares about you"; "My peace I give to you" (1 Pet 5:7; Jn 14:27).

54

Here are a few of the saint's words:

I find my consolation in the only companion of mine who never leaves me, that is, our divine Savior in the holy Eucharist.

It is at the foot of the altar that we find the strength we need in our isolation. Without the Blessed Sacrament, a situation like mine would not be sustainable. But with our Lord at my side, well then! I continue to be always happy and content. With this gaiety of heart and a smile on my lips, I work with zeal for the good of the poor unfortunate lepers, and little by little, without much fuss, good is done. . . . [Jesus in the Blessed Sacrament] is the most tender of friends with souls that seek to please him. His goodness knows how to proportion itself to the littlest of his creatures as to the greatest. Do not fear, then, in solitary conversations, to speak to him of your woes, your fears, your troubles, those who are dear to you, your plans, your hopes; do it confidently and with an open heart.[1]

The Eucharist, invention of love: at the end of his life on earth, Jesus so loved us that he did not wish to desert us and leave us alone. However, he had to die on the Cross to give us the gift of eternal life so that we might spend eternity with him in heaven in an indescribable joy. So Jesus made the greatest invention of all time, love's invention par excellence. The eve of his Passion, he took bread and said: "This is my body", then he took wine and said: "This is my blood." Take, eat, and drink. Jesus literally changed the bread and the wine into his own person. Why? To come dwell in our heart. This heart is so precious to him that he makes of it his new heaven on earth!

Immediately after having given his body to be eaten and his blood to be drunk, Jesus left for the Garden of Olives. He then asked his apostles to keep watch with him that they might not enter into temptation: Jesus came and found his disciples sleeping, "and he said to Peter, 'Simon, are you asleep? Could you not watch one hour? Watch and pray that you may not enter into temptation; the spirit indeed is willing, but the flesh is weak'" (Mk 14:37–38). In the Blessed Sacrament, Jesus remains with us to console us in our afflictions, accompany us in our solitudes, and make us victorious in our trials. He calls us to himself

---

[1] Saint Damien of Molokai, *Un étrange bonheur* (Paris: Éditions du Cerf, 1994), letter to his brother, December 13, 1881.

that he might give us the strength to persevere and the charity to love to the end. In other words, Jesus in the tabernacle is our traveling companion, our most faithful friend on earth.

Here are the words of Jesus to a woman religious, Josefa Menendez, who lived in Poitiers at the beginning of the twentieth century:

The Eucharist is the invention of Love! . . . Yet how few souls correspond to that love which spends and consumes itself for them! I live in the midst of sinners that I may be their life, their physician, and the remedy of the diseases bred by corrupt nature. And in return they forsake, insult, and despise me. . . . Poor pitiable sinners, do not turn away from me. . . . Day and night, I am on the watch for you in the tabernacle. I will not reproach you . . . I will not cast your sins in your face. . . . But I will wash them in My Blood and in My Wounds. No need to be afraid. . . . Come to Me. . . . If you but knew how dearly I love you. And you, dear souls, why this coldness and indifference on your part? . . . Do I not know that family cares, . . . household concerns, . . . and the requirements of your position in life make continual calls upon you? . . . But can not you spare a few minutes in which to come and prove your affection and your gratitude? Do not allow yourselves to be involved in useless and incessant cares, but spare a few moments to visit and receive this Prisoner of Love![2]

Some spiritual advice: Let us love Jesus passionately, not only with our feelings, but also with our entire will. "So long as we do not have a passionate love for our Lord in the Most Blessed Sacrament, we will have done nothing."[3] "It is said: all that, it is just exaggeration. But love is nothing but exaggeration! To exaggerate is to go beyond the law. Well, love must go beyond the law."[4]

~

[2] Sister Josefa Menendez, *The Way of Divine Love, or the Message of the Sacred Heart to the World, and a Short Biography of His Messenger* (Charlotte, N.C.: Saint Benedict Press, 2006), 271–72.

[3] Saint Peter Julian Eymard, *Adorer en esprit et en vérité* (Paris: Éditions F.-X. de Guibert, 2009), 178.

[4] Ibid., 182.

Here is the first part of Saint Anthony Mary Claret's meditation:[5]

Jesus speaks to me: My child, you do not need to know greatly in order to please me. It is enough to love me greatly. Tell me what you would say to your mother if she were here and she drew you upon her knees. Recount to me what you would recount to an intimate friend with whom you could never become bored. If, however, you desire some topics of conversation, here are some that you may find useful for each day of the week.

Have you no one to ask me to look after? Tell me the name of your parents, of your benefactors, of your friends. After each of these names, add what you would like me to do for them. Ask a lot, really a lot. I love generous hearts that forget themselves for others. Speak to me of all those who do you good, of the poor you would like to relieve, of the sick you have seen suffering, of the mean-spirited you would like to convert, of persons who have distanced themselves from you and whom you would like to bring back to your affection. For all of them, recite a fervent prayer; remind me that I promised graciously to hear every prayer that comes from the heart, and is it not a prayer from the heart that we make for those persons whom we love and who love us?

Have you no graces to ask me to grant you? If you wish, write a list of all your desires and come read it to me! Love of prayer would make you more fervent; humility would make you less touchy; patience would strengthen you against the fits of anger to which you let yourself give way; diligent work would prevent a host of angry mutterings; charity would make you more lovable. . . . Have you no need of all these virtues? Tell me all these things, and entreat me to help you in the efforts you wish to make; I am the master of the goods of the soul; the goods of the body are also in my possession, ask me for them: health, intelligence, success. I can give everything, and I give it always, when these goods are useful for making souls more holy. . . . What then do you wish, my child?

Have you no plans preoccupying you? Tell them to me in detail. . . . Is it about your vocation? What do you think about? What would you

---

[5] Saint Anthony Mary Claret, *Un quart d'heure en présence du Saint Sacrement* (Hauteville: Éditions du Parvis, 1988).

like? Is it a question of pleasing your family? What do you want to do for them all? And for me, have you not a few ardent thoughts? Do you not wish to do some good to those around you? Tell me in whom you are interested, what is the motive driving you? What are the means you want to take? Reveal your lack of success to me; I will show you the reason for it. Whom do you wish to interest in your work? I am the master of hearts, my child, and I lead them sweetly wherever I wish. I shall place near you those whom you will need, be at peace. . . .

Have you no troubles? Oh, my child, tell me your troubles with lots of details! Who has hurt you, who has injured your pride, who has hated you? Tell me everything; and then finish by adding that you forgive, that you forget, and I, I will bless you! Are you dreading something difficult? Is there in your soul that vague terror which is not rational but that torments you? Entrust yourself fully to my Providence. I am there; I am listening; I will not leave you. . . . Are there hearts around you that seem less good to you, and whose indifference or forgetfulness distances them from you without your being aware of having done anything to hurt them? Implore me heartily for them. . . . I will bring them back if they are useful for your sanctification.

(*Continuation of the meditation is in Stage 11.*)

⁓

I Respond, by Faith, to His Love

The Anointing at Bethany
The Great Service of Adoration

And while he was at Bethany in the house of Simon the leper, as he sat at table, a woman came with an alabaster jar of ointment of pure nard, very costly, and she broke the jar and poured it over his head. But there were some who said to themselves indignantly, "Why was the ointment thus wasted? For this ointment might have been sold for more than three hundred denarii, and given to the poor." And they reproached her. But Jesus said, "Let her alone; why do you trouble her? She has done a beautiful thing to me. For you always have the poor with you, and whenever you will, you can do good to them; but you will not always have me. She has done what she could; she has anointed my body beforehand for burying. And truly, I say to you, wherever the gospel is preached in the whole world, what she has done will be told in memory of her." (Mk 14:3–9)

Each hour of adoration is like a very pure ointment that we offer to Jesus. Why did the woman break a jar of very pure nard to pour over the head of Jesus? Note that the quality of the ointment expresses the quality of the love. Rather than keeping it for herself, she chooses to give it to Jesus. In the same vein, rather than keeping an hour of our week for ourselves, to attend to our own personal affairs, we can give it to Jesus by coming to adore him. And Judas becomes indignant: "What good can come of this waste?"—as the spirit of the world affirms today that spending time before the Blessed Sacrament is a waste or a loss of time. There are so many other ways to use our time. Yet Jesus responds: "Wherever the gospel is preached in the whole world, what she has done will be told." This act was so precious in the eyes of God and brought such glory to Jesus that the Holy Spirit wished this episode to be part of the Gospel! Likewise for us, for all eternity,

God the Father will bless us for having loved his Son here on earth by spending an hour each week with him to give him love for love in the sacrament of his Love!

Adoration is a service. A service to the Divine Person of Jesus AND a great service to mankind.

- Jesus remains in the Blessed Sacrament to give us the privilege of approaching him personally as so many people were able to do two thousand years ago in Galilee and Judea. By our adoration, we can love Jesus today, like the humble shepherds of Bethlehem, like the magi who brought their gifts, or like Mary of Bethany who poured very pure nard over the head of the Christ. Adoring the Eucharist *is serving the Divine Person of Jesus today*, as the disciples did in their time. In this vein, Saint John Chrysostom said: "How many say: I would like to see his face, his features, his beauty. . . . But in the Eucharist, it is he himself whom you see, he himself whom you touch, he himself whom you eat. Think of that and adore, for it is the same who is in heaven and whom the angels adore!"[1]

- Also, in adoring, we *render a great service to mankind*: "Through adoration the Christian contributes mysteriously to the radical transformation of the world and the germination of the Gospel. Every person who prays to the Lord brings the whole world along with him, raising the world to God. Thus those who remain before the Lord fulfill a great service; they present to Christ all those who do not know him or who are far from him; in their name they keep vigil before him."[2] On the Cross, Jesus took our place. We take the place of him who has the greatest need of divine mercy by going to Jesus in a holy hour. Our adoration makes the Precious Blood of Jesus descend upon this person. The person obtains the graces necessary to return to God. In the Eucharist, Jesus says: "It is the will of my Father that no one be lost" (cf. Jn 6:39–40). Paul VI wrote: "The Eucharist is supremely effective for the transformation of the world into a world of justice, holiness, and peace."[3]

[1] Saint John Chrysostom, *Homily on Saint Matthew*, 82, 4.

[2] John Paul II, letter to Bishop Albert Houssiau of Liège for the 750th anniversary of Corpus Christi, May 28, 1996.

[3] Paul VI, Discourse for the Inauguration of International Eucharistic Social Works at Dos Hermanas.

John Paul II encouraged all to "meet Him in adoration and in contemplation that is full of faith and ready to make reparation for the great faults and crimes of the world."[4]

Pascal Pingault, founder of the Bread of Life community, the "sixty-eighter" anarchist[5] who converted while prostrate before the sacred Host, was searching for a place to welcome the poor of our society. One day, during adoration, he was shattered by the passage of John's Gospel where Mary Magdalen anoints the feet of Christ with a precious ointment: "The poor you always have with you, but you do not always have me" (Jn 12:8).

> I understood that it was a prophecy for the persecuted Church, and our own, when his Eucharistic presence would be taken away from us. . . . The Lord undoubtedly wants us to begin adoring him day and night, him first of all. The poor you will always have with you, but me, you will not have always. I understood the urgency to adore Jesus in the mystery of the Encounter. It was by experiencing his presence in the Eucharist that we would end up discovering him, adoring him also in our brothers—men, and above all the poor. It was by living from the Eucharist and in his Presence that we would come to meet those times of intense poverty that will be the end times—with the anguish and blasphemies of men, with their fears, their enormous sins, and their refusal of God. It was by contemplating day and night his exposed Body—from which our eyes would be burned by light—that men who seek him would be deeply moved and would believe. Yes, it was time now to fulfill this mission that the Lord had assigned to us and to begin to prostrate ourselves day and night before him. I discovered at the same time that he was the poorest of all and that he desired us to take plenty of time beside him before letting us undertake whatever apostolate it would be and, above all, beside the poor.

From that instant, the community began perpetual adoration and obtained a house for welcoming the poor. God had put the priorities back

[4] John Paul II, Letter on the Mystery and Worship of the Eucharist *Dominicae Cenae,* February 24, 1980, no. 3.
[5] The expression "soixante-huitard" (literally, "sixty-eighter") is a noun and adjective referring to the socio-political upheavals marked by a radical revolutionary spirit that began in France in May 1968 and spread throughout much of Western Europe. —TRANS.

in order: "You shall love the Lord your God with all your heart, and with all your soul, and with all your mind. This is the great and first commandment. And a second is like it, You shall love your neighbor as yourself" (Mt 22:37–39).[6]

In a call for adoration, Peter Kreeft writes:

> Restoration of adoration of the Sacrament will heal our church, and thus our nation, and thus our world. It is one of Satan's most destructive lies that sitting alone in a dark church adoring Christ is irrelevant, impractical, a withdrawal from vital contemporary needs. Adoration touches everyone and everything in the world because it touches the Creator, who touches everything and everyone in the world from within, in fact, from their very center. When we adore, we plunge into the center of the hurricane, "the still point of the turning world"; we plug into infinite dynamism and power. Adoration is more powerful for construction than nuclear bombs for destruction.[7]

For if man with his created spirit can invent so powerful a weapon as the atomic bomb, how much more powerful will be the uncreated love of our resurrected Lord to bring eternal peace into the world!

~

Here is the second part of Saint Anthony Mary Claret's meditation (*from the end of Stage 10*).[8]

> *Jesus speaks to me: Have you no joys to tell me about?* Why not let me in on your joys? Tell me everything that has happened since yesterday to console you, make you smile, bring you joy. Was there an unexpected visit, a reward that you did not think you merited, a fear that dissipated all at once, a success that you worried you were unable to obtain, a mark of friendship, a letter, a memento you received. . . .

[6] Pascal Pingault, *Fioretti du Pain de Vie* (Paris: Éditions Le Sarment-Fayard, 1986), 79–80.

[7] Peter Kreeft, *The Angels and the Ants, Bringing Heaven Closer to Your Daily Life* (Ann Arbor, Mich.: Servant Publications, 1994), 92.

[8] Saint Anthony Mary Claret, *Un quart d'heure en présence du Saint-Sacrement* (Hauteville: Éditions du Parvis, 1988).

All of that, my child, it is I who have brought it about for you. Why would you not show yourself grateful for it . . . and would you not say again to me: Thank you! For gratefulness brings benefit, and the benefactor likes to be reminded of his generosities.

Have you no virtues to acquire, and have you no need of my help? Tell me your miseries, my child; confess yourself simply in my presence. . . . Show me, by citing your frailties, how very sensual, prideful, touchy, self-centered, weak, lazy you are. . . . Groan from how little you are familiar with renunciation, from how continually you abuse the graces that are accorded to you, from the pain that you give to your family, from the faults that perhaps you cause to be committed around you. My heart, my hands are full of treasures, and I want one thing only, to spread them with abundance. Ask me for my help. . . . Each time you have acted lightly, without consulting me, without praying a little first, have you not acted less well, have you not perhaps done foolish things? You can do nothing, nothing without my protection, but with me, my child, you can do all things. . . . Happy is the soul that feels me at its side, helping it, consoling it, protecting it!

Have you no promises to make me and orders to ask from me? I read to the depths of your heart, as you know. Men are fooled; God is not fooled. So be sincere. . . . Are you resolved not to expose yourself again to this occasion of sin, to deprive yourself of things that bring you to evil, no longer to read this book? Do you want immediately to be good for the sake of this person who has hurt you? Do you want to act simply with everyone? Good, my child. And now go take up your work again. Be quiet, modest, charitable. I am waiting for you tomorrow; tomorrow, bring me a very pure and very devoted heart; tomorrow, I will have new favors for you.

∼

I Respond, by Faith, to His Love

Martha and Mary
The Great Commandment of Love

[Jesus] entered a village; and a woman named Martha received him into her house. And she had a sister called Mary, who sat at the Lord's feet and listened to his teaching. But Martha was distracted with much serving; and she went to him and said, "Lord, do you not care that my sister has left me to serve alone? Tell her then to help me." But the Lord answered her, "Martha, Martha, you are anxious and troubled about many things; one thing is needful. Mary has chosen the good portion, which shall not be taken away from her." (Lk 10:38–42)

"You shall love the Lord your God with all your heart, and with all your soul, and with all your mind. This is the great and first commandment." (Mt 22:37–38) (heart-to-heart with God)

"And a second is like it, You shall love your neighbor as yourself." (Mt 22:39) (heart-to-heart with neighbor)

In this passage, Martha is presented as the mistress of the house. She wants to welcome her guests—Jesus and the disciples—in the best of conditions. Jesus will not reproach this obvious mark of Martha's charity. Her sister Mary chooses to serve Jesus himself by being entirely attentive to his presence and by listening to his Word. She offers this moment, for belonging entirely to Jesus. This other expression of charity focuses directly on the Divine Person of Jesus. He compliments her by showing that the service of God must always precede the service of our neighbor, even if the two are intrinsically linked. God is served first! The two commandments of love (cf. Mt 22:27–29) are applied by the two sisters. Mary loves God with all her heart, with all her soul, and with all her mind by "wasting" a little of her time on the Lord. She is the first contemplative. Martha loves her neighbors with all her strength by serving them as best she can. This is charity toward our neighbor. The double commandment finds its unity and source in the Divine Person of Jesus, at once true God and true man. Today, the Eucharist contains the Divine Person of Jesus. From this seat of charity, divine love comes to renew human love.

> Prayer, as a means of drawing ever new strength from Christ, is concretely and urgently needed. People who pray are not wasting their time, even though the situation appears desperate and seems to call for action alone. Piety does not undermine the struggle against the poverty of our neighbors, however extreme. In the example of Blessed Teresa of Calcutta we have a clear illustration of the fact that time devoted to God in prayer not only does not detract from effective and loving service to our neighbor but is in fact the inexhaustible source of that service.[1]

Here are a few quotations from Mother Teresa of Calcutta showing the link between the two great dimensions of the commandment of charity, or of the service to be rendered to God and to men.

1. *"You shall love the Lord your God with all your heart"*: "The time you spend with Jesus in the Blessed Sacrament is the best time that you can spend on earth. Each instant spent with Jesus will deepen your union with him, will make your immortal soul more glorious and more beautiful in heaven, and will contribute to bringing an eternal peace on earth." "To the question, 'What will save the world?' I respond prayer. Every parish must keep itself at the foot of Jesus in the Blessed Sacrament in hours of adoration."[2]

> We should strongly support perpetual adoration with exposition. Jesus made himself the Bread of Life to give us life. Day and night, He is there. If you really want to grow in love, return to the Eucharist, return to Eucharistic adoration. We must weave our lives around the

---

[1] Benedict XVI, Encyclical Letter *Deus Caritas Est* (2006), English translation: *God Is Love* (San Francisco: Ignatius Press, 2006), no. 36, pp. 89–90.

[2] Blessed Mother Teresa, *Tu m'apportes l'amour, Écrits spirituels* (Paris: Éditions du Centurion, 1975).

Eucharist. . . . Fix your eyes on the One who is light; put your hearts near his Divine Heart; ask him to grant you the grace of knowing him, the love of loving Him, the courage of serving him. Seek him fervently. Through Mary, the cause of our joy, you will discover that nowhere in the world are you better welcomed and nowhere in the world are you better loved than by Jesus living and truly present in the Most Blessed Sacrament. . . . He is truly there in Person, waiting for you.[3]

2. *"You shall love your neighbor as yourself"*: The Eucharist is the sacrament of love that strengthens our heart through divine charity. In the first paragraph, make note of the three quite distinct graces that Mother Teresa's religious sisters obtain by adoring the Blessed Sacrament daily. What is the great grace evoked in the fourth paragraph?

Each day, we expose the Blessed Sacrament, and we have perceived a change in our life. We have felt a deeper love for Christ through the distressing mask of the poor. We have been able to know ourselves better and to know the poor man better as a concrete expression of God. Since we began this adoration of the Blessed Sacrament, we have not reduced our work; we devote just as much time to it as before, but with more understanding. People accept us better. They are hungry for God. They have need, no longer of us, but of Jesus.[4]

The Eucharist is for us the sacrament of prayer, the source and summit of Christian life. The holy hour before the Eucharist must lead us to the holy hour with the poor, with those who will never have human accomplishments and for whom the sole consolation will be Jesus. Our Eucharist is incomplete if it does not lead us to the service and love of the poor. And by receiving the Communion of the poor, we discover our own poverty. That our hands must be pure in order to touch the Body of Christ, just as the priest touches it under the appearance of bread. . . . Think of the delicacy with which the priest treats the Body of Christ during the Mass. It is this Body that you will touch in the person of the poor.[5]

[3] Ibid.
[4] Ibid.
[5] Ibid.

When you contemplate the crucifix, you understand how much Jesus has loved you. When you contemplate the sacred Host, you understand how much Jesus loves you IN THIS MOMENT.[6]

Our daily hour of adoration is our family prayer where we come together before the Blessed Sacrament exposed in the monstrance. During the first half-hour, we recite the chaplet, and during the second half-hour, we pray in silence. Through our adoration, the number of our vocations has doubled. In 1963, we had one hour of adoration together each week, but it was only in 1973 when we began to do our daily hour of adoration that our community began to grow and prosper.[7]

⁓

[6] Ibid.
[7] Ibid.

I Respond, by Faith, to His Love

The Hemorrhaging Woman and the Act of Faith
Prolonging and Intensifying Mass

As he went, the people pressed round him. And a woman who had had a flow of blood for twelve years and had spent all her living upon physicians and could not be healed by any one, came up behind him, and touched the fringe of his garment; and immediately her flow of blood ceased. And Jesus said, "Who was it that touched me?" When all denied it, Peter said, "Master, the multitudes surround you and press upon you!" But Jesus said, "Some one touched me; for I perceive that power has gone forth from me." And when the woman saw that she was not hidden, she came trembling, and falling down before him declared in the presence of all the people why she had touched him, and how she had been immediately healed. And he said to her, "Daughter, your faith has made you well; go in peace." (Lk 8:42–48)

The multitudes press upon Jesus from all parts to hear him and see him perform signs and wonders. In this commotion, a woman touches Jesus with her faith, thus freeing his power. Jesus is conscious of the power that has gone forth from him and says: "Who was it that touched me?" Our faith touches the Heart of Jesus; it frees his power and his love, healing our being, our family, and the whole world, each time that we go to him in the Blessed Sacrament for an hour's adoration. Moreover, Saint John reminds us that "this is the victory that overcomes the world, our faith" (1 Jn 5:4). To the one who prays to him God gives faith. Nevertheless, it is possible to lose this inestimable gift. Paul warns Timothy of this: "Wage the good warfare, holding faith and a good conscience. By rejecting conscience, certain persons have made shipwreck of their faith" (1 Tim 1:18–19).

Faith is the pure act of the spirit, freed from the senses. For here (before the Blessed Sacrament), the senses are of no use; they have no part to play. It is the only mystery of Jesus Christ where the senses must be absolutely still. In all the others, in the Incarnation, the redemption, the senses see a child God, a dying God. Here, there is nothing but an impenetrable cloud for them. Faith alone must act; it is the kingdom of faith. This cloud asks of us a very meritorious sacrifice, the sacrifice of our reason and of our mind. It is necessary to believe as though against the witness of the senses, against ordinary laws of beings, against one's own experience. It is necessary to believe on the basis of the simple word of Jesus Christ; there is only one question to ask: "Who is there?" "Me", answers Jesus Christ. Let us fall to the ground and adore!

And this pure faith freed from the senses, free in its action, unites us simply to the truth of Jesus Christ in the Most Blessed Sacrament: "Faith is of no use, says the Savior; my words are spirit and life." The soul crosses the barrier of the senses and enters into the wonderful contemplation of the divine presence of God under the species, veiled enough so that we can handle the brightness, clear enough for the eyes of faith. Much more, rather than being a trial, this veil becomes, for a humble and sincere faith, a stimulus, an encouragement.

We like to penetrate a veiled truth, to discover a hidden treasure, to overcome a difficulty. Thus the faithful soul, in the presence of the Eucharistic veil, seeks her Lord, like Magdalen at the tomb: her desire grows; she calls him like the bride of the Canticle; she pleases herself in giving him all beauties, in decorating him with all glories. The Eucharist is for her what God is for the blessed: a truth, a beauty ever ancient, ever new, that one never wearies of contemplating, of penetrating. Only our Lord's wisdom and goodness could invent the Eucharistic veil.[1]

For Padre Pio, "It is easier for the world to survive without the sun than without the Holy Sacrifice of the Mass." If the celebration of the Mass is the center, source, and summit of every Christian life, why, some ask, is it still necessary to adore the Blessed Sacrament? Does the Mass not contain the entire Christian mystery? What is the good

---

[1] Saint Peter Julian Eymard, *Adorer en esprit et en vérité* (Paris: Éditions F.-X. de Guibert, 2009), 101–2.

of spending time in silence before the tabernacle? Certainly, nothing could supplant the Mass. Yet Eucharistic adoration is strongly encouraged by the Church. For Benedict XVI, "The act of adoration outside Mass *prolongs* and *intensifies* all that takes place during the liturgical celebration itself."[2] The two verbs "prolong" and "intensify" deserve our attention so that we can understand better why adoration is "not a luxury . . . but a priority"[3] in the Church today.

Prolong: "Eucharistic adoration is simply the natural consequence of the eucharistic celebration, which is itself the Church's supreme act of adoration. Receiving the Eucharist means adoring him whom we receive."[4] Adoration of the Blessed Sacrament finds its source and foundation in the Mass. That Christians are invited to prolong their adoration after Mass does not signify that they have not participated very well at Mass. Adoration would then be a kind of second chance, a "trump card" for absent-minded Christians, inattentive during Mass. No! The mystery celebrated at Mass is prolonged in the tabernacle. Here are two analogies that can clarify our understanding, even though they are insufficient to understand the mystery: just as the ground cannot absorb all of the water that falls from the sky during a heavy rain (the Mass), this very earth continues to absorb the water by letting it seep in over a long time (adoration). We could also say that adoration is like a freeze frame because everything goes so quickly at Mass! It is Jesus' entire work of redemption, from the Incarnation to Pentecost, which is made present and unfurled before us. The Mass will always offer more than we can ever receive. So let us know how to stop and take the time to contemplate all that is made present in the Mass in the silence of adoration! "Be still, and know that I am God" (Ps 46:10).

Intensify: What, in the Mass, can be intensified by Eucharistic adoration? Here, we must distinguish between the gift offered by God and our disposition to receive it. The gift offered, namely, the entire work

---

[2] Benedict XVI, Post-synodal Apostolic Exhortation *Sacramentum Caritatis* (2007), no. 66 (italics mine).

[3] Benedict XVI, Angelus, Castel Gandolfo: August 28, 2005, recalling his Address at the Meeting with German Bishops in the Piussaal of the Seminary in Cologne during World Youth Day (August 21, 2005).

[4] Benedict XVI, *Sacramentum Caritatis*, no. 66.

of redemption, finds its source in the Mass and is prolonged in adoration. So it is always the gift that is first at Mass. On the other hand, our interior disposition to receive this gift is directly linked to our faith. Our faith makes the gift of the Eucharist effective in us. Do we have to say that the adorer makes a more significant act of faith during his silent prayer before the Blessed Sacrament than when he participates at Mass? No, because faith is first of all made living in the liturgy of the Mass. Nevertheless, to give and adore, above all in the middle of the night, requires a different act of faith. This act is grounded in freedom, and no moral or spiritual obligation has been formulated by the Church in favor of Eucharistic adoration. We can also recognize that, during Mass, we are carried by the liturgy, while during an hour of silent adoration, we so often have occasion to ask ourselves what we are doing there! So it is necessary to direct acts of faith toward the Real Presence, which strengthens our faith and obtains an abundance of Eucharistic graces for us. Kneeling before the Eucharist is truly a profession of freedom. In the end, it is the most worthwhile and radical remedy against the idolatries of yesterday and of today.

> Adoring the Body of Christ, means believing that there, in that piece of Bread, Christ is really there, and gives true sense to life, to the immense universe as to the smallest creature, to the whole of human history as to the most brief existence. Adoration is prayer that prolongs the celebration and Eucharistic communion and in which the soul continues to be nourished: it is nourished with love, truth, peace; it is nourished with hope, because the One before whom we prostrate ourselves does not judge us, does not crush us but liberates and transforms us.[5]

∼

---

[5] Benedict XVI, homily for Corpus Christi, Rome: May 22, 2008.

I Respond, by Faith, to His Love

Modes of Christ's Presence
Extensions of the Incarnation

At the time of the Ascension, Jesus leaves his disciples in a paradox. What paradox (cf. Mt 28:20 and Acts 1:9)? How is it possible to leave and stay at the same time? But Jesus makes a promise. What promise (cf. Acts 1:8)? At the time of Pentecost, the Holy Spirit makes Jesus present to his Church in different ways. We are all called to meet Jesus in his different modes of presence each day. Connect the modes of presence and biblical verses below.

In the table below, link the boxes of the different columns by connecting the bullet points.

Recalling these different modes of presence, Paul VI writes:

These various ways in which Christ is present fill the mind with astonishment and offer the Church a mystery for her contemplation. But there is another way in which Christ is present in His Church, a way that surpasses all the others. It is His presence in the Sacrament of the Eucharist, which is, for this reason, "a more consoling source of devotion, a lovelier object of contemplation and holier in what it contains" than all the other sacraments; for it contains Christ Himself and it is "a kind of consummation of the spiritual life". . . . This presence is called "real" not to exclude the idea that the others are "real" too, but rather to indicate presence *par excellence*, because it is substantial and through it Christ becomes present whole and entire, God and man.[1]

Jesus extends his Incarnation to the Blessed Sacrament. All he did two thousand years ago in his natural life is prolonged for us in the

[1] Paul VI, Encyclical Letter *Mysterium Fidei* on the Holy Eucharist (1965), nos. 38–39.

Mode of Presence		Corresponding Biblical Verses		Biblical References
In the Church gathered together in the name of the Lord	• •	"As you did it to one of the least of these my brethren, you did it to me."	• •	(Mt 28:19) (Jn 20:22–23)
In the Church that prays; in the heart of the baptized	• •	"For where two or three are gathered in my name, there am I in the midst of them."	• •	(Jn 6:51)
In the Church that reads the Word of God	• •	"He who receives you receives me, and he who receives me receives him who sent me."	• •	(Mt 25:40)
In the Church that acts in charity	• •	"You are God's temple … God's spirit dwells in you." "Christ may dwell in your hearts through faith."	• •	(Jn 1:1; Heb 1:1–2; Rev 1:16)
In the Church that teaches	• •	"[Baptize] them in the name of the Father and of the Son and of the Holy Spirit." "Receive the Holy Spirit. If you forgive the sins of any, they are forgiven; if you retain the sins of any, they are retained."	• •	(Mt 18:20)
In the Church that celebrates the sacraments, through priests acting "in persona Christi"	• •	Jesus, Word of God incarnate, the spoken Word of God	• •	(Mt 10:40)
In the Eucharist	• •	"I am the living bread which came down from heaven."	• •	(1 Cor 3:16) (Eph 3:17)

sacramental mode. He wants to associate us with the mysteries of his own life. Scripture says, "Jesus Christ is the same yesterday and today and for ever" (Heb 13:8). In other words, he who became incarnate two thousand years ago is present today in the Eucharist in order to extend his salvation and the wonders of his love to our time. "For in this one mystery the entire supernatural order, with all its wealth and variety of wonders, is in a manner summed up and contained: . . . [the Eucharist] should be regarded as in a manner a continuation and extension of the Incarnation."[2]

He will come again one day in glory, "in the same way as you saw him go into heaven" (Acts 1:11). He was lifted up into a cloud (Acts 1:9). This cloud recalls the hidden presence of God in the midst of his people (cf. Ex 14:19; 16:10ff.) In the Eucharist, Jesus remains in the midst of his people, in a hidden manner, to guide and protect them. One day, he will come again in his glory. Then the cloud will recede and all will see him with their eyes . . .

In coming before the Blessed Sacrament, we go

to Bethlehem ("house of bread"): we have the same privilege as the shepherds and the Magi come from so far to prostrate themselves before the same Jesus that we can adore in the sacred Host . . . Let us not pay attention to the poor state of our soul, as Mary did not pay attention to the cold and miserable state of the stable. May our spirit, like that of Mary, find its joy in God its Savior!

to the temple: where Mary presented Jesus to the Father and consecrated him. Simeon's prophecy is realized anew: Jesus in the Eucharist is neglected and ignored. He is a stumbling block.

to Cana: just as Jesus changed water into wine, so, too, here in the Blessed Sacrament, he transforms our heart of stone into a heart of flesh, our deaths into life, and our failures into divine successes according to his words: "I will take out of your flesh the heart of stone and give you a heart of flesh" (Ezek 36:26). In the Blessed Sacrament, we drink from the source of living water that flows from his Heart.

to Jesus who preaches and heals: in the Blessed Sacrament, he heals us and leads us by his light. If we are ill, tired, he is the doctor. If we are

[2] Leo XIII, Encyclical Letter *Mirae Caritatis* (1902), no. 7.

sad, he gives us his joy. If we are under temptation, he gives us his peace, his strength. He awaits our response to his invitation of love, because "love is not loved!" (Saint Francis of Assisi). He who is rich makes himself poor to enrich us with his grace and clothe us with his glory each time we approach him in the Blessed Sacrament.

to the institution of the Eucharist: he gives us again this food for eternal life.

to Gethsemane: where he repeats: "Could you not watch one hour?" (Mk 14:37).

to the foot of the Cross: there, the good thief is forgiven. The Blessed Sacrament is divine mercy personified. He burns with the desire to forgive. The Eucharist is the fruit of the Passion of Christ. As wheat is ground to become bread, Jesus, in his Passion, is struck, beaten, pierced through to become our living bread. He awaits our total gift, in response to the gift of himself in the Eucharist.

to the Resurrection: we are in the presence of the Resurrected One, who repeats his words: "Peace be with you." In the Blessed Sacrament, the power of his Resurrection pours out on those who find themselves in his presence. He sends us off to bear witness to the marvels of his love.

∿

I Respond, by Faith, to His Love

The Shock of the Bodily Presence
of the Resurrected One

How are we to understand these words that travel down the centuries: "Where two or three are gathered in my name, there am I in the midst of them" (Mt 18:20)? He is there in the midst of them; he is present with a spiritual presence. In the uprightness of their hearts, the Word made flesh is present with a *spiritual presence* there where two or three are gathered in his name. But in the Eucharist, the Word made flesh is *present bodily*. Here a new dimension is added.

This bodily presence of Christ is not only when two or three are gathered in his name, so long as they are before the Blessed Sacrament. There is an important distinction to underline! By his bodily presence something like a *shock* is added to the spiritual presence of Christ.

For example, the evening in the Cenacle, the apostles are gripped by fear; they are afraid of persecution; and of whom are they thinking if not the Savior Jesus? They have no other horizon besides him; they are all preoccupied with him and with the persecution to be undergone for him. And then, all the doors being shut, Jesus appears in his body: "Peace be with you." Suddenly, something hits them, *it is a real shock, it is the bodily presence of Christ in their midst*; this is not just anything! The bodily presence of Christ is not going to diminish the intensity of his spiritual presence.

Another example: the apostle Thomas was not there when the resurrected Jesus appeared. Thomas the apostle says: "I will not believe unless I see." Thomas is a discouraged person. He had had so much con-

---

Cardinal Journet, *Entretien sur l'Eucharistie* (Saint-Maur: Parole et Silence), 51–56.

fidence in Christ that he said: "Lord, let us go and die with You." And then, everything fell apart, everything was broken; he is despairing. He is no braggart being bull-headed; no, he is crushed; "I will not believe unless I place my hand in his side." This is why Jesus comes toward him; if he had been bull-headed, Jesus would have left him to his certitude. And eight days later, Jesus comes again and says to Thomas: "Put your hand in the wound in my side and your finger in the wounds of my hands." Then, at the shock of the presence of Jesus, he falls on his knees: "My Lord and my God!"

In the resurrected Christ, there is at once a tangible certainty and the act of faith in his divinity. There is a tangible certainty: it is really he, it is his humanity that is there. So this is a historical fact, noted throughout history. The observation of the Christ's Resurrection is historical. He with whom the apostles shared their lives in Galilee, in Samaria, it is he who now is resurrected. But this historical observation of his humanity overflows, as it were, with the mystery of the glory of the resurrected Christ. Believing is necessary, believing in the divinity of Christ: "My Lord and my God!"

Some use the pretext of this language about the resurrected Christ to say that it is only a mystery and, consequently, that it was not historically manifest. But there is a historical root available, the witness of the apostles. During Christ's time of pilgrimage, it was no different: the apostles saw the humanity of Christ, but his divinity they had to believe. They had to ask for the same certainty of faith that we have to ask for today. The life of Christ, during the thirty-three years he lived in the midst of the world and the apostles, was the life of the Son of God. Consequently, he was the man whose divinity had to be believed in while grasping his humanity. And through his humanity, a kind of light made him shine in the midst of all the friends of God: "No one has spoken like this man."

So you can see how, at the Cenacle, the apostles suddenly felt the bodily presence of Christ; what richness! It is the same thing at Emmaus: Jesus speaks with them without making himself known; he tempers his glory. At Emmaus, if Christ had let out all the power of transfiguration in him, it would have been the end of the world. He himself, the disciples, and the whole world would have been transfigured. So when he appears, he is obliged to moderate the splendor of his divinity.

When we see him, it will be the transfiguration of the whole world. But even when he tempers his glory, the disciples at Emmaus divine that it is he, but they do not dare to ask him the question. They wait for a sign; it is really he who is present bodily, but not in order to continue his life of vulnerability. Something has changed in him. It is he himself in another state; so Jesus gives them a sign, the breaking of the bread. At that very moment, they have no more hesitation. They believe.

There is also the bodily presence of Jesus resurrected on the bank of the lake of Tiberias: they have fished all night and caught nothing. Then, toward morning, they notice Jesus on the shore. Immediately, the most intuitive of the apostles, the contemplative, he whom Jesus loves, says: "It is the Lord!" But he does not move; he has recognized him; he does not need to go to him because they have met through the heart. Saint Peter, the man of action, jumps immediately into the water; he never hesitates, Saint Peter, even if he is never the first to see! There again you have the appearance of Christ in the midst of them, and again it is a shock, the shock of the bodily presence of Christ in the midst of the apostles.

Do you see now what the bodily presence of the Word made flesh is going to signify for the bodily presence of Jesus in the tabernacle? That is what we have in the Eucharist.

And finally, we can meditate on the resurrection of Lazarus. At Bethany, the village of Martha and her sister, Mary, there was a sick man, Lazarus. This Mary was the one who anointed the Lord with perfume and wiped his feet with her hair. It was her brother, Lazarus, who was sick. Jesus had had to flee from Judea and go to the other side of the Jordan because his hour had not yet come; he smelled the persecution, the death that is near. So the two sisters sent to Jesus, saying: "Lord, he whom you love is ill." To this news, Jesus responded: "This illness is not unto death; it is for the glory of God, so that the Son of God may be glorified by means of it." Jesus loved Martha and her sister and Lazarus.

When he learned that this Lazarus was ill, he stayed two days longer in the place where he was; only then did he say to his disciples: "Let us go into Judea again." The disciples said to him: "Rabbi, the Jews

were but now seeking to stone you and you are going there again?"
There is a time for death and a time for life. Jesus wanted them to
understand this, so he added: "Our friend Lazarus has fallen asleep,
but I go to awake him out of sleep." The disciples said: "Lord, if he has
fallen asleep, he will recover." Jesus had spoken of his death, but they
thought he was speaking of sleep, of rest. So Jesus told them clearly:
"Lazarus is dead; and for your sake I am glad that I was not there, so
that you may believe." Then Jesus went to Lazarus. So Thomas, called
the Twin, said to his fellow disciples: "Let us also go, that we may die
with him." As I was telling you, Thomas was a generous man who
had put everything on Jesus, and everything fell apart. At his arrival,
Jesus found Lazarus entombed for four days already. Bethany is only
about fifteen furlongs away from Jerusalem. Many Jews had come to
Martha and Mary to console them concerning their brother. When
Martha learned of the arrival of Jesus, she went to meet him, while
Mary remained seated in the house. And Martha said to Jesus: "Lord,
if you had been here, my brother would not have died." If he had
been there, would he have been able to resist the prayers of Martha
and Mary? "If you had been here, my brother would not have died.
And even now I know that whatever you ask from God, God will give
you." With these words, she went to call her sister, Mary, and she said
to her quietly: "The Teacher is here and is calling for you." Mary,
at this news, rose quickly and went to him. Jesus had not yet entered
the village; he was at the place where Martha had met him. When the
Jews, who were with Mary in the house consoling her, saw her rise
quickly and go out, they followed her, thinking that she was going to
the tomb to weep there. When she came to the place where Jesus was,
as soon as she saw him, she fell at his feet and said to him: "Lord, if
you had been here, my brother would not have died" (cf. Jn 11).

Do you see now what the bodily presence of Jesus is? "If you had
been here . . ." There are, then, things he grants when we are gathered for and in the Eucharist and that he does not grant whenever two
or three are gathered in his name, where there is simply the spiritual
presence. The spiritual presence is an immense dimension, but there is
more; there is the bodily presence of the Word made flesh. The bodily
presence of Christ in glory is there in the most humble of our chapels,
waiting. And in a sense it remains true to say that he is there in agony

until the end of the world, in the heart of the tempests of history, and that we must not sleep during this time. Must the complaint still be made to us: "So, could you not watch with me one hour?" (Mt 26:40).

—Cardinal Journet

The Signs of the Covenant

Covenants in the Bible

After having meditated on the love of Jesus in the Eucharist and on his desire to be loved (cf. *first fifteen stages*), in this new phase, we follow some of the great biblical passages concerning the signs of the Covenant, or the sacraments. We will study how these passages are centered on the Eucharist and how we can be nourished from it through faith.

In these verses, find each one of the Persons of the Trinity at work in creation:

> In the beginning God created the heavens and the earth. The earth was without form and void, and darkness was upon the face of the deep; and the Spirit [wind] of God was moving over the face of the waters. And God said, "Let there be light"; and there was light. (Gen 1:1–3)

"God" is the Father; the "wind" indicates the Holy Spirit; "God said" indicates the Word, the speech of the Father (cf. Jn 1:1). God is not solitary, he is familial. He brings about the creation in order to share his life and joy.

The first story of creation (cf. Gen 1:1–2, 4) makes no claim to be a scientific text. This sacred text does not explain the "how" of creation, but the "why". Creation is presented as a dwelling that God carefully organizes. The numbered succession of days evokes a great liturgy that is realized in the Covenant of God with men. Days 1, 2, and 3 are similar to the exterior parts of a great dwelling (foundations, walls, frame of the roof). What is created during days 4, 5, and 6 is put in the interior of the dwelling. The story does not end with the creation of man and woman. On the seventh day, God "rests". The final end of creation, this day is the day of the Covenant when God comes to visit the first family with whom he wants to make a covenant.

Day 1: Light and darkness
Day 2: Firmament[1] (water from the heavens and from the earth)
Day 3: Land and vegetation
Day 4: Celestial bodies (sun, moon, stars)
Day 5: Birds, fish
Day 6: Animals and men/women (image of God)
Day 7: God's rest: Time of the Covenant

The Covenant, dwelling of God in the midst of his people: "And I will make my abode among you, and my soul shall not abhor you. And I will walk among you, and will be your God, and you shall be my people" (Lev 26:11–12). According to Leviticus 26, what is a covenant? How does a covenant involve God? How does it involve man? What is the difference between a contract and a covenant? What is given in a contract? In a covenant? For how long? Covenants involve the person, the heart, for life.

> God, infinitely perfect and blessed in himself, in a plan of sheer goodness freely created man to make him share in his own blessed life. For this reason, at every time and in every place, God draws close to man. He calls man to seek him, to know him, to love him with all his strength. He calls together all men, scattered and divided by sin, into the unity of his family, the Church. To accomplish this, when the fullness of time had come, God sent his Son as Redeemer and Savior. In his Son and through him, he invites men to become, in the Holy Spirit, his adopted children and thus heirs of his blessed life.[2]

Throughout the whole of sacred history, God comes to live with his people. He was present during the Exodus in the tent of meeting, then at Jerusalem in the temple of Solomon. He came to live among us by taking a body: "Consequently, when Christ came into the world, he said, 'Sacrifices and offerings you have not desired, but a body have you prepared for me'" (Heb 10:5). Or again: "The Word became flesh and dwelt among us" (Jn 1:14), literally: "He pitched his tent among us." At the end of his life on earth, the Heart of Jesus invents the Eucharist to continue to dwell in the midst of his people until the end

---

[1] The firmament represents the apparent "vault" of the sky, which was for the ancient Semites, a solid dome, holding back the waters above. Through its openings the flood will stream down (cf. Gen 7:11).

[2] CCC 1.

of the world because the Shepherd does not abandon his flock with the passing of time. John Paul II explained: "The Lord Jesus has pitched His tent among us and, from this His Eucharistic dwelling, He repeats to each man and each woman, 'Come to me, all you who labor and are overburdened, and I shall give you rest' (Mt 11:28)."[3]

Let us look more closely at the first five covenants in the Old Testament and the new and eternal Covenant sealed in the Eucharist, presented in the New Testament: "God said, 'Let us make man in our image, after our likeness. . . .' So God created man in his own image, in the image of God he created him; male and female he created them. And God blessed them, and God said to them, 'Be fruitful and multiply, and fill the earth and subdue it; and have dominion over the fish of the sea and over the birds of the air and over every living thing that moves upon the earth'" (Gen 1:26–28). Here we have the first covenant with a couple. The couple is called to cooperate with the plan of God in the gift of life. While reading the following texts, find what God promises in each of the covenants. With whom does God conclude them? A family (Adam and Eve), three families (Noah), a clan or tribe (Abraham), twelve tribes (Moses), an empire (David). Note the numerical progression of the persons implicated in each of the covenants. Toward what are we progressing?

> "But I will establish my covenant with you; and you shall come into the ark, you, your sons, your wife, and your sons' wives with you." (Gen 6:18)

> God said, "This is the sign of the covenant. . . . I set my bow in the cloud, and it shall be a sign of the covenant between me and the earth. When I bring clouds over the earth and the bow is seen in the clouds, I will remember my covenant which is between me and you and every living creature of all flesh; and the waters shall never again become a flood to destroy all flesh." (Gen 9:12–15)

> When Abram was ninety-nine years old, the LORD appeared to Abram, and said to him, "I am God Almighty; walk before me, and be blameless. . . ." Then Abram fell on his face; and God said to him, "Behold, my covenant is with you, and you shall be the father of a multitude

---

[3] John Paul II, Message for the 37th World Day of Prayer for Vocations, May 14, 2000.

of nations. No longer shall your name be Abram, but your name shall
be Abraham; for I have made you the father of a multitude of nations.
I will make you exceedingly fruitful; and I will make nations of you,
and kings shall come forth from you. And I will establish my covenant
between me and you and your descendants after you throughout their
generations for an everlasting covenant, to be God to you and to your
descendants after you. And I will give to you, and to your descendants
after you, the land of your sojournings, all the land of Canaan, for an
everlasting possession; and I will be their God." (Gen 17:1, 3–8)

The LORD said to Moses, "Write these words; in accordance with
these words I have made a covenant with you and with Israel." And
he was there with the LORD forty days and forty nights; he neither
ate bread nor drank water. And he wrote upon the tables the words
of the covenant, the ten commandments. (Ex 34:27–28)

God addresses David through the intermediary of the prophet Nathan:

"When your days are fulfilled and you lie down with your fathers,
I will raise up your offspring after you, who shall come forth from
your body, and I will establish his kingdom. He shall build a house
for my name, and I will establish the throne of his kingdom for ever.
I will be his father, and he shall be my son. . . . And your house and
your kingdom shall be made sure for ever before me; your throne
shall be established for ever." (2 Sam 7:12–14, 16)

This text presents the Covenant with David and his dynasty. As the
Jerusalem Bible notes, the prophecy is constructed around an opposition: it is not David who will make a *house* (a temple) for the Lord,
but it is the Lord who will make a *house* (a dynasty) for David.

Now as they were eating, Jesus took bread, and blessed, and broke it,
and gave it to the disciples and said, "Take, eat; this is my body." And
he took a chalice, and when he had given thanks he gave it to them,
saying, "Drink of it, all of you; for this is my blood of the covenant,
which is poured out for many for the forgiveness of sins." (Mt 26:
26–28)

With whom does God conclude the New Covenant? In the Old
Testament, God concluded covenants with his people. What do we
call the new people of God? How does this people, the Church, come
into being? The Church is the Body of Christ. As Pseudo-Jerome af-

firms, "The Eucharist makes the Church, and the Church makes the Eucharist."

Saint Augustine develops this idea: "This bread that you see on the altar, once sanctified by the Word of God, is the Body of Christ. This cup, or rather the drink it contains, once sanctified by the Word of God, is the Blood of Christ. Our Lord Jesus Christ wanted to bestow here his Body and Blood, which he shed for us in remission of sins. If you have received them well, you are yourself what you have received."[4] Consequently, "we have become not only Christians, but Christ himself."[5] "Christ is not in the head without being in the body, Christ is entirely in the head and in the body."[6]

> The Eucharist, as the sacrifice of the New Covenant, is the development and fulfillment of the covenant celebrated on Sinai when Moses poured half the blood of the sacrificial victims on the altar, the symbol of God, and half on the assembly of the children of Israel (cf. Ex 24:5–8). This "blood of the covenant" closely united God and man in a bond of solidarity. With the Eucharist the intimacy becomes total; the embrace between God and man reaches its apex. This is the fulfillment of that "new covenant" which Jeremiah had foretold (cf. 31:31–34): a pact in the spirit and in the heart, which the Letter to the Hebrews extols precisely by taking the prophet's oracle and linking it to Christ's one definitive sacrifice (cf. Heb 10:14–17).[7]

～

---

[4] Saint Augustine, sermon 227, 1; PL 38:1099.
[5] Saint Augustine, PL 35:1568.
[6] Saint Augustine, PL 35:1622.
[7] John Paul II, General Audience, "Eucharist Is Perfect Sacrifice of Praise", October 11, 2000.

The Signs of the Covenant

STAGE 17

The Memorial

The LORD said to Moses and Aaron in the land of Egypt, "This month shall be for you the beginning of months; it shall be the first month of the year for you. Tell all the congregation of Israel that on the tenth day of this month they shall take every man a lamb according to their fathers' houses, a lamb for a household. . . . This day shall be for you a memorial day, and you shall keep it as a feast to the LORD; throughout your generations you shall observe it as an ordinance for ever." (Ex 12:1–3, 14)

At each benediction of the Blessed Sacrament, the priest prays like this:

Lord Jesus Christ, you gave us the Eucharist as *the memorial of suffering and death.* May our worship of this sacrament of your body and blood help us to experience the salvation you won for us and the peace of the kingdom where you live with the Father and the Holy Spirit for ever and ever. Amen.

The Eucharist is the memorial of the suffering and death of Christ. In the Bible and the liturgy, the memorial is not only a memory or a place of memory as we hear it said today. The memorial comprises three distinct dimensions:

- First *it recalls the liberating action* of God for his people. "Remember this day, in which you came out from Egypt, out of the house of bondage, for by the strength of hand the LORD brought you out from this place" (Ex 13:3).

- Next, the memorial makes present and effective for his people what God has done in the past. Thus, each year, the people of Israel celebrated the Passover (cf. Ex 12:25–27), *making present the salvation of God* from the new forms of slavery suffered by Israel.

• Lastly, the memorial anticipates the Day of the Lord, that is, the total and definitive liberation from all evil, from all bondage, and from death, when at the end of time, all things will be subjected to God and he will be everything to everyone (cf. 1 Cor 15:28).

In the Bible, celebrating the Passover is remembering the wonders of God. In the verses from Saint Luke below, find first what belongs to the ancient rite (the Jewish Passover that Jesus celebrates in the Jewish tradition, the memorial of the God's liberation of his people). Then find what belongs to the new rite of the Christian Eucharist, the memorial of his Passion, celebrated at each Mass.

[The disciples] prepared the Passover. And when the hour came, he sat at table and the apostles with him. And he said to them, "I have earnestly desired to eat this Passover with you before I suffer; for I tell you I shall not eat it until it is fulfilled in the kingdom of God." And he took a chalice, and when he had given thanks he said, "Take this, and divide it among yourselves; for I tell you that from now on I shall not drink of the fruit of the vine until the kingdom of God comes."

And he took bread, and when he had given thanks he broke it and gave it to them, saying, "This is my body which is given for you. Do this in remembrance of me." And likewise the chalice after supper, saying, "This chalice which is poured out for you is the new covenant in my blood." (Lk 22:13–20)

The Jewish Passover was the memorial of God's action of liberation from the political slavery of Pharaoh. But Jesus came to free man from another form of slavery. Since it is not from political servitude (cf. Jn 6:15), what is this slavery of which man is at once victim and guilty? And what is its direct consequence for man? "The wages of sin is death" (Rom 6:23). The word "passover" recalls "passage". To what passage of the Jewish people does this refer? What is the Passover (the passage) of Jesus? And for us, what is our Passover? "If the Spirit of him who raised Jesus from the dead dwells in you, he who raised Christ Jesus from the dead will give life to your mortal bodies also through his Spirit who dwells in you" (Rom 8:11).

Thus, in prolonging the Jewish Passover, Jesus celebrates the new Passover that fully accomplishes what the old one could not achieve: "When Christ appeared as a high priest of the good things that have come, then through the greater and more perfect tent (not made with hands, that is, not of this creation) he entered once for all into the Holy Place, taking not the blood of goats and calves but his own blood, thus securing an eternal redemption" (Heb 9:11-12).

Jesus, celebrating his Passover, leaves us the Eucharist, the memorial of his Passion. In the verses of Saint Paul, find the three dimensions of the memorial celebrated at each Eucharist:

> For I received from the Lord what I also delivered to you, that the Lord Jesus on the night when he was betrayed took bread, and when he had given thanks, he broke it, and said, "This is my body which is for you. Do this in remembrance of me." In the same way also the chalice, after supper, saying, "This chalice is the new covenant in my blood. Do this, as often as you drink it, in remembrance of me." For as often as you eat this bread and drink the chalice, you proclaim the Lord's death until he comes. (1 Cor 11:23-26)

Through the Mass, the Church responds to the explicit request of Jesus, at the time of his Last Supper, to celebrate his Passover in his memory. The anamnesis (Greek for "memorial") proclaimed by the assembly just after the Consecration, recalls the three dimensions of the memorial precisely, according to the following traditional formulas:

> *The mystery of faith:* We proclaim your Death, O Lord, and profess your Resurrection, until you come again.

> *The mystery of faith:* When we eat this Bread and drink this Cup, we proclaim your Death, O Lord, until you come again.

> *The mystery of faith:* Save us, Savior of the world, for by your Cross and Resurrection you have set us free.

A remark on the Blood of Christ, shed upon those who approach the Eucharist in faith:

After having given the Decalogue as the foundation of the Covenant between God and the people, Moses sacrifices an animal. With the blood, he sprinkles one part on the altar from which God receives the offering and the other part on the people. The aim of this gesture is to confirm the Covenant: "And Moses took the blood and threw it upon the people, and said, 'Behold the blood of the covenant which the Lord has made with you in accordance with all these words'" (Ex 24:8). In Matthew 27:25 and in John 11:50, find the two Gospel passages where the Blood of Jesus is called upon the people so that all may live. What passages are these? The characters who call for the Blood of Christ upon themselves act with hate, ignorance, or jealousy. It is for this reason that Christ died for all. He came to save all sinners through the New Covenant in his Blood. The Blood spilled upon the Cross is made present in the Eucharist. "This is the chalice of my Blood . . . poured out . . . for many." Each time the Host is elevated or adored during the Mass, Jesus mystically sheds his Blood which saves, heals, and liberates upon all of mankind.

ANIMA CHRISTI

Soul of Christ, sanctify me.
Body of Christ, save me.
Blood of Christ, inebriate me.
Water from the side of Christ, wash me.
Passion of Christ, strengthen me.
O good Jesus, hear me.
Within Thy wounds, hide me.
Suffer me not to be separated from Thee.
From the malignant enemy defend me.
In the hour of my death call me.
And bid me to come to Thee,
That with Thy Saints I may praise Thee,
For ever and ever. Amen.[1]

---

[1] A traditional Catholic prayer dating back at least to the fourteenth century (perhaps Pope John XXII) and often attributed incorrectly to Saint Ignatius of Loyola.—TRANS.

The Signs of the Covenant

STAGE 18

The Holy Sacrifice of the Mass

The LORD said to Moses and Aaron in the land of Egypt, "This month shall be for you the beginning of months; it shall be the first month of the year for you. Tell all the congregation of Israel that on the tenth day of this month they shall take every man a lamb according to their fathers' houses, a lamb for a household. . . . Your lamb shall be without blemish, a male a year old; you shall take it from the sheep or from the goats; and you shall keep it until the fourteenth day of this month, when the whole assembly of the congregation of Israel shall kill their lambs in the evening. Then they shall take some of the blood, and put it on the two doorposts and the lintel of the houses in which they eat them. They shall eat the flesh that night, roasted; with unleavened bread and bitter herbs they shall eat it. . . . In this manner you shall eat it: your loins girded, your sandals on your feet, and your staff in your hand; and you shall eat it in haste. It is the LORD's Passover. For I will pass through the land of Egypt that night, and I will strike all the first-born in the land of Egypt, both man and beast; and on all the gods of Egypt I will execute judgments; I am the LORD. The blood shall be a sign for you, upon the houses where you are; and when I see the blood, I will pass over you, and no plague shall fall upon you to destroy you, when I strike the land of Egypt. This day shall be for you a memorial day, and you shall keep it as a feast to the LORD; throughout your generations you shall observe it as an ordinance for ever." (Ex 12:1–3, 5–8, 11–14)

In the Jewish calendar, the first month of the year is Nisan, which corresponds to March–April in our calendar. This is the month when the people of Israel celebrate their Passover. Starting with the text above, find the links between the Jewish Passover, the Passover of Jesus, and the Christian Passover, celebrated at each Mass and culminating at the Paschal Vigil.

Jewish Passover (Ex 12)	Passover of Jesus (Passion)	Christian Passover (Mass)
First month of the year (Nisan)	During the Jewish Passover	March-April: beginning of the Paschal season; new Paschal candle
Male yearling without blemish	Jesus, unstained victim (Heb 7:26), Paschal Lamb	In the sacred Host, it is the Lamb of God who takes away the sin of the world
Throat slit at twilight	Jesus expiring at the ninth hour	Paschal Vigil at twilight
Blood spilled on the lintels (protection against death)	Christ saves us by his blood (1 Jn 2:2)	The Blood of Christ shed in the Eucharist: "who eats my flesh and drinks my blood has eternal life" (Jn 6:54)
The blood is a sign (Ex 12:13)	The Cross of Jesus	The appearances of bread are a sign
Flesh roasted over a fire	Sufferings and sacrifice of Christ on the Cross	The Mass makes present the sacrifice of Christ
Your loins girded, your sandals on your feet: passage from slavery to freedom	Christ descends into death and opens the gates of heaven	The Eucharist is the sacrament of eternal life

The Passover of the Jews was at hand, and Jesus went up to Jerusalem. In the temple he found those who were selling oxen and sheep and pigeons, and the money-changers at their business. And making a whip of cords, he drove them all, with the sheep and oxen, out of the temple; and he poured out the coins of the money-changers and overturned their tables. And he told those who sold the pigeons, "Take these things away; you shall not make my Father's house a house of trade." His disciples remembered that it was written, "Zeal for your house will consume me." The Jews then said to him, "What sign have you to show us for doing this?" Jesus answered them, "Destroy this temple, and in three days I will raise it up." The Jews then said, "It has taken forty-six years to build this temple, and will you raise it up in three days?" But he spoke of the temple of his body. When therefore he was raised from the dead, his disciples remembered that he had said this; and they believed the Scripture and the word which Jesus had spoken. (Jn 2:13–22)

Jesus enters the temple for the Passover and drives away the animals that were sold for sacrifice. By this gesture, Jesus signifies that he is himself the true Lamb, who offers itself freely in sacrifice, accomplishing what the blood of the animals could not: "But when Christ appeared as a high priest of the good things that have come, then through the greater and more perfect tent (not made with hands, that is, not of this creation) he entered once for all into the Holy Place, taking not the blood of goats and calves but his own blood, thus securing an eternal redemption" (Heb 9:11–12).

"Destroy this temple, and in three days I will raise it up": the temple is the place where God dwells in the midst of his people. Of what temple is Jesus speaking? Here is the testimony of John the Baptist at the Jordan: "I saw the Spirit descend as a dove from heaven and remain on him" (Jn 1:32). At what time will this temple be destroyed and then raised up again? As wheat is ground to become bread, the Body of Jesus is whipped, thrashed, pierced by the spear and ground by hate, to become the living bread come down from heaven that gives life to the world (Jn 6:51). What then is the fruit of the Passion? How should we respond today to this prayer—"Zeal for your house will consume me"—in relation to the Eucharist, the Body of Christ that is given, and new temple (or house) of God among men?

"And he took bread, and when he had given thanks he broke it and gave it to them, saying, 'This is my body which is given for you. Do this in remembrance of me.' And likewise the chalice after supper, saying, 'This chalice which is poured out for you is the new covenant in my blood'" (Lk 22:19–20). This passage makes clear the sacrificial character of the Eucharist. What are the two verbs that Jesus uses to express the offering that he makes of his Body and Blood? These verbs must be understood in their literal sense. Given, that is, sacrificed; poured out, that is, shed unto death. "Body", in Semitic languages, recalls the person, with all he has done, said, and been throughout his life. "Blood" is the seat of life (cf. Gen 9:4). During the Last Supper, Jesus gives his blood separately from the body. This anticipates his death. In giving over his body and his blood, Jesus gives all he has, all he is, his life and his death. His offering is total. In commanding his apostles: "Do this in remembrance of me", Jesus makes of the Eucharistic celebration a sacrifice. The Mass is the unbloody re-presentation of the bloody sacrifice of Jesus on the Cross. It makes present and effective the fruit of redemption for the Church and for the world.

In the text below, Benedict XVI shows how the Mass is a sacrifice that saves the world. Find in this text the four great transformations worked by Christ. What is their source?

In their hearts, people always and everywhere have somehow expected a change, a transformation of the world. Here now is the central act of transformation that alone can truly renew the world: violence is transformed into love, and death into life. Since this act transmutes death into love, death as such is already conquered from within, the Resurrection is already present in it. Death is, so to speak, mortally wounded, so that it can no longer have the last word. To use an image well known to us today, this is like inducing nuclear fission in the very heart of being—the victory of love over hatred, the victory of love over death. Only this intimate explosion of good conquering evil can then trigger off the series of transformations that little by little will change the world. All other changes remain superficial and cannot save. For this reason we speak of redemption: what had to happen at the most intimate level has indeed happened, and we can enter into its dynamic. Jesus can distribute his Body, because he truly gives himself. This first fundamental transformation of violence into

love, of death into life, brings other changes in its wake. Bread and
wine become his Body and Blood. But it must not stop there; on the
contrary, the process of transformation must now gather momentum.
The Body and Blood of Christ are given to us so that we ourselves will
be transformed in our turn. We are to become the Body of Christ, his
own Flesh and Blood. We all eat the one bread, and this means that
we ourselves become one. In this way, adoration, as we said earlier,
becomes union. God no longer simply stands before us as the One
who is totally Other. He is within us, and we are in him. His dynamic
enters into us and then seeks to spread outward to others until it fills
the world, so that his love can truly become the dominant measure
of the world.[1]

A related question: Can we speak of several "offerings" of the redemptive sacrifice? "Melchizedek king of Salem brought out bread and
wine; he was priest of God Most High. And he blessed him and said,
'Blessed be Abram by God Most High, maker of heaven and earth'"
(Gen 14:18–19).

The word offering has two meanings. It can designate the sacrificial
rite that makes present for us the one Sacrifice. So each Mass celebrated throughout time in fidelity to the commandment called for by
Christ, "Do this in remembrance of me", is a new offering of his
sacrifice. And it can signify the sacrificial act of Christ offering himself "with loud cries and tears" and becoming "the source of eternal
salvation to all who obey him" (Heb 5:7, 9). And so all Masses refer
us back to the one redemptive Offering. The enveloping offering is
renewed, the enveloped offering remains unchanged.[2]

∽

---

[1] Benedict XVI, homily, World Youth Day, Cologne, Marienfeld, August 21, 2005.
[2] Cardinal Journet, *Le mystère de l'Eucharistie* (Paris: Pierre Téqui, 1981), 32–33.

The Signs of the Covenant

STAGE 19

The Paschal Lamb

[God] said, "Take your son, your only-begotten son Isaac, whom you love, and go to the land of Moriah, and offer him there as a burnt offering upon one of the mountains of which I shall tell you." So Abraham rose early in the morning, saddled his donkey, and took two of his young men with him, and his son Isaac; and . . . went to the place of which God had told him. . . . And Abraham took the wood of the burnt offering, and laid it on Isaac his son; and he took in his hand the fire and the knife. So they went both of them together. And Isaac said to his father Abraham, "My father!" And he said, "Here am I, my son." He said, "Behold, the fire and the wood; but where is the lamb for a burnt offering?" And Abraham said, "God will provide himself the lamb for a burnt offering, my son." So they went both of them together. When they came to the place of which God had told him, Abraham built an altar there, and laid the wood in order, and bound Isaac his son, and laid him on the altar, upon the wood.

Then Abraham put forth his hand, and took the knife to slay his son. But the angel of the LORD called to him from heaven, and said, "Abraham, Abraham!" And he said, "Here am I." He said, "Do not lay your hand on the lad or do anything to him; for now I know that you fear God, seeing you have not withheld your son, your only-begotten son, from me." And Abraham lifted up his eyes and looked, and behold, behind him was a ram, caught in a thicket by his horns; and Abraham went and took the ram, and offered it up as a burnt offering instead of his son. So Abraham called the name of that place The LORD will provide; as it is said to this day, "On the mount of the LORD it shall be provided."

And the angel of the LORD called to Abraham a second time from heaven, and said, "By myself I have sworn, says the LORD, because you have done this, and have not withheld your son, your only-begotten son, I will indeed bless you, and I will multiply your descendants as the stars of heaven and as the sand which is on the seashore. And your descendants shall possess the gate of their enemies, and by your descendants shall all the nations of the earth bless themselves, because you have obeyed my voice." (Gen 22:2–3, 6–18)

What is Isaac's dramatic question to his father Abraham? It is in fact the question that dwells in the heart of every man: What must be done to have eternal life? By what offering can I avoid death? Who will die in my place so that I may live? Isaac's question about the lamb that must be sacrificed finds no answer in the Old Testament, "for it is impossible that the blood of bulls and goats should take away sins" (Heb 10:4). Abraham responds mysteriously to Isaac: "God will provide." In other words, God will give the Lamb when the time is come.

"This took place in Bethany beyond the Jordan, where John was baptizing. . . . He saw Jesus coming toward him, and said, 'Behold, the Lamb of God, who takes away the sin of the world!' . . . John bore witness, 'I saw the Spirit descend as a dove from heaven and remain on him'" (Jn 1:28–29, 32). Thus it is John the Baptist who "answers" Isaac's great question—two thousand years later. He points out Jesus as the Lamb of God, who takes away the sin of the world. John the Baptist's term "behold" must be understood as the fulfillment of a hopeful expectation: "He is here at last."

"And when he came up out of the water, immediately he saw the heavens opened and the Spirit descending upon him like a dove; and a voice came from heaven, 'You are my beloved Son; with you I am well pleased'" (Mk 1:10–11). To evangelize is to announce the Good News. Jesus is the Good News. He alone can take away the sin of man and fill his heart. Thus John the Baptist is evangelized by God when he sees the Spirit descending upon Jesus and when he hears the Father point out the Son so that all may go to him. In his turn, John the Baptist will invite the crowds to follow Jesus the Christ, he who is the true Lamb, who will die for the sins of the world. This is the Father's evangelization, taken up by John the Baptist, the evangelization that we in turn must continue: announcing Jesus, he who comes to free us from sin and fill us with his life-giving Spirit.

The following passage brings out the link between "adoration" and "mission" with the verbs "look" and "say". In order to announce, it is first necessary to contemplate. "He *looked* at Jesus as he walked, and *said*, 'Behold, the Lamb of God!' The two disciples heard him say this, and they followed Jesus. Jesus turned, and saw them following, and said to them, 'What do you seek?' And they said to him, 'Rabbi' (which means Teacher), 'where are you staying?' He said to them, 'Come and see.' They came and saw where he was staying; and they stayed with him that day, for it was about the tenth hour" (Jn 1:36–39).

Thanks to John the Baptist's evangelization, two of his disciples follow Jesus. What question do they ask Jesus? As with Abraham's response to Isaac, Jesus' response will be understood later. He tells them only: "Come and see." In other words, you are going to see what you are looking for if you come follow me. Yet Saint John gives a major detail: it was about the tenth hour.

It was now about the sixth hour, and there was darkness over the whole land until the ninth hour. (Lk 23:44)

When they came to Jesus and saw that he was already dead, they did not break his legs. But one of the soldiers pierced his side with a spear, and at once there came out blood and water. (Jn 19:33–34)

Jesus is crucified at the sixth hour; he dies at the ninth. About the tenth hour, his Heart is pierced! This is where Jesus invites his disciples. He invites them to contemplate his Heart, this Heart which expresses the love of God, this Heart which, receiving hate, gives only love in response. The whole mystery of our God of love is revealed when Christ is nailed to the Cross with his open Heart, from which flows water and blood. It is the birth of the Church and the sacraments. It is the place of encounter between God and mankind. This encounter is made through the infinite mercy in the Heart of God revealed at the tenth hour.

Thus, the episode of the sacrifice of Isaac makes sense in light of the baptism of Jesus, which in turn makes sense in light of the open Heart of Christ on the Cross. Let us note other links between these three texts:

1. Mount Moriah, the place where Abraham goes to sacrifice Isaac, is in Jerusalem. "Then Solomon began to build the house of the Lᴏʀᴅ in Jerusalem on Mount Moriah, where the Lᴏʀᴅ had appeared to David his father" (2 Chron 3:1). In the center of the temple in Jerusalem was the "Holy of Holies", the place where God dwelled among his people. It was there that the people went to adore God. It was there that they offered sacrifices to ask forgiveness for their sins. It was at this same place that Jesus would be sacrificed, offering his life for the forgiveness of sins and revealing, through his pierced Heart, the love of God our Father.

2. Isaac carries the wood for the sacrifice in Genesis 22. He prefigures Christ, who will carry his Cross during his Passion.

3. The ram, sacrificed by Abraham in place of Isaac, is caught by his horns in a bush of thorns. What link can be found with Jesus on the Cross?

4. What does the following verse about Abraham's love for Isaac reveal? "Take your son, your only-begotten son Isaac, whom you love, and go to the land of Moriah, and offer him there as a burnt offering upon one of the mountains." What conclusion can be drawn about the Father's love for his Son Jesus, who will really be sacrificed and not spared, so that every person may live eternally? What can be deduced about God's love for us (cf. Jn 15:9)?

5. What sort of blessing does God promise Abraham because of his faith? What blessings will the Father grant to all generations who believe that Jesus died for their sins?

Thus, John the Baptist answers Isaac's question—"Where is the lamb for a burnt offering?"—by pointing out Jesus and declaring: "Behold, the Lamb of God who takes away the sin of the world." These words of the forerunner are taken up again by each priest at the elevation of the Host for the adoration of all. In the sacred Host, the Lamb of God takes away our sins by pouring out divine mercy on us and on the world. He comes to fill our heart with Holy Communion. Through Mass and adoration, the Lord gives his open Heart in the Eucharist. There, we draw abundantly from the living sources of salvation.

"The sacrifice of Christ and the sacrifice of the Eucharist are *one single sacrifice*" [CCC 1367]. Saint John Chrysostom put it well: "We always offer the same Lamb, not one today and another tomorrow, but always the same one. For this reason the sacrifice is always only one. . . . Even now we offer that victim who was once offered and who will never be consumed."[1]

Mother Marie-Thérèse Dubouché [1809–1863] wrote, when founding the Congregation of the Adoration of Reparation: "Human misery! The way is sought everywhere: we question science, read lengthy books, consult experience, observe, reflect, consider the creature in the physical and moral orders, all of this in search of life! And the principle of life is here, he is available to us, and we disdain him to go drink from all these streams that cannot quench our thirst! How sad it is to see men who move about in vain to discover the means of finding God, when they have him so close to them in this divine sacrament!"[2]

~

---

[1] John Paul II, Encyclical Letter *Ecclesia de Eucharistia* (2003), no. 12.

[2] Théodelinde Dubouché, *L'adoration au soleil de Dieu: Fragments spirituels*, ed. Sisters of the Adoration of Reparation, p. 40.

The Signs of the Covenant

Divine Mercy (Hosea)

The book of Hosea shows God's infinite mercy. The etymology of the Latin word for mercy, *misericordia*, contains two words: *miseria* (misery) and *cor* (heart). It is God who loves what is not lovable in man. Mankind's only hope, mercy, is the expression of God's love that comes to love and save what is wounded in man. What attracts God to man is not first of all his fine qualities or his virtues, but his wounds and his sin. Our good qualities are due to the new man, saved by grace. Our vices are due to the old man in us, not yet saved, but calling out for divine mercy.

God asks Hosea to take a prostitute for his wife. She continues her infidelities with her husband. Despite everything, Hosea remains faithful to her. By analogy, this story exalts the faithfulness of God, the Bridegroom, who never rejects his bride, Israel, despite her numerous infidelities. The marriage between God and his people is realized through the Covenant. So often the people will reject the Covenant with their God by worshipping other gods, the Baals. God reproaches his people for carrying on like Hosea's ungrateful bride by neglecting the Covenant and forgetting that the Covenant is the source of all goods and blessings. The first paragraph of the text sets out the list of the bride's infidelities and the just condemnation merited. We await the sentence, but instead God applies mercy. This is how God treats his children.

> "Plead with your mother, plead—for she is not my wife, and I am not her husband. . . . Therefore I will hedge up her way with thorns; and I will build a wall against her, so that she cannot find her paths. She shall pursue her lovers, but not overtake them; and she shall seek

them, but shall not find them. Then she shall say, 'I will go and return to my first husband, for it was better with me then than now.' And she did not know that it was I who gave her the grain, the wine, and the oil, and who lavished upon her silver and gold which they used for Baal. Therefore I will take back my grain in its time, and my wine in its season; and I will take away my wool and my flax, which were to cover her nakedness. Now I will uncover her lewdness in the sight of her lovers, and no one shall rescue her out of my hand. And I will put an end to all her mirth, her feasts, her new moons, her sabbaths, and all her appointed feasts. And I will lay waste her vines and her fig trees, of which she said, 'These are my hire, which my lovers have given me.' I will make them a forest, and the beasts of the field shall devour them. And I will punish her for the feast days of the Baals when she burned incense to them and decked herself with her ring and jewelry, and went after her lovers, and forgot me, says the Lord.

"*Therefore*, behold, I will allure her, and bring her into the wilderness, and speak tenderly to her. And there I will give her her vineyards, and make the Valley of Achor a door of hope. And there she shall answer as in the days of her youth, as at the time when she came out of the land of Egypt. And in that day, says the Lord, you will call me, 'My husband,' and no longer will you call me, 'My Baal.' For I will remove the names of the Baals from her mouth, and they shall be mentioned by name no more. And I will make for you a covenant on that day with the beasts of the field, the birds of the air, and the creeping things of the ground; and I will abolish the bow, the sword, and war from the land; and I will make you lie down in safety. And I will espouse you for ever; I will espouse you in righteousness and in justice, in steadfast love, and in mercy." (Hos 2:2, 6–19)

The passage above is structured around the adverb "therefore". Rather than justly condemning, God gives proof of his mercy. Unceasingly, despite everything, he continues to love his bride, his people with whom he sealed a covenant in the desert. God's faithfulness to his people rests, not on Israel's response, but on God's promise. This is how Jesus acts in the Eucharist, the sacrament of the New Covenant. Whatever our infidelities, our ingratitude, our coldness, the Heart of Jesus would never be able to condemn, but continues to pursue us with his mercy. "How can I give you up, O Ephraim! How can I hand

Mercy in Hosea	Mercy in the Eucharist (according to Saint Peter Julian Eymard)
I will allure her	He hides his divine and bodily glory so as not to dazzle and blind you. He veils his majesty so that you might dare go to him and speak to him as a friend speaks to his friend; he even tempers the ardor of his Heart and his love for you, because you could not withstand its strength and tenderness; he lets you see only that goodness which leaks out and escapes through the sacred species, like rays of the sun through a light cloud.[1]
I will bring her into the wilderness	Faith is the pure act of the spirit, freed from the senses. For here (before the Blessed Sacrament), the senses are of no use; they have no part to play. It is the only mystery of Jesus Christ where the senses must be absolutely still. In all the others, in the Incarnation, the redemption, the senses see a child God, a dying God. Here, there is nothing but an impenetrable cloud for them. Faith alone must act; it is the kingdom of faith. This cloud asks of us a very meritorious sacrifice, the sacrifice of our reason and of our mind. It is necessary to believe as though against the witness of the senses, against ordinary laws of beings, against one's own experience. It is necessary to believe on the basis of the simple word of Jesus Christ; there is only one question to ask: "Who is there?" "I am", answers Jesus Christ. Let us fall to the ground and adore![2]
I will speak tenderly to her; I will give her vineyards; I will be a door of hope	Our Lord, to maintain and make more effective in us the hope of heaven, to make us patiently await heaven and glory and lead us there, created the beautiful heaven of the Eucharist. For the Eucharist is a beautiful heaven, heaven begun. Is it not Jesus in glory coming from heaven to "earth" and bringing heaven with him? He comes and remains bodily in our hearts as long as the Sacrament lasts; then, the species having been destroyed, he goes up again to heaven, but remains in us through his grace and through his loving presence.... The Eucharist is the ladder, not of Jacob, but of Jesus, who mounts to heaven and descends continually for us. He is in an unceasing movement toward us.[3]

[1] Saint Peter Julian Eymard, *Adorer en esprit et vérité* (Paris: F.-X. de Guibert, 2009), 37.
[2] Ibid., 101–2.
[3] Ibid., 261.

I will answer as in the days of her youth	He is there, this Heart, to defend us from our enemies, as a mother, in order to save her child from a danger, holds him against her heart so that the child may not be reached without reaching the mother. And, Jesus tells us, even if a mother could forget her child, I will never abandon you.[4]
You will call me "my husband"	Jesus will have two thrones, one of glory in heaven, another of sweetness and goodness on earth; two courts: the celestial and triumphant court and the court of his redeemed ones here below. In what state does Jesus remain with us? In a state of change, from one time to another? No, rather in a state of perseverance. He stays forever until the end of the world.[5]
I will remove the names of the Baals from your mouth	"It is not only that Penance leads to the Eucharist, but that the Eucharist also leads to Penance."[6]
I will abolish the bow, the sword, war	Jesus said to Faustina: "Mankind will not find Peace so long as it does not turn with confidence to my Mercy."[7] "The throne of Mercy is the Tabernacle."[8]
I will make for you a covenant; I will espouse you forever in steadfast love and mercy	We like to penetrate a veiled truth, to discover a hidden treasure, to overcome a difficulty. Thus the faithful soul, in the presence of the Eucharistic veil, seeks her Lord, like Magdalen at the tomb: her desire grows, she calls him like the bride of the Canticle, she pleases herself in giving him all beauties, in decorating him with all glories. The Eucharist is for her what God is for the blessed, a truth, a beauty ever ancient, ever new, that one never wearies of contemplating, of penetrating. Only our Lord's wisdom and goodness could invent the Eucharistic veil.[9]

[4] Ibid., 257.
[5] Ibid., 53.
[6] John Paul II, Apostolic Letter *Dominicae Cenae* (1980), no. 7.
[7] Saint Faustina, *Petit journal*, 300.
[8] Ibid., 1484.
[9] Saint Peter-Julian Eymard, *Adorer en esprit et vérité*, 102.

you over, O Israel! . . . My heart recoils within me, my compassion grows warm and tender" (Hos 11:8).

God's mercy shows itself in the book of Hosea through the words noted in the left-hand column. The right-hand column sets out how this same mercy is realized today in the Eucharist (see the table on the preceding pages).

When leaving his parish, a holy priest, whose difficult character his parishioners knew well, gave this account: "All you have loved in me comes from the time I spent in front of the Blessed Sacrament. All that has disappointed you in me comes from the time I should have spent in front of the Blessed Sacrament."

∼

The Signs of the Covenant

Parable of the Marriage Feast
Baptism and Confession

"Have you never read in the Scriptures: 'The very stone which the builders rejected has become the cornerstone; this was the Lord's doing, and it is marvelous in our eyes'? Therefore I tell you, the kingdom of God will be taken away from you and given to a nation producing the fruits of it". . . . And again Jesus spoke to them in parables, saying, "The kingdom of heaven may be compared to a king who gave a marriage feast for his son, and sent his servants to call those who were invited to the marriage feast; but they would not come. Again he sent other servants, saying, 'Tell those who are invited, Behold, I have made ready my dinner, my oxen and my fat calves are killed, and everything is ready; come to the marriage feast.' But they made light of it and went off, one to his farm, another to his business, while the rest seized his servants, treated them shamefully, and killed them. The king was angry, and he sent his troops and destroyed those murderers and burned their city. Then he said to his servants, 'The wedding is ready, but those invited were not worthy. Go therefore to the streets, and invite to the marriage feast as many as you find.' And those servants went out into the streets and gathered all whom they found, both bad and good; so the wedding hall was filled with guests. But when the king came in to look at the guests, he saw there a man who had no wedding garment; and he said to him, 'Friend, how did you get in here without a wedding garment?' And he was speechless. Then the king said to the attendants, 'Bind him hand and foot, and cast him into the outer darkness, where there will be weeping and gnashing of teeth.' For many are called, but few are chosen." (Mt 21:42–43; 22:1–14)

In Matthew 21:42, Jesus cites the passage of Psalm 118 (22–24) about the stone rejected by the builders but chosen by God. What parable immediately follows? Why does the evangelist illustrate the passage of Psalm 118 with the wedding banquet?

Those invited show themselves to be unworthy to participate in the wedding feast of the King's Son because they put their priorities elsewhere. In finding excuses for turning down the invitation, those invited show contempt for the man who invited them as well as for the prepared banquet. For us today, what is the wedding meal? In this wedding, who is the bridegroom? Who is the bride? What food do we receive? How do we respond to this invitation?

One of the guests is not wearing the wedding attire. What does this wedding garment represent? By the sacrament of baptism, the baptized is dressed in the wedding garment and receives the dignity of a child of God. While putting on the white garment, the priest says to the newly baptized: "You have become a new creation, and have clothed yourself in Christ. Receive this baptismal garment and bring it unstained to the judgment seat of our Lord Jesus Christ so that you may have everlasting life." The soul of the baptized becomes the bride, chosen by Christ, who is the spouse. The wedding is inaugurated by baptism. The wedding is consummated by the Eucharist. Thus baptism and Eucharist seal the covenant between the soul and Jesus for eternal life.

He who has not put on the garment at the feast is excluded from it: "Bind him hand and foot, and cast him into the outer darkness." By baptism, we are uprooted from original sin and freed from the power of the demon. The priest makes this prayer of exorcism: "Almighty God, . . . your Son died and rose again to save us. By his victory over sin and death, bring this child out of the power of darkness." Later, the baptized receives the light of Christ with this warning: "Receive the light of Christ. . . . This child . . . has been enlightened by Christ. He is to walk always as a child of light."

Nevertheless the new life received at baptism "has not abolished the frailty and weakness of human nature, nor the inclination to sin that tradition calls *concupiscence*" (CCC 1426).

Saint Paul expressed his interior combat between good and evil like thus: "For I do not do the good I want, but the evil I do not want is what I do" (Rom 7:19). Saint John reminds us that we are all sinners: "If we say we have not sinned, we make him a liar, and his word is not in us. My little children, I am writing this to you so that you may not sin; but if any one does sin, we have an advocate with the Father, Jesus Christ the righteous" (1 Jn 1:10—2:1). Recognizing that man would sin despite his baptism and despite the light of the Word of God, Jesus instituted in his mercy the sacrament of confession or reconciliation for "all sinful members of his Church: above all for those who, since Baptism, have fallen into grave sin, and have thus lost their baptismal grace and wounded ecclesial communion" (CCC 1446). The Resurrected One, conqueror of sin and death, said to his apostles, his first priests: "Peace be with you. . . . Receive the Holy Spirit. If you forgive the sins of any, they are forgiven" (Jn 20:21–23).

Being excluded from the feast means passing up the grace that the feast is ordered to give. In our Eucharistic interpretation, this is equivalent to not receiving the grace that the sacrament of the Eucharist is ordered to transmit. In other words, if someone communicates in a state of grave sin without first having been purified in the sacrament of reconciliation, the Eucharist will not bear the desired fruit. On the contrary, his Communion will be sterile. "Communicating without being in communion" could only hurt his incorporation into the Church. How miserable this is! This is why the Church asks believers to confess once a year at a minimum, but strongly encourages frequent confession with individual absolution, to enable approaching the sacrament of the Eucharist worthily, following the words of Saint Paul: "Let a man examine himself, and so eat of the bread and drink of the cup" (1 Cor 11:28). In the sacrament of confession, we of course confess our sins by admitting them according to number and kind, but above all we confess the love of God, conqueror of our sins! Divine mercy finds its source in the Eucharist but transmits itself in a unique way through reconciliation. John Paul II shows the intimate link between the sacrament of reconciliation or penance and the Eucharist.

"Let a man examine himself, and so eat of the bread and drink of the cup." This call by the Apostle indicates at least indirectly the close link between the Eucharist and Penance. Indeed, if the first word of Christ's teaching, the first phrase of the Gospel Good News, was "Repent, and believe in the gospel" (*metanoeite*), the Sacrament of the Passion, Cross and Resurrection seems to strengthen and consolidate in an altogether special way this call in our souls. The Eucharist and Penance thus become in a sense two closely connected dimensions of authentic life in accordance with the spirit of the Gospel, of truly Christian life. The Christ who calls to the Eucharistic banquet is always the same Christ who exhorts us to penance and repeats his "Repent." Without this constant ever renewed endeavor for conversion, partaking of the Eucharist would lack its full redeeming effectiveness and there would be a loss or at least a weakening of the special readiness to offer God the spiritual sacrifice in which our sharing in the priesthood of Christ is expressed in an essential and universal manner. In Christ, priesthood is linked with his Sacrifice, his self-giving to the Father; and, precisely because it is without limit, that self-giving gives rise in us human beings subject to numerous limitations to the need to turn to God in an ever more mature way and with a constant, ever more profound, conversion.[1]

Let us welcome divine mercy as often as possible through the sacrament of reconciliation. This sacrament deploys in the soul not only God's forgiveness but also interior healing and the strength to fight against the soul's imperfections. It helps us to love God and our neighbor better. Above all it reveals to us the true face of the Father, the face of mercy and tenderness.

Many priests who have set up perpetual adoration in their parish testify to a growing demand for the sacrament of reconciliation as a fruit of Eucharistic adoration. The growth is not only in quantity but also in quality. One cannot stay before the Blessed Sacrament without the light of Christ profoundly illuminating the soul and enlightening the conscience.

Unless the LORD builds the house, those who build it labor in vain. Unless the LORD watches over the city, the watchman stays awake in vain. (Ps 127:1)

---

[1] John Paul II, Encyclical Letter *Redemptor Hominis* (1979), no. 20.

STAGE 22

Marriage in the Bible

The man gave names to all cattle, and to the birds of the air, and to every beast of the field; but for the man there was not found a helper fit for him. So the LORD God caused a deep sleep to fall upon the man, and while he slept took one of his ribs and closed up its place with flesh; and the rib which the LORD God had taken from the man he made into a woman and brought her to the man. Then the man said, "This at last is bone of my bones and flesh of my flesh; she shall be called Woman, because she was taken out of Man." Therefore a man leaves his father and his mother and clings to his wife, and they become one flesh. (Gen 2:20–24)

This passage from the second story of creation recalls the "day that the LORD God made the earth and the heavens" (Gen 2:4). The two stories of creation (Gen 1 and 2) are complementary; each sheds a unique light on man, on what he must do, where he comes from, and where he is going. Genesis does not claim to give a scientific explanation of the origin of the world; rather, it speaks to us about man, God, his love, and the work of God so that man might live with him forever. With regard to the biblical texts that precede Abraham, we should avoid two extreme positions: that which claims that all that is contained in the biblical texts must be read as modern scientific descriptions AND that which, on the contrary, claims that these texts are but a series of tales or legends devoid of historical ties. No, the first chapters of Genesis do not evoke historical facts, even though they are told with ancient images in a Semitic language more than three thousand years old. The sacred authors were looking, not for scientific truth, but for the profound truth about man and God.

At issue here is marriage between the first man and the first woman. The book of Genesis reminds us that this natural marriage is not a human invention. It is the first covenant sealed by God. The two are now one! God wanted this to be so and not otherwise. Behind this first marriage, another covenant emerges throughout revelation: that between God, who is the Bridegroom, and mankind, who is the bride. All the vocabulary of the Bible is nuptial. Scripture describes a series of covenants (cf. *Stage 16*) that lead up to the great Covenant, new and eternal, that is fulfilled in Jesus Christ. The Old Testament (Covenant) gives way to the New Testament (New Covenant).

The Covenant between God and mankind is eternally sealed when Jesus gives his body to his Bride. On the Cross, he, the Bridegroom, hands over his body to the Church, the chosen Bride. Just as Eve is taken from the side of Adam, so too, on the Cross, *the Church is born from the open side of Christ*, from which flows water and blood. About the pierced side of Christ, Saint Ambrose said: "It is now that the Church is founded, now that she is formed, now that she appears, now that she is created."[1] Likewise, Adam's mysterious sleep prefigures Christ's death on the Cross before his glorious Resurrection. Through his Incarnation, Jesus is united to all mankind. Through his suffering, Jesus saves men: he makes of them children of God. We become his people, acquired at great price: "taking . . . his own blood, thus securing an eternal redemption" (Heb 9:12, cf. 1 Pet 2:9).

The sacrament of marriage possesses the particularity among the other sacraments of sanctifying a natural reality that existed before the coming of Christ. In the natural love of man and woman God put an image of his faithful love for men. Even though sin has come and darkened the consciousness of what a true love implies, the spouses are naturally called to a reciprocal and indissoluble gift of their person. This reality of natural marriage has received a new dimension through the coming of Christ, who not only restored the initial order of creation but, in handing himself over, has loved the Church as her only Bridegroom. So that Christian marriage is truly the sign of the New Covenant between God and men, and it can only be this sign if it does not lie about the reality that it designates: the union between Christ and the Church is indissoluble. This is the foundation of the

[1] Saint Ambrose, *Sur saint Luc*, II, 87; PL 15:1585, (Paris: Éditions du Cerf, 1958).

sacrament of marriage and what Christian spouses bear witness to for the world. "What therefore God has joined together, let no man put asunder" (Mt 19:6): in taking this commandment of Christ seriously, the Church reaffirms its mystery and calls Christians to live from it in the sacrament that makes it manifest, sure that God has provided in it an irreplaceable means of sanctification.[2]

Pharisees came up and in order to test him asked, "Is it lawful for a man to divorce his wife?" He answered them, "What did Moses command you?" They said, "Moses allowed a man to write a certificate of divorce, and to put her away." But Jesus said to them, "For your hardness of heart he wrote you this commandment. But from the beginning of creation, 'God made them male and female.' 'For this reason a man shall leave his father and mother and be joined to his wife, and the two shall become one flesh.' So they are no longer two but one flesh. What therefore God has joined together, let not man put asunder." (Mk 10:2–9)

Jesus is asked to clarify himself on the thorny question of the indissolubility of marriage. First Jesus recalls a prescription of Moses authorizing divorce under certain conditions. But he recalls that at the time of Moses, man did not have access to the fullness of grace and truth. "For the law was given through Moses; grace and truth came through Jesus Christ" (Jn 1:17). This allowed for a tolerance about divorce. From now on, the presence of Jesus in the heart of his Church is the source of all grace. He promises to give the necessary help to those who ask it of him. It is by prayer and conversion that we obtain the graces to stay fast in love, to learn to forgive, to achieve sanctity in doing the will of God to the very end.

Jesus thus recalls that marriage, according to the plan of God, is indissoluble: "What therefore God has joined together, let not man put asunder." Some ask why the Church does not want to bless a new union between two people who are seeking to rebuild their lives after the failure of their marriages. One might ask oneself why priests do not show more compassion or mercy, since Jesus forgave all sins and since the priest is there to give divine mercy freely. These biblical texts show

[2] Brother Emmanuel Perrier, O.P., for Liberté-Politique.com; cf. CCC 1601ff.; Vatican Council II, *Gaudium et spes* (1965), nos. 47ff.; Apostolic Exhortation *Familiaris consortio* (1981), nos. 11ff., 20 on indissolubility.

that Jesus speaks of marriage in another register. Christ united himself
to humanity in an indissoluble way in an eternal marriage by dying on
the Cross. Sacramental marriage is sealed in the absolutely indissoluble
covenant of Christ with his Church. Saint Paul writes: "Neither death,
nor life, . . . nor things present, nor things to come, . . . nor anything
else in all creation, will be able to separate us from the love of God in
Christ Jesus our Lord" (Rom 8:38–39).

To conclude, let us listen to Saint Paul speaking to us about the
Church, Body of Christ, and marriage:

> Be subject to one another out of reverence for Christ. Wives, be sub-
> ject to your husbands, as to the Lord. For the husband is the head of
> the wife as Christ is the head of the Church, his body, and is himself
> its Savior. As the Church is subject to Christ, so let wives also be
> subject in everything to their husbands. Husbands, love your wives,
> as Christ loved the Church and gave himself up for her, that he might
> sanctify her, having cleansed her by the washing of water with the
> word, that he might present the Church to himself in splendor, with-
> out spot or wrinkle or any such thing, that she might be holy and
> without blemish. Even so husbands should love their wives as their
> own bodies. He who loves his wife loves himself. For no man ever
> hates his own flesh, but nourishes and cherishes it, as Christ does the
> Church, because we are members of his body. "For this reason a man
> shall leave his father and mother and be joined to his wife, and the
> two shall become one flesh." This is a great mystery, and I mean in
> reference to Christ and the Church. (Eph 5:21–32)

The submission of which Saint Paul speaks in the text is not a kind
of servility or abasement of one partner in relation to the other. It recalls the spirit of charity and service that must animate every Christian.
Find what Saint Paul asks of the woman, then of the man. The mutual
requirements are of the order of total gift. Find the link between the
sacrament of marriage and the marriage of Christ with his Church.

～

STAGE 23

The Eucharist Makes the Church
Incorporation into the Church
Pharaoh's Dream Interpreted by Joseph

Then Pharaoh said to Joseph, "Behold, in my dream I was standing on the banks of the Nile; . . . I also saw in my dream seven ears growing on one stalk, full and good; and seven ears, withered, thin, and blighted by the east wind, sprouted after them, and the thin ears swallowed up the seven good ears." . . . Joseph said to Pharaoh, . . . "God has revealed to Pharaoh what he is about to do. . . . The seven good ears are seven years [of plenty] . . . the seven empty ears blighted by the east wind are also seven years of famine [which will follow]. . . . Let Pharaoh proceed to appoint overseers over the land, and take the fifth part of the produce of the land of Egypt during the seven plenteous years. And let them gather all the food of these good years that are coming, and lay up grain . . . for food in the cities, and let them keep it. That food shall be a reserve for the land against the seven years of famine which are to befall the land of Egypt, so that the land may not perish through the famine." (Gen 41:17–36)

In this text we can see a prefiguration of the Eucharistic Sacrifice: the seven years of plenty in Egypt can be compared to the abundance of graces obtained by Jesus during his work of redemption. On the Cross, Christ obtained all the graces necessary for the salvation of all men, without exception, of all places and all times. This is prefigured by the Egyptian storehouses that contain the wheat necessary for the survival of Egypt and the neighboring nations for the years of famine. During the years of famine, the nations came to Egypt to buy their food. Likewise, in coming to Mass today, we go and draw from the abundance of graces obtained by Jesus on the Cross. In instituting the sacrament of the Eucharist, Jesus anticipates and integrates the sacrifice of the Cross and the victory of the Resurrection. Thus, the Eucharist celebrated (the Mass) and contemplated (adoration within and outside of Mass) transmits all the graces necessary for our sanctification and the salvation of the world. The Eucharist celebrated and adored makes us *contemporaries* of the work of redemption. Through the Mass, we draw from the living fonts of salvation, as the Council affirms:

> The Most Blessed Eucharist contains the entire spiritual [bounty] of the Church, that is, Christ himself, our Pasch and Living Bread, whose flesh, which lives and creates life through the Holy Spirit, gives life to men.[1]

> The foundation and wellspring [of the Church] is the whole *Triduum paschale*, but this is as it were gathered up, foreshadowed and "concentrated" for ever in the gift of the Eucharist. In this gift, Jesus Christ entrusted to his Church the perennial making present of the paschal mystery. With it he brought about a mysterious "oneness in time" between that *Triduum* and the passage of the centuries.[2]

Here now are a few reminders about the nature of the Church, the universal sacrament of salvation, and about our incorporation into her through faith and the seven sacraments.

> The Lord Jesus, the only Savior, did not only establish a simple community of disciples, but constituted the Church as a *salvific mystery*: he himself is in the Church and the Church is in him. . . . Therefore the fullness of Christ's salvific mystery belongs also to the Church, inseparably united to her Lord. Indeed, Jesus Christ continues his presence and his work of salvation in the Church and by means of the Church . . . , which is his body. . . . And thus, just as the head and the members of a living body, though not identical, are inseparable, so too Christ and the Church can neither be confused nor separated, and constitute a single "whole Christ".[3]

What is the "whole Christ"? The Church is the Body of Christ. Christ is the Head of it, we his members. Through faith in Jesus Christ, the divine life circulates from the Head to the members of the Body. This divine life flows from the redemption.

[1] Vatican Council II, Decree *Presbyterorum ordinis* (1965), no. 5.
[2] John Paul II, Encyclical Letter *Ecclesia de Eucharistia* (2003), no. 5.
[3] Joseph Ratzinger, Declaration *Dominus Iesus* (2000), no. 16.

Above all else, it must be *firmly believed* that "the Church, a pilgrim now on earth, is necessary for salvation: the one Christ is the mediator and the way of salvation; he is present to us in his body which is the Church. He himself explicitly asserted the necessity of faith and baptism (cf. Mk 16:16; Jn 3:5), and thereby affirmed at the same time the necessity of the Church which men enter through baptism as through a door."[4]

In this passage, what are the ties between the Church and salvation? What are the two conditions for being incorporated into the Church, the Body of Christ?

The Church is "the universal sacrament of salvation", since, united always in a mysterious way to the Savior Jesus Christ, her Head, and subordinated to him, she has, in God's plan, an indispensable relationship with the salvation of every human being. For those who are not formally and visibly members of the Church, salvation in Christ is accessible by virtue of a grace which, while having a mysterious relationship to the Church, does not make them formally part of the Church, but enlightens them in a way which is accommodated to their spiritual and material situation. This grace comes from Christ; it is the fruit of his sacrifice and is communicated by the Holy Spirit"; it has a relationship with the Church.[5]

It is in the Mass, then, celebrated on all the altars of the world, that the grace of redemption is made present. This grace is poured out first upon those who participate in the Eucharist, but also, more broadly, upon all men of goodwill.

With respect to the *way* in which the salvific grace of God—which is always given by means of Christ in the Spirit and has a mysterious relationship to the Church—comes to individual non-Christians, the Second Vatican Council limited itself to the statement that God bestows it "in ways known to himself".[6]

"The bread which I shall give for the life of the world is my flesh" (Jn 6:51). The Eucharist is the spiritual sun of the world. As the sun

---

[4] Ibid., no. 20; quotation from Vatican Council II, Dogmatic Constitution *Lumen gentium* (1964), no. 14.

[5] Ibid.; quotation from John Paul II, Encyclical Letter *Redemptoris missio* (1990), no. 10.

[6] Ibid., no. 21; quotation from Vatican Council II, Decree *Ad gentes* (1975), no. 7.

gives life to nature through its heat and light, the Eucharist gives divine life to our souls and its spiritual light to our world. "The world could live without the sun, but not without the Holy Mass" (Saint Padre Pio).

"The Church draws her life from Christ in the Eucharist; by him she is fed and by him she is enlightened."[7] The incorporation into the Church sealed at baptism is extended by virtue of the following sacraments: confirmation, sacramental confession, matrimony, anointing of the sick, Holy Orders. But above all, by sacramental Communion. Let us recall the three distinct dimensions of the Eucharist: the Holy Sacrifice of the Mass, Holy Communion, and adoration outside of Mass (cf. *Stage 1*). Through sacramental Communion, the Lord weds the soul that he comes to visit in giving himself to her: "Blessed are those who are invited to the marriage supper of the Lamb" (Rev 19:9). "Take, eat; this is my body" (Mt 26:26); "He who eats my flesh and drinks my blood abides in me, and I in him" (Jn 6:56).

> Communion is the complete development, the blooming of the Incarnation. The Body of Jesus Christ thus unites itself to our body, his soul to our soul, and his divinity hovers over both. Our body is, as it were, inserted within the Body of our Lord. . . . Our body takes strength, grace, integrity, morals from his. Let us then leave our body to be reformed in this divine mold and germinate in him for glory. But the soul? Jesus Christ goes directly to our soul. He says to her: "I want to wed you forever." Above all, the soul is the object Jesus is aiming for in us. The body is but an antechamber: it is the first to be honored, yet our Lord only passes through it. The soul receives Jesus and transmits his divine life: she is as though lost within our Lord.[8]

The two following passages clarify the extent to which sacramental Communion strengthens incorporation into Christ, which begins with baptism and faith. What are the fruits of sacramental Communion evoked by John Paul II?

> Incorporation into Christ, which is brought about by Baptism, is constantly renewed and consolidated by sharing in the Eucharistic Sacrifice, especially by that full sharing which takes place in sacramental

---

[7] John Paul II, *Ecclesia de Eucharistia*, no. 6.

[8] Saint Peter Julian Eymard, *La Divine Eucharistie*, 2nd series, 15th ed. (Paris: Desclée de Brouwer, 1922), 146.

communion. We can say not only that *each of us receives Christ*, but also that *Christ receives each of us*. He enters into friendship with us: "You are my friends" (Jn 15:14). Indeed, it is because of him that we have life: "He who eats me will live because of me" (Jn 6:57). Eucharistic communion brings about in a sublime way the mutual abiding of Christ and each of his followers: "Abide in me, and I in you" (Jn 15:4).[9]

The saving efficacy of the sacrifice is fully realized when the Lord's body and blood are received in communion. The Eucharistic Sacrifice is intrinsically directed to the inward union of the faithful with Christ through communion; we receive the very One who offered himself for us, we receive his body which he gave up for us on the Cross and his blood which he "poured out for many for the forgiveness of sins" (Mt 26:28). We are reminded of his words: "As the living Father sent me, and I live because of the Father, so he who eats me will live because of me" (Jn 6:57).[10]

Let us now consider the difficult question of the relation of those divorced and remarried to the Eucharist.

Divorced and remarried persons "find themselves in a situation that objectively contravenes God's law":[11] "What therefore God has joined together, let not man put asunder" (Mk 10:9). The Church does not judge consciences and does not condemn persons. She knows how painful their personal story often is. Nevertheless, divorced and remarried persons cannot be admitted to Eucharistic Communion because "their state and condition of life objectively contradict that union of love between Christ and the Church which signified and effected by the Eucharist."[12] These persons can feel a real suffering, all the stronger given their great desire to receive the Lord. Those who abstain from receiving Communion through fidelity to the Church do not distance themselves from Christ. On the contrary, they come closer to him.

Even though they cannot, for the time being, receive Eucharistic Communion, as baptized persons, they remain members of the Church.

[9] John Paul II, *Ecclesia de Eucharistia*, no. 22.
[10] Ibid., no. 16.
[11] CCC 1650.
[12] John Paul II, Apostolic Exhortation *Familiaris consortio* (1981), no. 84.

The imprint of baptism is not erased. They are thus invited to participate in the life of the Church: "to listen to the word of God, to attend the Sacrifice of the Mass, to persevere in prayer, to contribute to works of charity".[13] Thus, they are called to draw abundantly from the graces that flow from the Eucharist, not by sacramental Communion, but by spiritual communion during Mass and also in adoration of the Blessed Sacrament.

Despite a suffering that will always remain sharp, by their persevering faith that pushes them to come to Mass all the same, and by their witness of obedience to the Church who asks them to abstain from Communion, they remind others of the grace they are granted in being able to unite themselves to Christ through sacramental Communion and of how much this is a gift and never something owed them.

> With firm confidence, [the Church] believes that even those who have rejected the Lord's command and are still living in this state will be able to obtain from God the grace of conversion and salvation, provided that they have persevered in prayer, penance and charity.[14]

> Contemplation prolongs Communion and enables one to encounter Christ, true God and true man, in a lasting way, to let oneself be looked upon by him, and to experience his presence. When we contemplate him present in the Blessed Sacrament of the altar, Christ draws near and more intimate to us than we are to ourselves: he gives us a part of his divine life in a transforming union and, through the Spirit, he gives us access to the Father, as he himself said to Philip: "He who has seen me has seen the Father" (Jn 14:9). Contemplation, which is also a communion of desire, intimately associates us with Christ and, in a very special way, associates those who are prevented from receiving him.[15]

> Salvation comes from God alone; but because we receive the life of faith through the Church, she is our mother: "We believe the Church as the mother of our new birth, and not *in* the Church as if she were

[13] Ibid.

[14] Ibid.

[15] John Paul II, letter to Bishop Houssiau for the 750th anniversary of Corpus Christi, May 28, 1996.

the author of our salvation." Because she is our mother, she is also our teacher in the faith.[16]

The marriage that Jesus Christ desires to enter into with our soul . . . through the most adorable Eucharist. . . . Where is the banquet of this royal wedding held? It is in the bosom of your soul, which is a magnificent palace that the heavenly King has had adorned with his wonderful riches, which are his divine virtues, his gifts, and his mercies. There in surplus are all the graces and merits of Jesus the Bridegroom that he gives as a gift to your soul. The witnesses to this holy marriage are the Divine Persons of the Father and the Holy Spirit, and the eternal Word pronounces these mysterious words found in holy Scripture, speaking to your soul: "I marry you in faith." This is so profound and so true that this holy marriage is renewed each time you receive Communion. . . . Prefer nothing to the love of Jesus Christ, but be careful not to come without your wedding gown, which shows the purity of the heart . . . or the purity of our intentions. Let us do all things according to the divine will. This intent keeps our soul apart from all that is not God and arrays it in the holy dispositions of Jesus Christ. And for the time being she is dressed in the wedding gown and able to be admitted to the magnificent and sublime banquet in which she is satisfied by God himself with such abundance that the soul that has once eaten him as she should, with the necessary dispositions, will never again hunger for the things of the earth. Oh! How well does the soul that in faith eats Jesus Christ in the sacred Host understand what I am saying! All creatures become tasteless to her, and she can only delight in the one taste of Jesus her Bridegroom, which she finds better than wine.[17]

Eucharistic Communion strengthens the unity of the Church, the Body of Christ. "The bread which we break, is it not a participation in the body of Christ? Because there is one bread, we who are many are one body, for we all partake of the one bread" (1 Cor 10:16–17). Saint John Chrysostom is more specific: "For what is this bread? It is the Body of Christ. And what do those who receive it become? The Body of Christ—not many bodies but one body. For as bread is completely

[16] CCC 169, quoting Faustus of Riez, *De Spiritu Sancto* 1, 2: PL 62:11.

[17] Catherine de Bar (Mechtilde of the Blessed Sacrament), *Adorer et adhérer* (Paris: Cerf, 1994), 102.

one, though made up of many grains of wheat, and these albeit unseen, remain nonetheless present, in such a way that their difference is not apparent since they have been made a perfect whole, so too are we mutually joined to one another and together united with Christ."[18] "The seeds of disunity, which daily experience shows to be so deeply rooted in humanity as a result of sin, are countered by *the unifying power* of the body of Christ. The Eucharist, precisely by building up the Church, creates human community."[19]

~

---

[18] Homily on the First Letter to the Corinthians 24, 2: PG 61:200, quoted in John Paul II, *Ecclesia de Eucharistia*, no. 23.

[19] John Paul II, *Ecclesia de Eucharistia*, no. 24.

The Signs of the Covenant

STAGE 24

The Suffering Servant and Kenosis

He had no form or comeliness that we should look at him, and no beauty that we should desire him. He was despised and rejected by men; a man of sorrows, and acquainted with grief; and as one from whom men hide their faces he was despised, and we esteemed him not. Surely he has borne our griefs and carried our sorrows; yet we esteemed him stricken, struck down by God, and afflicted. But he was wounded for our transgressions, he was bruised for our iniquities; upon him was the chastisement that made us whole, and with his stripes we are healed. All we like sheep have gone astray; we have turned every one to his own way; and the LORD has laid on him the iniquity of us all. He was oppressed, and he was afflicted, yet he opened not his mouth; like a lamb that is led to the slaughter, and like a sheep that before its shearers is silent, so he opened not his mouth. By oppression and judgment he was taken away; and as for his generation, who considered that he was cut off out of the land of the living, stricken for the transgression of my people? And they made his grave with the wicked and with a rich man in his death, although he had done no violence, and there was no deceit in his mouth. Yet it was the will of the LORD to bruise him; he has put him to grief; when he makes himself an offering for sin, he shall see his offspring, he shall prolong his days; the will of the LORD shall prosper in his hand; he shall see the fruit of the travail of his soul and be satisfied; by his knowledge shall the righteous one, my servant, make many to be accounted righteous; and he shall bear their iniquities. Therefore I will divide him a portion with the great, and he shall divide the spoil with the strong; because he poured out his soul to death, and was numbered with the transgressors; yet he bore the sin of many, and made intercession for the transgressors. (Is 53:2–12)

The table below shows the parallels between the prophecy of the suffering servant (Is 53), the bloody Passion of Jesus on his bloody way to Golgotha (Jn 19), and the permanent presence of Jesus the Host on his mystical Calvary in the tabernacles of the world. These parallels only take up the first part of Isaiah 53. Others can be established by glancing through the end of Isaiah 53.

By kenosis, God empties himself of his glory in order to meet fallen man:

> Though he was in the form of God, [he] did not count equality with God a thing to be grasped, but emptied himself, taking the form of a servant, being born in the likeness of men. And being found in human form he humbled himself and became obedient unto death, even death on a cross. Therefore God has highly exalted him and bestowed on him the name which is above every name, that at the name of Jesus every knee should bow, in heaven and on earth and under the earth, and every tongue confess that Jesus Christ is Lord, to the glory of God the Father. (Phil 2:6–11)

> That the Son of God so loved the world that he made himself man, we understand: the Creator must have it in his heart to repair the work of his hands. That the Man-God died on the Cross, we still understand through an excess of love. But what stops being understandable, what amazes those weak in faith and scandalizes unbelievers, is that Jesus Christ, glorious, crowned, having achieved his mission here below, still desires to remain with us, and in a state more humbled, more dejected than at Bethlehem, or even than at Calvary. Let us raise with respect the mysterious veil that covers the Holy of Holies and try to understand the excess of love that the Lord shows for us.[1]

On the Cross Christ lowered himself in the extreme in order to show us his love. All the same, in the Blessed Sacrament, he lowers himself even more. There, we no longer even see the Divine Person, but only the appearances of bread. We no longer hear his voice that rang from the Cross: "I thirst." In coming to the Blessed Sacrament, he leaves his glory and majesty in heaven and takes the risk of being ignored and forgotten under insignificant appearances. He comes but with his

---

[1] Saint Peter Julian Eymard, *Adorer en esprit et vérité* (Paris: Éditions F.-X. de Guibert, 2009), 99.

Song of the Suffering Servant (Is 53)	Jesus during his Passion (Jn 19)	Jesus present in the Eucharist, memorial of the Passion
"no form or comeliness that we should look at him"	"Here is the man" (Jn 19:5)	the still Host
"no beauty that we should desire him"	"Crucify him" (Jn 19:6)	Jesus truly present, under the appearances of bread
"despised"	"Hail, King of the Jews" (Jn 19:3)	too often considered as a thing, or at best a simple food
"rejected by men"	abandoned by those he healed, fed, taught	abandoned in the tabernacles of the world
"A man of sorrows, and acquainted with grief; and as one from whom men hide their faces he was despised, and we esteemed him not"	betrayed by Judas; denied by Peter; a criminal is preferred to the sweet Savior who says: "I thirst" (Jn 19:28)	"What does he do in the Blessed Sacrament? He awaits us" (Curé of Ars). "My thirst to be loved in the Blessed Sacrament is so great that it consumes me" (Jesus to Saint Margaret Mary).
"Surely he has borne our griefs and carried our sorrows"	"He went out, bearing his own cross" (Jn 19:17)	Eucharist is the Lamb of God, who bears the sin of the world, my sin
"He was wounded for our transgressions, he was bruised for our iniquities"	"One of the soldiers pierced his side with a spear, and at once there came out blood and water" (Jn 19:34)	Eucharist flows from the pierced Heart of Jesus; he gives love for hate
"Upon him was the chastisement that made us whole, and with his stripes we are healed"	He shows his glorious wounds (Jn 20:27)	He gives his resurrected Body in the Eucharist that heals us
"All we like sheep have gone astray; we have turned every one to his own way"	"Jesus should die ... to gather into one the children of God who are scattered abroad" (Jn 11:51–52)	He is our Shepherd in the Eucharist; his people are the Church; "the Eucharist makes the Church."

love and his mercy. He seeks souls who will love him for himself. But love is not loved. Saint Thérèse of Lisieux said: "The nature of love is to humble oneself. . . . Yes, in order that Love be fully satisfied, it is necessary that It lower Itself, and that It lower Itself to nothingness and transform this nothingness into *fire*."[2]

The following witness helps in understanding why God pushes his Son to such an annihilation: a young woman who had spent a number of years in the street, after having been abandoned by her family, abused by men, and broken by the trials of life, tells how her encounter with Jesus during a period of Eucharistic adoration transformed her life: "I had descended so low, like someone fallen from a precipice into the depths. Darkness surrounded me on all sides. But, at the greatest depth of the abyss, I crashed into Jesus, who took me in his arms and raised me up again toward God my Father. Thank you Jesus!"

Here is how kenosis unfurls in the Eucharist, the memorial of Jesus' Passion:

> 1. Christ hands himself over in a freely accepted offering. The Eucharist is instituted on *Holy Thursday*, "This is my body given for you, this is my blood poured out for you!" In sovereign freedom, Jesus gives himself.

> 2. The love freely offered is handed over in the Passion. Jesus undergoes the torments that are inflicted upon him. He freely carries his Cross, lowers his head, and gives up his spirit. Love consents to be handed over: "No one takes [my life] from me, but I lay it down of my own accord" (Jn 10:18). It is a silent sheep that hands itself over! It is the passivity of the Passion: he allows himself to be led! It is a life given up to the last drop of blood. This is *Good Friday*.

> 3. The offering is accomplished to the end; it is the ultimate abasement of the One who is handed over, in total passivity, to death. It is this state of the Son dead among the dead. He descended to hell in the hell of death. This is the silence of *Holy Saturday*. Jesus is in the tomb.

[2] Saint Thérèse of Lisieux, *Story of a Soul: The Autobiography of St. Thérèse of Lisieux*, trans. John Clark, O.C.D., 2nd ed. (Washington, D.C.: ICS Publications, Institute of Carmelite Studies, 1976), 14, 195.

4. Christ is resurrected *Easter Sunday*. He remains present in his Church until the end of time to pass on his victory over death and the glory of his Resurrection. After the Consecration, the Real Presence of Jesus remains in the Eucharist. "The tabernacle is there to show the definitive state of the Son's offering to the Father and gift to the world. We are pathetically passive. Jesus is present and supremely active. The Prince of Life is intensely active, and it is up to us to attune ourselves to Jesus' transfiguring and deeply moving presence."[3] But to the Real Presence of Jesus we often respond with our real absence!

Jesus will have two thrones, one of glory in heaven, another of sweetness and goodness on earth; two courts: the celestial and triumphant court and the court of his redeemed ones here below. In what state does Jesus remain with us? In a state of change, from one time to another? No, rather, in a state of perseverance. He stays forever until the end of the world.

But, O marvel of the Eucharist! Through his sacramental state, Jesus gives new homage to his Father such as the Father has never received from any creature; a greater homage, so to say, than all that the Word incarnate could do on earth. What, then, is this extraordinary homage? It is the homage of the King of glory, consummated in power and the majesty of heaven, who comes in his Sacrament to immolate to his Father, not only his divine glory as in the Incarnation, but even his human glory, the glorious qualities of his resurrected humanity![4]

---

[3] Conference by Bishop Léonard during the Congress of Adoration, Paray-le-Monial, 2005.

[4] Saint Peter Julian Eymard, *Adorer en esprit et en vérité*, 53.

The Signs of the Covenant

STAGE 25

"I Am the Living Bread"
(John 6)

For this stage, use your New Testament at chapter 6 of Saint John's Gospel.

Part 1: vv. 1–15, The multiplication of the loaves: Jesus shows his desire to feed mankind. He does not accomplish the miracle out of nothing; rather, he uses a child's five loaves and two fishes. This offering, insignificant to the apostles, the Lord welcomes favorably. He multiplies it to feed the large crowd. Likewise, in the offertory during Mass, we give a part of our material goods to the collection. Nevertheless, it is first of all our person and our heart that we offer to the Lord. This offering is brought to the altar in the form of bread and wine. Jesus, in the person of the priest, changes it into his Body and Blood to feed the faithful who are present. Likewise, in adoration, the Lord welcomes the offering of our time and our person, which he uses to bless and spiritually feed so many people who receive a new effect of divine grace: "Through adoration, the Christian contributes to the radical transformation of the world. Every person who prays to the Lord brings the whole world with him, raising the world to God."[1]

For having received bread from him, the crowd wants to make Jesus its king (Jn 6:15). But he did not come for a social kingship that consists in giving bread to all. "My kingship is not of this world" (Jn 18:36). His kingship is first of all spiritual. In fact, the episode of the multiplication of the loaves prepares the crowds to welcome another food, which does not satisfy the body but gives life to the soul: it is the Eucharist, God's gift for the life of the world. Through the Eucharist,

---

[1] John Paul II, letter to Bishop Houssiau for the 750th anniversary of Corpus Christi, May 28, 1996.

126

Jesus comes to reign in hearts. His kingdom, although spiritual, must nevertheless have social repercussions, particularly in civil laws, and become concrete through gestures of charity. This episode can be considered the first Eucharistic miracle in the history of the Church.

Part 2: vv. 16–21, Jesus walks on water: While Providence moves first and normally through the natural laws that God has fixed, God is not limited by his laws and can, in his sovereign freedom, act in a supernatural way. In walking on water, Jesus prepares his disciples for his Eucharistic discourse, whose content surpasses the scope of natural laws. In the Eucharist, Jesus gives himself under the sacramental mode, a mode unique in its type and having no equivalent in nature.

Part 3: vv. 22–71, The Eucharistic discourse at Capernaum: In verse 26, the crowds do not grasp that the multiplication of the loaves and Jesus' walking on water were but precursory signs of the discourse on the bread of life. The disciples do not manage to see farther than the earthly food that has satisfied their bodies. They make of the sign an end in itself. It can happen that we, too, through a lack of faith, see in the Eucharist only the sign or the appearances of bread, without discerning the real, bodily, substantial presence of Jesus.

In verse 27, Jesus invites his disciples to seek first the "food which endures to eternal life". This is why the Church has always desired that Sunday be a public holiday, so that every Christian might have the time to go and receive the true food at Mass, given by God himself, more essential for man than the "food which perishes" (Jn 6:27).

"This is the work of God, that you *believe* in him whom he has sent" (Jn 6:29). In the context of the Eucharistic discourse, it is not only about *believing* in Jesus seated at the right hand of the Father, about *believing* precisely in Jesus who gives himself in the Eucharist. This is what God desires for us and what he accomplishes by his grace.

In rereading verses 29, 32, 38, 44, and 45, note the verbs used by Jesus to speak of the Father's action toward him. The work of the Father is to render all glory to the Son—this glory that the Son gives to him in perfectly doing his will. It is the Father who gives this food. He gives faith for believing in this presence. He leads toward Jesus, draws us to him, and glorifies him.

Remember that before the Son became incarnate and gave himself in the Eucharist on earth, "He was from all eternity in a position of (Eucharistic) 'availability' to the Father, an attitude of offering so absolute that in the eyes of the Father it appeared as the prefiguration of the Cross. Saint Peter expresses this in his first epistle: Christ was known beforehand by the Father as the Lamb giving his blood for us, even before the creation of the world (1 Pet 1:20), thus, precisely when he put himself at the disposal of the Father for us; when he, as it were, 'interposed' himself so that the arrows of sin that the world sends to God reach, not the Father, but himself (Adrienne von Speyr)."[2]

In verses 32–34, Jesus explains that the manna received from God during the Exodus prefigured the Eucharist. Jesus is himself the new manna that gives what the old manna could not: eternal life.

Preliminary reflections on faith: Faith is first of all a grace, a gift of God: when Peter confesses that Jesus is the Christ, the Son of the living God, Jesus declares to him that this revelation has come to him, not from "flesh and blood . . . , but [from] my Father who is in heaven" (Mt 16:17). Faith is a gift of God, a supernatural virtue infused by him. "To make this act of faith, the grace of God and the interior help of the Holy Spirit must precede and assist, moving the heart and turning it to God, opening the eyes of the mind and giving 'joy and ease to everyone in assenting to the truth and believing it.' "[3]

Faith is also the adequate response of man to the Father's invitation: by his revelation, "the invisible God . . . speaks to men as friends and lives among them, so that He may invite and take them into fellowship with Himself."[4]

Just after the Consecration, the priest proclaims: "The mystery of faith". The Church's faith finds its culmination in the Eucharist. The Eucharist recapitulates, concentrates, and makes present anew all the

[2] Father Anthony Birot, the House of Trinitarian Love community, conference on *L'Eucharistie comme mystère trinitaire* at the colloquium *Communion-Évangélisation* (Hyères: April 19, 2009). The author has since developed this whole point, with its theological references, in *La Dramatique trinitaire de l'Amour* (Saint-Maur: Parole et Silence—Lethielleux, 2009), 100–113.

[3] Vatican Council II, Dogmatic Constitution *Dei Verbum* (1964), no. 5; the quote is in fact from the Second Council of Orange, canon 7.

[4] Ibid., no. 2.

mysteries of the life of Christ. In welcoming faith in the Eucharist, we believe that the Son became incarnate in Jesus, died for our sins, was resurrected to give us eternal life, and leads us through his Spirit. We believe that the Holy Sacrifice of the Mass, celebrated in the Church, makes redemption present. We believe that Jesus gives himself in food to fortify the divine life received at baptism. We believe that he remains among us in the tabernacle as our travel companion and that he pushes us to love one another: "Greater love has no man than this, that a man lay down his life for his friends" (Jn 15:13). He asks us to become witnesses of his love that gives itself to the end in the Eucharist. For the fullness of the divine life is transmitted by his Body, which is the Church and whose heart is the Eucharist: "For in him the whole fulness of deity dwells bodily" (Col 2:9).

The holy Eucharist is truly the Sacrament of faith. The Eucharist roots our faith ever more in the Passion of Christ and in his pierced Heart. This is the source of the authentic faith that gives us this assurance: "Faith is the assurance of things hoped for, the conviction of things not seen" (Heb 11:1). And when doubt seems to carry it away, let us approach nearer to the Eucharist, at Mass and in adoration. Faith, while radiant, is often lived in darkness, because "we walk by faith, not by sight" (2 Cor 5:7). Faith is never tangible, but the Eucharist fortifies it in such a way that it makes us able to move mountains!

Vv. 35–47: Spiritual communion and adoration: For the Eucharist to strengthen the divine life in the soul, faith in the Real Presence is indispensable. The greater the intensity of a man's faith, the preparation of his heart, and his desire to receive Jesus, the more does the Eucharist nourish his heart. Be sure to note that in this passage the question is not yet of receiving sacramental Communion. Rather the elements of spiritual communion are brought together. These are three verbs that Jesus uses for spiritually communicating with his Eucharistic Body: come, see, and believe.

"For this is the will of my Father, that every one who sees the Son and believes in him should have eternal life" (Jn 6:40). This verse is made clear by the passage about the bronze serpent in Numbers 21:4–9. The Israelites, who had sinned, were bitten by serpents. In order not to die, they had to direct their gaze toward a sign: "And as Moses lifted up the serpent in the wilderness, so must the Son of man be lifted up, that whoever believes in him may have eternal life" (Jn 3:14). In what way can Jesus compare himself to a serpent when he was suspended from the wood of the Cross? John 3:14 recalls that the salvation offered by Jesus comes from the Cross. John 6:40, the heart of the Eucharistic discourse, shows that the salvation offered on the Cross is realized in the soul by approaching the Eucharist with faith. Through the Eucharist, Jesus desires to save every man, without exception, for "this is the will of him who sent me, that I should lose nothing of all that he has given me" (Jn 6:39). Thus the salvation of mankind is received through the Eucharist, which makes present for us the victory of Jesus on the Cross, a victory prefigured by the bronze serpent in the desert. The Eucharist is truly the memorial of the Passion.

~

STAGE 26

"I Am the Living Bread"
(John 6, *continued*)

For this stage, use your New Testament at chapter 6 of Saint John's Gospel.

Vv. 51–58, Sacramental communion (banquet): In these verses, the verb used is "to eat". In Greek, the verb *trôgô* is translated literally as "to chew", "to masticate". Thus, after having discerned through faith the Body of Christ in the Eucharist and after having contemplated and adored it, it is necessary to "eat" this food. It nourishes and fortifies the baptismal life, also called eternal life, supernatural life, or divine life. The Eucharist is the ordinary food that God gives to his children to fortify his divine life in them. The sacramental mode is unique in creation. God uses this mode to strengthen the indwelling of the Divine Persons in the soul of the just man. Through sacramental Communion, the indwelling of the Divine Persons becomes more interior, more intimate.

Saint Augustine puts these words in the mouth of Jesus: I am the food of adults. Grow, and you shall eat me, yet without my being transformed into you, as with food for your flesh, rather you shall be transformed into me.[1] "It is no longer I who live, but Christ who lives in me" (Gal 2:20). Through Eucharistic Communion, we remain in Jesus (cf. Jn 6:56). This life is not in us like water in a container, rather it is we who are like a sponge in an ocean of divine life.

Following Leviticus 9:4, it was forbidden to drink the blood of an animal. All the more reason why drinking the blood of a man (cf. Jn 6:53) provokes a scandal with the Jews. In fact, Jesus announces the

[1] Saint Augustine, *Confessions* VII, 10, 16.

New Covenant, sealed by his Blood spilled on the Cross and made present in each Eucharist. This covenant, while prefigured by the former covenants, brings with it a radically new dimension: it is necessary to drink the Blood of Christ. The blood, in the Semitic language, is the seat of life. It is the soul. When Jesus gives his Body, he gives himself in person, with all he is and all he has. In giving his Blood separately from the Body, he gives, in addition, his death. More precisely, he gives his love that extends to offering his life. He cannot give more than his Body and his Blood. Note Jesus' sacrificial vocabulary: to eat the Body that has been given up and drink from the spilled Blood recalls that the Mass is *first of all a sacrifice and, then, a meal*, like the fruit that a tree bears.

On three occasions (vv. 41, 52, 61), the Jews "murmur", as they did many times during the Exodus. The following verses explain the gravity of murmuring, unveiling this spirit of contestation that attracts divine wrath: "The people became impatient on the way. And the people spoke against God and against Moses, 'Why have you brought us up out of Egypt to die in the wilderness? For there is no food and no water, and we loathe this worthless food'" (Num 21:4–5). God can do nothing more for his people if they are disgusted by the manna, this food that is supposed to enable them to reach the Promised Land. Likewise for us, if we are scandalized or revolted by the Eucharist, what can give us eternal life and enable us to reach the heavenly city?

This same form of contestation about the bread of life stirs up the crowds listening to the Eucharistic discourse. They are scandalized by the "realism" of this food that Jesus announces. There is no other alternative: either Jesus is speaking in a *symbolic or metaphorical* way (for example, we can say: he is as strong as a lion, or he eats like an ogre, without for all that being a lion or an ogre!), or what Jesus is saying must be interpreted *literally*, which is in fact the faith of the Church. Jesus is truly the "bread of life"; we must eat his flesh and drink his blood to grow in divine life. If Jesus was speaking symbolically, the Jews would have accepted his words. No, Jesus prefers to lose his disciples, those he has fed, healed, those who have accompanied him from the beginning of his ministry. Jesus cannot compromise on this truth. So we sadly note the first schism in the Church as yet being born:

"After this many of his disciples drew back and no longer walked with him" (Jn 6:66). For the first time, it is his disciples and no longer those opposing him who separate themselves from him. They cannot receive the truth about the Eucharist.

"It is the Spirit that gives life, the flesh is of no avail; the words that I have spoken to you are Spirit and life" (Jn 6:63). The words about the Eucharist scandalize them. Jesus reproaches them for listening to the spoken Word in too human and fleshly a way and not spiritually. It is the Spirit that is going to give life to the body of Christ in the tomb and who will resurrect him from the dead. In Communion, we receive sacramentally the body of Jesus dead and resurrected, and not his body in its natural presence. Only the Spirit can give understanding about this food.

"Lord, to whom shall we go? You have the words of eternal life" (Jn 6:68). That is the greatness of Peter's faith! He does not understand everything, but he welcomes this truth, for he knows that "with God nothing will be impossible" (Lk 1:37). It is this assent of faith that we must imitate. By faith, man submits his intellect and his will to God. With all his being, man gives his assent to the God who reveals himself. No one can understand the Eucharist intellectually or scientifically, because the sacramental mode surpasses natural laws. Nevertheless, Jesus is the Truth; thus, he cannot lie. The Eucharist is the Sacrament of faith par excellence.

During the creation of the world, what the Word commands is immediately achieved. He said "let there be light" and "there was light" (Gen 1:3). Likewise, when the Word incarnate, Jesus, said: "This is my body", the intellect understands only that God is capable of it, and, if Jesus works this miracle, it is for our salvation. The intellect can only adore this mystery. Our faith is nourished on it!

We need the Church in order to believe in the Real Presence. Without her, it is not possible to believe in it. For this reason, Peter does not speak in the first person singular but uses the first person plural: "We have believed, and have come to know, that you are the Holy One of God" (Jn 6:69). It is the faith of the Church that we receive. It is in the Church that we believe. The Church lives from the Eucharist, and the Eucharist makes the Church.

Faith is a personal act—the free response of the human person to the initiative of God who reveals himself. But faith is not an isolated act. No one can believe alone, just as no one can live alone. You have not given yourself faith as you have not given yourself life. The believer has received faith from others and should hand it on to others. Our love for Jesus and for our neighbor impels us to speak to others about our faith. Each believer is thus a link in the great chain of believers. I cannot believe without being carried by the faith of others, and by my faith I help support others in the faith.[2]

Faith is *certain*. It is more certain than all human knowledge because it is founded on the very word of God who cannot lie. To be sure, revealed truths can seem obscure to human reason and experience, but "the certainty that the divine light gives is greater than that which the light of natural reason gives." "Ten thousand difficulties do not make one doubt."[3]

During Communion, we receive neither bread nor a symbol, but the reality itself of the Body of Christ, Jesus himself in person. This divine food is without price! A single Communion has more value than all the world's gold, because through it, Christ resurrected gives himself completely. Saint John Chrysostom said: "Terrible, truly terrible are the mysteries of the Church, terrible is the altar. Without the special help of the grace of God, no soul could withstand the fire of this food without being entirely destroyed." And he also said that after Communion, "the Christian is like a fearsome lion with flames coming forth from his mouth. The devil cannot withstand the sight of him."

To distinguish and not risk confusing the "bread of life" and the bread that nourishes the body, Benedict XVI invites adoration of this heavenly food. He says, taking up the words of Saint Augustine:

"No one should eat this flesh without first adoring it; . . . we should sin were we not to adore it." . . . Indeed, we do not merely receive something in the Eucharist. It is the encounter and unification of persons; the person, however, who comes to meet us and desires to unite himself to us is the Son of God. Such unification can only be

[2] CCC 166.
[3] Ibid., 157, quoting, first: Saint Thomas Aquinas, *Summa Theologiae* II-II, 171, 5, obj. 3, and, second: Blessed John Henry Cardinal Newman, *Apologia pro vita sua* (London: Longman, 1878), 239.

brought about by means of adoration. Receiving the Eucharist means adoring the One whom we receive.[4]

The Word feeds the soul, but the Word incarnate feeds the body by giving it a seed of immortality.

～

[4] Benedict XVI, Christmas Address to the Roman Curia, December 22, 2005, quoting Saint Augustine, *Enarr. in Ps* 98:9, CCL XXXIX 1385.

STAGE 27

Isaac's Blessing (Gen 27)
and Transubstantiation

Saint Thomas Aquinas, termed the Doctor of the Eucharist, is part of the line of great witnesses who were truly penetrated by this mystery of the Eucharist. One day while celebrating Mass at Naples, he was so profoundly overwhelmed that he no longer had any desire to write. He suspended the writing of the *Summa Theologiae*. His brother Reginald asked him why he was interrupting such a work. Thomas answered him: "I cannot go on, because all I have written appears to me so much straw! So much straw compared to what has been shown and revealed to me [at the Mass]." And yet, had God not said to him: "Thomas, you have spoken well of me"?[1]

Thomas had just set out in his *Summa* the nine great wonders of the Eucharist presented below. For these wonders, it is necessary to distinguish clearly the substance of a thing (what exists in itself, the profound being) and the accidents or appearance or species of this thing (what is accessible to our senses and enables us to understand the substance):

1. The first wonder is that under the appearance of bread the true Body of Christ is present, under the species of the humble host is found the Creator of heaven and earth;

2. The substance of the bread is changed into the true Body of Christ. This Body is the same that was formed in the womb of the Virgin Mary, because there is only one Jesus, who really took flesh from the Virgin Mary;

3. Nothing of the bread is left, except for an appearance. But the appearance does not make bread bread: it is its substance. Yet, the

---

[1] Nicolas Buttet, *L'Eucharistie à l'école des saints* (Paris: Éditions de l'Émmanuel, 2000), 25.

substance of the bread has been entirely changed into the Body of Jesus without altering the appearances of bread—the color, taste, exterior form;

4. It is not a small bit of Jesus that we find in the Host; the Body of Christ in its entirety is under the appearance of a small host;

5. Another wonder of the Eucharist: one and the same Body is in its entirety in many places, in many Hosts, in many portions;

6. This Body of Jesus in many places, however, remains one. It is not divided or broken into pieces, but remains whole and undivided;

7. When we take the Body of Christ to be nourished from it, it is not at all diminished;

8. If the Body of Christ is not eaten, it is in some way diminished insofar as we are all together one same Body since we participate in one bread (1 Cor 10:17). And when Christians able to communicate do not do so, they prevent the construction of the mystical Body of Christ. . . . The Body of Christ in the Host thus builds the Body of Christ that is the Church. It is by communicating and receiving the grace of Communion that the Church is built up and becomes an ever more visible sign of God's Real Presence in the heart of mankind.

9. The Body of Christ is increased when we communicate, because those who communicate are called to convert themselves and will be changed into the Body of Christ. It is thus the holy Church, whose border is located in our hearts, that grows (cf. Eph 4:10).[2]

All these wonders concerning the Eucharist, which the Church sums up in the word *transubstantiation,* call for our wonder and demand our assent of faith. The tradition distinguishes the literal and spiritual senses of the great biblical texts.[3] Saint Thomas Aquinas presents a spiritual interpretation of chapter 27 of Genesis (reread the chapter in your Bible). He sees a type of the discrepancy between faith and the senses in the blessing of Jacob:

> What then has happened? Isaac is ill, agonizing, and almost blind. He desires to pass on the blessing to his eldest son, Esau. But his wife,

[2] Ibid., 24.
[3] CCC 115.

Rebecca, sees things differently and arranges everything so that it is Jacob, the younger son, who receives the blessing and thus his Father's mission. What at first sight appears a terrible trick is interpreted differently—spiritually—by Saint Thomas Aquinas. It is not Isaac as such who is deceived, it is his senses: he thought he was blessing Esau when he was touching Jacob, who resembled Esau because of the veil with which he had covered himself.

How then is this applied to the mystery of the Eucharist? In an allegorical interpretation that does not exclude other understandings of the text, Jacob is the type of the Body of the Lord. Isaac and Rebecca, his wife, signify the two natures that are in us: body and soul. The male figure, Isaac, represents the exterior man, the senses. Rebecca, the wife who resides at home and governs the family, represents the soul who cares for its salvation and that of others. Jacob, lovable and good, dwelling in the tent, Rebecca's favorite—that is, the favorite of the faithful soul—signifies the true Body of Jesus. Esau, loved by Isaac, type of the body, signifies the substance of the bread with its accidents: flavor, color, and its other qualities.

While Isaac—that is, the exterior man—is working the consecration, Esau—or the substance of the bread—is no longer there. But Esau's likeness remains: the clothes, the hairy skins, the food with his particular flavor. It is here that Isaac's darkened sight—that is, our senses too weak to grasp this invisible mystery of transubstantiation— finds itself deceived. Isaac indeed thinks he has Esau—or the bread— under his eyes, but all that remains are his clothes—that is, the species of bread. And under this appearance, hidden, as though disguised, is Jacob—that is, the Body of Christ. His sense of taste is also deceived, since Isaac believes he is eating Esau's food—that is, the bread—but he is only tasting its appearance. Equally deceived is the sense of smell, since Isaac thinks he smells Esau's odor—or that of the bread—which is no longer really there. Rather, he smells the odor of Esau's clothes in which Jacob is dressed—that is, the form of the bread, in which the Body of Christ is dressed.

Isaac was wise, but he is deceived by the judgment he made, believing he recognized Esau when it was really Jacob. In the same way, the exterior man in us is also deceived when judging the bread of the altar other than with faith. This is why Isaac says: "The voice is Jacob's voice, but the hands are the hands of Esau." The hands are the hands

BLESSING OF JACOB		CONSECRATION	
Before the blessing	*During the blessing*	*Before the Consecration*	*During the Con-secration*
Esau	Appearances of Esau (hairy hands, taste, smell)	Bread	Appearances of bread
	JACOB		BODY OF CHRIST
Isaac: *exterior man: loves Esau; deceived senses (except hearing)*		My Body: *exterior man; the deceived senses (except hearing)*	
Rebecca: *interiority: loves Jacob; undeceived heart*		My Soul: *interior man; faith that recognizes the Body of Christ*	

of Esau: nothing could be more false since Isaac is in fact touching the hands of Jacob. But the voice that says: "It is I" is really the voice of Jacob. Nothing could be more true. Likewise, is the Sacrament that I touch the substance of the bread? Nothing could be more false. But nothing could be more true than the voice of Jesus Christ who says, through the mouth of the priest: "This is my Body." Rebecca, that is, the soul, believes what is true, that Jacob is in the mysterious benediction—that is, that the Body of Jesus is veiled under the clothes of Esau, which is to say, under the appearance of bread.[4]

Saint Cyril of Jerusalem wrote: "Do not then attach yourself to the bread and wine as to natural elements, for they are, according to the declaration of the Master, Body and Blood. This is, it is true, what the senses suggest to you; but let faith reassure you."[5]

~

---

[4] Cf. Saint Thomas Aquinas, *Opuscules spirituelles sur l'admirable Sacrement de l'Eucharistie,* cited in Nicolas Buttet, *L'Eucharistie à l'école des saints,* 91.

[5] Saint Cyril of Jerusalem, *Catéchèses baptismales et mystagogiques,* IV, 6: SCh 126, 138, Les Pères dans la foi (Paris: Migne, 1993).

The Tree of Life Recovered

And out of the ground the LORD God made to grow every tree that is pleasant to the sight and good for food, the tree of life also in the midst of the garden, and the tree of the knowledge of good and evil. A river flowed out of Eden to water the garden, and there it divided and became four rivers. . . . And the LORD God commanded the man, saying, "You may freely eat of every tree of the garden; but of the tree of the knowledge of good and evil you shall not eat, for in the day that you eat of it you shall die." (Gen 2:9–10, 16–17)

The tree of life symbolizes immortality. The tree of the knowledge of good and evil gives a privilege that God reserves for himself, namely, the faculty of deciding for himself what is good and evil and of acting accordingly. The serpent tempts Adam and Eve like this: "When you eat of it your eyes will be opened, and you will be like God, knowing good and evil" (Gen 3:5). This is an assertion of moral autonomy by which man denies his creaturely state and wishes to equal or be like God. It is the sin of pride, represented by the symbol of the forbidden fruit.

In the beginning, man finds himself in a perfect harmony: harmony with his Creator, harmony within himself, harmony with his neighbor, and harmony with the whole of creation:

- *With his Creator:* God seals a covenant with men (cf. *Stage 16*). He frequently visits man in the garden to speak to him.

- *Within himself:* man is created in the image of God. God saw that this was very good (Gen 1:31). Man's heart is whole, holy. It is neither wounded nor sullied nor divided. Man has access to the tree of life that represents immortality.

- *With his neighbor* in general, and in particular here with his wife: "Therefore a man leaves his father and his mother and clings to his wife, and they become one flesh" (Gen 2:24).

- *With creation:* through his work, he subdues creation by cultivating and keeping the garden (Gen 2:15).

This harmony is wounded by original sin:

- *With his Creator:* Adam and Eve are afraid of God. He becomes a rival: "And they heard the sound of the LORD God walking in the garden in the cool of the day, and the man and his wife hid themselves from the presence of the LORD God" (Gen 3:8).

- *Within himself:* the man and the woman discover that they are naked (cf. Gen 2:25). "The control of the soul's spiritual faculties over the body is shattered. . . . The world is virtually inundated by sin."[1] Death makes its entrance into the history of mankind (cf. Rom 5:12). Through his disobedience, man cuts himself off from the tree of life: "In the day that you eat of it you shall die." God "drove out the man; and at the east of the garden of Eden he placed the cherubim, and a flaming sword which turned every way, to guard the way to the tree of life" (Gen 3:24).

- *With his neighbor:* interpersonal relations are subjected to tensions and divisions. The man/woman relationship is subjected to lust and domination: "Your desire shall be for your husband, and he shall rule over you" (Gen 3:16).

- *With creation:* creation becomes hostile, foreign. Work becomes trying and painstaking: "In toil you shall eat of it all the days of your life; thorns and thistles it shall bring forth to you" (Gen 3:17).

The Eucharist reestablishes what sin destroyed and reinforces the harmony desired by God at the origin:

- *With the Creator:* communion between God and men. "He who eats my flesh and drinks my blood abides in me, and I in him" (Jn 6:56).

- *Within himself:* although marked by the original wound, man find peace in himself again by receiving eternal life at baptism. The Eu-

[1] CCC 400–401.

charist fortifies it: "He who eats my flesh and drinks my blood has eternal life" (Jn 6:54). The Word feeds the soul, but the Word incarnate feeds the body by giving it a seed of immortality. "With the Eucharist we digest, as it were, the 'secret' of the resurrection. For this reason Saint Ignatius of Antioch rightly defined the Eucharistic Bread as 'a medicine of immortality, an antidote to death.'"[2]

• *With the neighbor:* we receive the same food, we form the same body, we are animated by the same Spirit.

• *With creation:* according to Teilhard de Chardin's reflections in *The Divine Milieu*, the mystery of transubstantiation is not a change in which the Lord enters under the appearances of bread and wine. Rather it is a change in which he elevates the created realities of the bread and wine to himself, where he is found with his eternal Father. He attracts them to himself in transforming the realities of the bread and wine in an ascending spiral and converts them into his glorious Body and Blood. Thus Jesus maintains his corporeal unity by elevating to himself all these elements scattered about on earth. He leaves only the appearances of earthly realities so as not to appear glorious during the Consecration. These appearances are the vehicles of supernatural realities through which he comes physically as our food, thus attracting us to himself and letting himself be adored without manifesting his glory. This is the grace of recapitulation: All comes from God, all must return to God, all must be reconciled to Jesus, in such a way that Jesus may give back his kingdom to his Father (cf. 1 Cor 15:25).

In fact, the Eucharist is the "retribution for original sin: in the earthly paradise, the soul was deceived by the senses in tasting the forbidden fruit that appeared seductive to see and good to eat. Here, it is the senses that are deceived by what they see. Only the soul believes, and the soul alone can taste how good God is, under the trifling appearance of the bread."[3] Also, our first parents wanted to be *gods*: "You will be like God" (Gen 3:5). But instead, their prideful disobedience brought them death by separating them from the tree of life and the Creator.

[2] John Paul II, Encyclical Letter *Ecclesia de Eucharistia* (2003), no. 18, quoting Saint Ignatius: *Ad Ephesios* 20, PG 5:661.
[3] Nicolas Buttet, *L'Eucharistie à l'école des saints* (Paris: Éditions de l'Émmanuel, 2000), 92.

By contrast, the Eucharist makes us *children of God*. By the "bread of life", we become "partakers of the divine nature" (2 Pet 1:4). The dry wood of the Cross, which represents sin and death, becomes the new tree of Life that bears as fruit the Eucharist, living and life-giving food. What was lost by the first sin is recovered by the Eucharist, and to a greater degree. The liturgy of Easter acclaims: "O happy fault which gained for us so great a Redeemer!" Find what more the Eucharist gives us than our first parents had before original sin.

The first pages of the Bible evoke the dramatic situation of man separated from the tree of life and, thus, subjected to the power of eternal death. The last page of the Bible, in the book of Revelation, shows how man recovers access to the tree of life: the Angel "showed me the river of the water of life, bright as crystal, flowing from the throne of God and of the Lamb through the middle of the street of the city; also, on either side of the river, the tree of life with its twelve kinds of fruit, yielding its fruit each month; and the leaves of the tree were for the healing of the nations" (Rev 22:1–2). "Blessed are those who wash their robes, that they may have the right to the tree of life and that they may enter the city by the gates" (Rev 22:14).

The river of life, bright as crystal, flows from the throne of God and of the Lamb. The Lamb evokes the sacrificial presence of Christ in the Eucharist (cf. *Stage 19*). From the throne of the Lamb, that is to say, from the Eucharist (celebrated, received, adored), flows a river of living water, healing the nations. It is the realization of what Genesis 2:9–10 prefigured with the river divided into four branches that flowed out of the garden of Eden and the tree of life.

This corresponds to the vision of Saint Faustina:

One evening upon entering my cell, I saw Jesus exposed in the monstrance. It seemed to me that this was in the open air. At the feet of Jesus, I saw my confessor and behind him a great number of dignitaries of the Church. . . . Still farther, I saw great crowds that I could not encompass with a glance of the eye. I saw these two rays coming out from the Host, the same as in the image. They were closely united but not mixed up. They passed through the hands of my confessor, then through the hands of the clergy, from their hands to the crowd, and then returned to the Host.[4]

---

[4] Saint Faustina, *Petit Journal*, 343.

The Eucharist is truly a glimpse of heaven appearing on earth. It is a glorious ray of the heavenly Jerusalem which pierces the clouds of our history and lights up our journey.[5]

~

TRANSITION

- In Stages 1 to 15 (Part I), we meditated on the love of Jesus, the One sent by the Father, who *comes to us, who calls us to him.*

- In Stages 16 to 28, we have just recalled what the *signs of the Covenant* are. We have clarified what the Eucharist is and how to approach it in faith in order to be truly nourished by it.

- In Stages 29 to 38 (Part II), *let us allow Jesus, the Good Shepherd, to lead us to the Father.* Let us allow ourselves to be transformed by his love in trust and faithfulness, despite inevitable periods of spiritual dryness.

- The final fourteen stages evoke *life in the Spirit* (Part III): we adore the Father, through the Son present in the Eucharist, who gives us the Spirit and sends us on a mission in the Church following Mary.

∼

"To the angel of the Church in Ephesus write: 'The words of him who holds the seven stars in his right hand, who walks among the seven golden lampstands. I know your works, your toil and your patient endurance, and how you cannot bear evil men but have tested those who call themselves apostles but are not, and found them to be false; I know you are enduring patiently and bearing up for my name's sake, and you have not grown weary. But I have this against you, that you have abandoned the love you had at first. Remember then from what you have fallen, repent and do the works you did at first. If not, I will come to you and remove your lampstand from its place, unless you repent. . . . He who has an ear, let him hear what the Spirit says to the churches. To him who conquers I will grant to eat of the tree of life, which is in the paradise of God.' " (Rev 2:1−5, 7)

"I have this against you, that you have abandoned the love you had at first." Even if we know that Jesus is really present in the Eucharist, it can happen that we become spiritually lukewarm. The following stages help us to persevere in the spiritual battle, to overcome droughts or trials by letting ourselves be transformed by this Eucharistic fire. It is the Son who leads us to the Father and who gives us access to the tree of life. "True worshipers will worship the Father in spirit and truth, for such the Father seeks to worship him" (Jn 4:23).

~

II. THE FATHER

Through the Son, Ascending to the Father and Letting Oneself Be Transformed by His Love

He Is the Good Shepherd Who
Leads Me to the Father

STAGE 29

Cain's and Abel's Offerings
The Offering of Oneself

Now Abel was a keeper of sheep, and Cain a tiller of the ground. In
the course of time Cain brought to the LORD an offering of the fruit
of the ground, and Abel brought some of the firstlings of his flock
and of their fat portions. And the LORD had regard for Abel and his
offering, but for Cain and his offering he had no regard. So Cain was
very angry, and his countenance fell. The LORD said to Cain, "Why
are you angry, and why has your countenance fallen? If you do well,
will you not be accepted? And if you do not do well, sin is lurking at
the door; its desire is for you, but you must master it." Cain said to
Abel his brother, "Let us go out to the field." And when they were
in the field, Cain rose up against his brother Abel, and killed him.
(Gen 4:2–8)

No reason is indicated to justify the Lord's preference: it depends on
his free will. Cain's subsequent attitude manifests the bad disposition
of his heart. This mysterious passage can enlighten us about our adoration. The Lord did not have regard for Cain's offering. For Cain wor-
ships God, but he keeps one eye on his brother; his heart is not entirely
God's. God sees first the person, the heart, and not the offering. Later,
the Lord will say to Samuel:

> Do not look on his appearance or on the height of his stature, because
> I have rejected him; for the LORD sees not as man sees; man looks
> on the outward appearance, but the LORD looks on the heart. (1 Sam
> 16:7)

Adoration brings us into the truth. It turns us entirely to our Father
by decentering us from ourselves. It is about giving to God the worship that is his by right: "You shall worship the Lord your God and
him only shall you serve" (Mt 4:10). This implies adoring God as the

Lord of all that exists; giving him the worship due to him individually and communally; praying to him with praise, thanksgiving, and supplication; offering sacrifices to him—above all, the spiritual sacrifice of our life—united to the perfect sacrifice of Christ. In the parable of the Pharisee and the Publican, the Pharisee offers his good acts, while the tax collector humbly presents his own life to God, despite its flaws. Jesus declares: "This man went down to his house justified rather than the other" (Lk 18:9–14).

When we come to adore Jesus in the Blessed Sacrament, we present ourselves to him as we are truly! His presence frees us, heals us, and establishes us in the truth. We can then order our life in God's light and let ourselves be put at peace. This will be reflected in our behavior toward our brothers. Saint Paul encourages us to offer our bodies to God. This is the true spiritual worship that leads to conversion of the heart. This "transformation" consists in renewing our judgment in order to discern the will of God in all things: "I appeal to you therefore, brethren, by the mercies of God, to present your bodies as a living sacrifice, holy and acceptable to God, which is your spiritual worship. Do not be conformed to this world but be transformed by the renewal of your mind, that you may prove what is the will of God, what is good and acceptable and perfect" (Rom 12:1–2). Adoration, when it becomes the offering of oneself renews one's way of thinking and judging. Changing one's way of looking at others, the world, and oneself makes us receptive to welcoming the divine will: this is true conversion. For it, one must abandon oneself entirely to the Lord and even die to oneself.

For Saint Thérèse of Lisieux, "the nature of love is to humble oneself. . . . In order that Love be fully satisfied, it is necessary that It lower Itself . . . to nothingness and transform this nothingness into fire."[1] Sister Marie-Thérèse Dubouché said: "Eucharistic adoration is being there like a flower before its sun. If you knew who it is who watches you through these veils. . . . Do nothing, no matter what! A virtue will come forth from him."[2]

---

[1] Saint Thérèse of Lisieux, *Story of a Soul: The Autobiography of St. Thérèse of Lisieux*, trans. John Clark, O.C.D., 2nd ed. (Washington, D.C.: ICS Publications, Institute of Carmelite Studies, 1976), 14, 195.

[2] Théodelinde Dubouché, *L'Adoration au soleil de Dieu: Fragments spirituels*, ed. by the Sisters of Adoration for Reparation, 63.

Here is the testimony of an adorer who, through a very serious illness, carries the world by her heroic offering:

Is life worth living? This is what I was asking myself in 1998 when, at the age of 33, I was informed that I would live all my life in palliative care, but with a normal life expectancy, with the sciatic nerve alive, in unceasing pain day and night that even continual infusions of morphine are insufficient to relieve. It was in adoration and offering of myself that I found the answer to this question. I discovered adoration during a retreat. From questioning I passed to marveling: I had entered into adoration. That day in March 1998, I received the grace of a vital need to meet Jesus each day in the Blessed Sacrament, and I have remained faithful to it to this day.

For me adoration is a time of light and healing: In adoration, Jesus heals me by showing me how I hurt him. I welcome this light with joy because it allows me to undo an attitude that displeases his Father, by confessing my misery as soon as I am conscience of it. And each time it is a feast to be able to confess the mercy of God that heals me. In adoration, I give Jesus the only thing I fully possess: my unworthiness. In his eyes this has more value than my successes, which do not belong to me. "Your love makes me dance with joy: You see my misery and you know my adversity" (Ps 31:7 [Vulg.]).

Adoration, a time of offering, intercession, and spiritual motherhood: Offering my sufferings to the Father by uniting them to those of Christ for the redemption of sinners takes on all its meaning in adoration. For this reason, adoration made me understand that I had a real spiritual motherhood to exercise within the Church and that adoration was at the heart of evangelization. The Father calls us all to be an offering —that is, to offer our everyday life, following Jesus, the first to have offered himself.

In Eucharistic adoration, then, one must offer one's person to Jesus. All the same, in the first place it is Jesus himself who remains in a permanent state of offering to his Father. His offering is made present in the tabernacle. The adorer, then, must enter into this offering. Jesus desires to let us share in his great offering to the Father. His whole life was a life of adoration and offering to the Father. Jesus leaves his great adoration of the Father to his Church in the tabernacle. In the Eucharist, he adores the Father and "always lives to make intercession for [us]" (Heb 7:25). In the Mystical Body, Jesus is the Head, and we the members. We must, then, enter into the same movement as the Head and unite ourselves to Jesus' permanent adoration of his Father, for "true worshipers will worship the Father in spirit and truth, for such the Father seeks to worship him" (Jn 4:23). Paul VI said: "And it is our very sweet duty to honor and adore in the blessed Host which our eyes see, the Incarnate Word whom they cannot see, and who, without leaving heaven, is made present before us."[3]

> What does the Savior do in the Eucharist? He continues his charge as adorer, as glorifier of his Father. He will make himself the Sacrament of God's glory. Do you see him, Jesus, on the altar? in the tabernacle? He is there; what is he doing there? He is adoring his Father, giving him thanks, and continuing his charge as the intercessor of men. . . . He remains on his mystical Calvary repeating his sublime words: Father, forgive them! For them I offer you my blood, my wounds! He multiplies himself everywhere, everywhere where there is something to expiate. In whatever place that a Christian family establishes itself, Jesus comes to make a society of adoration with him and glorifies his Father by adoring him and making him to be adored in spirit and in truth. God the Father, satisfied, glorified as much as he deserves, cries out: My name is great among the nations; for from the rising of the sun unto its setting, a host of pleasing fragrance is offered to me!"[4]

~

---

[3] Paul VI, *Solemni Hac Liturgia* (1968), no. 26.

[4] Saint Peter Julian Eymard, *Adorer en esprit et en vérité* (Paris: Éditions F.-X. de Guibert, 2009), 93.

He Is the Good Shepherd Who
Leads Me to the Father

STAGE 30

"The Lord Is My Shepherd"
The Evangelization of My Being

"I am the good shepherd. The good shepherd lays down his life for the sheep. He who is a hireling and not a shepherd, whose own the sheep are not, sees the wolf coming and leaves the sheep and flees; and the wolf snatches them and scatters them. He flees because he is a hireling and cares nothing for the sheep. I am the good shepherd; I know my own and my own know me, as the Father knows me and I know the Father; and I lay down my life for the sheep." (Jn 10:11–15)

See the table on the following page.

"In giving you my presence in the tabernacle until the end of the centuries, I am giving you an infinite gift, . . . but I am giving you two other infinite gifts as well. In the second place, I am giving myself to you as your food, and in the third place, to be offered for you in sacrifice to my Father." (Blessed Charles de Foucauld)

The LORD is my shepherd, I shall not want; he makes me lie down in green pastures. He leads me beside still waters; he restores my soul. He leads me in paths of righteousness for his name's sake. Even though I walk through the valley of the shadow of death, I fear no evil; for you are with me; your rod and your staff, they comfort me. You prepare a table before me in the presence of my enemies; you anoint my head with oil, my cup overflows. Surely goodness and mercy shall follow me all the days of my life; and I shall dwell in the house of the LORD for ever. (Ps 23)

When the soul approaches the Eucharist with faith, Jesus acts toward it as a shepherd to his sheep. He leads it, feeds it, heals it. In short, Jesus evangelizes the whole interior being. For this, Jesus expects only that

What does a shepherd do for his sheep?	*Jesus is the good shepherd (Jn 10)*	*Jesus in the Blessed Sacrament is our Shepherd*
He feeds them.	"I came that they may have life, and have it abundantly" (Jn 10:10).	The Bread of Life strengthens the divine life in us (Holy Communion).
He leads them. He knows them, and they know his voice.	"If any one enters by me, he will be saved, and will go in and out and find pasture" (Jn 10:9). "I know my own and my own know me" (Jn 10:14).	In Eucharistic adoration, Jesus reveals himself to the heart. He lets himself be known. He leads and enlightens souls.
He protects them.	"I lay down my life for my sheep" (cf. Jn 10:11).	In the Holy Sacrifice of the Mass, Jesus offers himself as the spotless victim for the salvation of the world.

the soul have an interior predisposition that does not put up a barrier to the transformative power of Eucharistic grace.

a. Evangelization of the body: "Adoration" (derived from the Latin "os": the mouth). Adoration includes a prostration whose goal is to attain and kiss the object of veneration. To adore, then, signifies: to bow profoundly in a sign of extreme respect. It is the natural attitude of man when he finds himself confronted with someone greater than himself. This posture is manifest throughout the book of Revelation: "The twenty-four elders fall down before him who is seated on the throne and worship him who lives for ever and ever; they cast their crowns before the throne" (Rev 4:10). Yes, we have the grace to know someone before whom we fall to our knees. The exterior posture conveys the interior devotion. Cf. Stage 2 on the bodily position to take before the Blessed Sacrament.

> Etty Hillesum was a young Dutch Jewish woman. She was deported to Auschwitz, where she died in the last days of November 1943. A professor of Russian in Amsterdam, a refined intellectual, she found herself in the heart of the Nazi torment. When the atrocities against the Jews began, she too was arrested. From the camps where she stayed, Etty was able to write a few letters and a journal in each of which love always appears stronger than death. From the heart of suffering, she wrote: "My whole being is being transformed into a great prayer." Thomas of Celano reported this about Francis of Assisi: "Francis did not pray; he was prayer." In the midst of the hell of deportation, when the horror became unbearable, Etty left this last message: "I had the desire to kneel down on the tiles in the midst of all these people. The only gesture of human dignity that we still have in this terrible era: kneeling down before God."[1]

Bowing down to adore—this is man's ultimate goal.

b. Evangelization of the gaze and of memory: Advertising campaigns unceasingly bombard our spirit with images, marked very often by sensuality, indeed, eroticism. Few major film productions are without any erotic or violent scenes. These images profoundly imprint themselves on the memory and harm our relationship with the Father. It takes years to be freed of this poison that pollutes the spirit and taints the

---

[1] Jean Puyo, *Dieu les a séduits* (Paris: Desclée de Brouwer, 1994), 59.

heart. Jesus said: "Blessed are the pure in heart, for they shall see God" (Mt 5:8). In contemplating the Host, the resurrected Body of Christ, the Lord heals the heart, purifies the gaze, frees the unconscious from the most pernicious images, erases what is harmful from the memory, and renews the capacity to marvel at true beauty. Under the light of the Resurrected One, Christ touches our interior senses and chases away all darkness, because "the sun of righteousness shall rise, with healing in its wings" (Mal 4:2).

c. Evangelization of the intellect: Let us enter into God's humility through the Eucharist. Faced with the incomprehensibility of the Eucharistic mystery, our intellect makes the words of Peter its own: "Lord, to whom shall we go? You have the words of eternal life; and we have believed, and have come to know, that you are the Holy One of God" (Jn 6:68–69). Since Jesus is the Truth, he cannot deceive us. He makes himself present in the Eucharist to enlighten our intellect. The *intellect* makes possible the study of theology, that is, the study of God. *Faith* pushes us to go before the Blessed Sacrament. One is the academic study of love, the other the sweet experience of Love embodied. At the end of her life, Pauline-Marie Jaricot wrote these poignant lines as her spiritual testament:

> It is at the feet of your holy tabernacles that my heart, hardened by the harshest trials, has constantly found the strength necessary to endure their rigor; it is there that my struggles turned into victories, my weakness into courage, my lukewarmness into fervor, my uncertainties into lights, my sadness into joy, my obstacles into success, my desires into willpower, my dislikes, my jealousies, my resentments of my neighbor into ardent charity. All that I know, I have learned at your feet, Lord. Receive, then, the homage of all that I am, all that I have, all the good that I could ever think, say, and do.[2]

This is the homage of our intellect to the supreme divine intellect.

d. Evangelization of the will: Let us enter into God's poverty. Although the universe cannot contain God, the Lord chooses to be contained bodily in a little Host, because love always tends to self-abasement

---

[2] Pauline-Marie Jaricot, *L'Amour infini dans la Divine Eucharistie* (Lyon: Imp. St Joseph), 85–86.

beside the beloved person. To adore is to adhere, that is, freely to welcome God's will and his plan of love that unveils itself through Divine Providence. "Thy will be done" and not my own. Through adoration of the Blessed Sacrament, the Christian entirely gives back his own will to the Lord and lets God inspire his heart and put his supreme will in it. Adoration makes us enter into Jesus' prayer: "Abba, Father, all things are possible to you; remove this chalice from me; yet not what I will, but what you will" (Mk 14:36). The more faithful we are to God's will, the more our apostolic activity will be fruitful, for Jesus said: "Apart from me you can do nothing" (Jn 15:5).

Jesus is the Good Shepherd. We must learn to let ourselves be led and to abandon ourselves with confidence. Why should we not expect everything from him, for he said: "I myself will be the shepherd of my sheep, and I will make them lie down. . . . I will seek the lost, and I will bring back the strayed, and I will bind up the crippled, and I will strengthen the weak" (Ezek 34:15–16). Our deepest wounds often prevent us from going toward others to serve them or announce the love of God to them. Jesus comes to heal these wounds when we approach the Eucharist with faith. He visits our heart and comes to fill it with his power and his healing love.

> My Father, I abandon myself to you, do with me what
>   you will.
> Whatever you do with me, I thank you.
> I am ready for everything, I accept everything.
> So long as your will is done in me,
> in all your creatures,
> I desire nothing else, my God.
> I give back my soul into your hands.
> I give it to you, my God,
> with all the love of my heart,
> because I love you,
> and because for me it is a necessity of love to give myself,
> to give myself back into your hands without measure,
> with an infinite confidence,
> for you are my Father.
>
> — Blessed Charles de Foucauld

He Is the Good Shepherd Who
Leads Me to the Father

STAGE 31

"The Clay in the Potter's Hand"

"Like the clay in the potter's hand, so are you in my hand, O house of Israel" (Jer 18:6). We are the clay. God is the potter. God uses all of life's events to achieve the masterpiece he desires to accomplish in our souls. What is the masterpiece in question? "We know that in everything God works for good with those who love him. . . . For those whom he foreknew he also predestined *to be conformed to the image of his Son*, in order that he might be the first-born among many brethren" (Rom 8:28–29).

> The witness of Scripture is unanimous that the solicitude of divine providence is *concrete* and *immediate*; God cares for all, from the least things to the great events of the world and its history. The sacred books powerfully affirm God's absolute sovereignty over the course of events: "Our God is in the heavens; he does whatever he pleases." [Ps 115:3] And so it is with Christ, "who opens and no one shall shut, who shuts and no one opens" [Rev 3:7]. As the book of Proverbs states: "Many are the plans in the mind of a man, but it is the purpose of the Lord that will be established" [19:21].[1]

Jesus demands a filial abandonment to the Providence of the heavenly Father, who cares for his children's least needs: "Therefore do not be anxious, saying, 'What shall we eat?' or 'What shall we drink?' . . . Your heavenly Father knows that you need [all these things]. . . . But seek first his kingdom and his righteousness, and all these things shall be yours as well" (Mt 6:31–33; cf. 10:29–31). Jesus reminds us that the Divine Persons act unceasingly: "My Father is working still, and I am working" (Jn 5:17). The following verses make clear how

[1] CCC 303.

God acts in the soul (Jn 15:2), for what end (Jn 15:8), and what our responses should be (Jn 15:4):

> I am the true vine, and my Father is the vinedresser. Every branch of mine that bears no fruit, he takes away, and every branch that does bear fruit he prunes, that it may bear more fruit. (Jn 15:1-2)

> Abide in me, and I in you. As the branch cannot bear fruit by itself, unless it abides in the vine, neither can you, unless you abide in me. (Jn 15:4)

> By this my Father is glorified, that you bear much fruit, and so prove to be my disciples. (Jn 15:8)

The verb "prune" evokes the work that God carries out in the soul of one who has begun to follow Jesus. To "abide in the vine" is to establish oneself in a communion of love with Jesus. This new life makes the faithful person able to bear "fruit". The vinedresser prunes the branches so that he may bear ever more fruit. It is the call to sanctity, the noblest and most beautiful adventure that a man can complete: "You shall be holy; for I the LORD your God am holy" (Lev 19:2).

Thus God uses all of life's events, the happy ones as well as the sad ones, to fortify us in his love and to reproduce the image of his Son in us. He desires to make of us "another Christ". It is often by the most dramatic events of life, like a personal failure, illness, or the loss of someone dear to us, that God prunes the soul by renewing our hope and our confidence in him. The greater our confidence, the greater will be the wonders worked in the soul by God: he uproots pride from our heart; he unbinds us from our self-satisfaction; he frees us from our attachments to the goods of this world. For this, Jesus left us Mary, one of whose titles is "Mother of Confidence". According to Saint Louis-Marie Grignon de Montfort, Mary is the "living mold of God" who reproduces her Son in us "without great pain or cost".

> A sculptor has two ways of making a lifelike statue or figure: He may carve the figure out of some hard, shapeless material, using for this purpose his professional skill and knowledge, his strength and the necessary instruments, or he may cast it in a mold. The first manner is long and difficult and subject to many mishaps; a single blow of the hammer or the chisel, awkwardly given, may spoil the whole work. The second is short, easy and smooth; it requires but little work and slight expense,

provided the mold be perfect and made to reproduce the figure exactly; provided, moreover, the material used offer no resistance to the hand of the artist.

Mary is the great mold of God, made by the Holy Ghost to form a true God-Man by the Hypostatic Union and to form also a man-God by grace. In that mold none of the features of the Godhead is wanting. Whoever is cast in it, and allows himself be molded, receives all the features of Jesus Christ, true God. The work is done gently, in a manner proportioned to human weakness, without much pain or labor, in a sure manner, free from all illusion. . . . How many stains and defects and illusions, how much darkness and how much human nature is there in [the soul who trusts in its own skill and ingenuity]; and oh how pure, how heavenly and how Christlike is [the soul that is thoroughly tractable and casts itself into Mary to be molded by the Holy Spirit].[2]

Adoration is a school of fervor in prayer. Whatever discipline we practice (physical, intellectual, or spiritual), regularity proves fundamental. No spiritual progress is possible without faithfulness in prayer. Without it, prayer would risk becoming sentimental: "I pray when I feel like it, or rather, if I have time after all my daily activities . . ." And our love for Jesus would come after everything else! Remember Jesus' words to Martha: "Martha, Martha, you are anxious and troubled about many things; one thing is needful. Mary has chosen the good portion, which shall not be taken away from her" (Lk 10:41–42). Mary was seated at Jesus' feet. For a moment, she leaves everything to belong entirely to Jesus. Through our regularity in prayer of adoration, we let God act in the soul, whatever the states of our souls! In parishes where continuous Eucharistic adoration is organized, the parishioners, who agree to commit themselves to a fixed hour of adoration every week, grow in faithfulness and attentiveness. Their commitment allows them not to be discouraged in moments of trial and spiritual dryness.

Also: a more limited commitment—for example, one hour of adoration per month—remains insufficient for letting this time of prayer transform us. Since Mass is a weekly commitment, and since adoration "prolongs and intensifies all that takes place during the liturgical

[2] Saint Louis-Marie Grignon de Montfort, *The Secret of Mary* (London: Catholic Way Pub., 2013), 8–9.

celebration itself",[3] it makes sense to adore for an hour each week! As a practical matter, it is easier to free an hour per week than an hour per month since our schedules are established on a weekly basis.

Some state that they prefer to pray at home! Experience shows that it is more difficult to pray at home because of noise, distractions, or many inconveniences than in a chapel dedicated solely to silent prayer of adoration. The Eucharist is the sublime means that God, in the superabundance of his love, gives us so that man might unite himself to him. The Church today strongly encourages the practice of Eucharistic adoration. It would be a shame to neglect it! To want to meet God in us in a "heart-to-heart" without passing through the "face to face" of adoration requires a purification of the inner self and a solid formation without which prayer risks leading us back to ourselves and not to God present in us. In the "face to face" of adoration, the resurrected Body of Jesus purifies us, transforms us, and divinizes us. To contemplate the Host leads us to the "heart-to-heart" with Jesus and the Divine Persons (cf. *Stage 6 of this itinerary*).

A monstrance in barbed wire: Brother Claude Humbert, O.P., testifies about his stay at Dachau: "Among the 4,000 priests who were at Dachau, a few had secretly fashioned a monstrance with barbed wire. For us, who were entirely surrounded with barbed wire, this monstrance took on an extraordinary meaning. It was Christ crowned with thorns and sharing our own. And the Body of Christ was often exposed in it. Like many priests, I spent long hours of adoration before him and Our Lady of Dachau at his right. This has marked me for life."[4]

~

---

[3] Benedict XVI, Post-synodal Apostolic Exhortation *Sacramentum Caritatis* (2007), no. 66.

[4] *Présences mariales, scènes de guerre*, Marian collection, ed. by the Marist Brothers (Varennes-sur-Allier, 1987), 95.

He Is the Good Shepherd Who
Leads Me to the Father

STAGE 32

"Not What I Will, but What You Will"

And they went to a place which was called Gethsemane; and he said to his disciples, "Sit here, while I pray." And he took with him Peter and James and John, and began to be greatly distressed and troubled. And he said to them, "My soul is very sorrowful, even to death; remain here, and watch." And going a little farther, he fell on the ground and prayed that, if it were possible, the hour might pass from him. And he said, "Abba, Father, all things are possible to you; remove this chalice from me; yet not what I will, but what you will." And he came and found them sleeping, and he said to Peter, "Simon, are you asleep? Could you not watch one hour? Watch and pray that you may not enter into temptation; the spirit indeed is willing, but the flesh is weak." And again he went away and prayed, saying the same words. (Mk 14:32–39)

Scripture says that when Jesus was at Gethsemane, his "soul was very sorrowful, even to death". He came to give his very self to mankind through the gift of the Holy Eucharist. But so many will reject this love! This rejection pierces his heart: "I looked for pity, but there was none; and for comforters, but I found none" (Ps 69:20). He called upon his apostles to comfort him, but they preferred to sleep, for it was already late at night. They slept during Christ's greatest agony, even after he had expressly called upon them: "So, could you not watch with me one hour?" (Mt 26:40). So, someone sent by the Father descended from heaven to console him. This angel comforted Jesus by showing him all our acts of love toward the Eucharist in the ages to come. Among other things, Jesus saw the numerous sacrifices of all those who would faithfully come to pray day and night, each week, to keep him company in the Blessed Sacrament. These sacrifices comforted, consoled, strengthened, and encouraged our Savior. He knew then that his love would be requited, because "greater love has no man than this, that a man lay down his life for his friends" (Jn 15:13).

In Eucharistic adoration, the adorer learns to do no longer "his will for God", but "God's will". Every baptized person must live out this conversion of the will. Too often Christians generously exert themselves in many acts of service that they have chosen. At the end of the week, beyond physical fatigue, they experience a feeling of spiritual dissatisfaction, because they did their will for God. Jesus reminded us that the Father's will is true food: "My food is to do the will of him who sent me, and to accomplish his work" (Jn 4:34). Before acting, we must get on our knees, to receive from God not only his will, but also the strength to persevere in accomplishing it. Beyond this, prayer is a powerful defense against daily temptations: "Pray that you may not enter into temptation" (Mk 14:38).

"Abba, Father, all things are possible to you; remove this chalice from me; yet not what I will, but what you will" (Mk 14:36)! At Gethsemane, Jesus accepts the Father's will, even if it seems to be opposed to his personal will and leads him to the Cross. But it is in handing his life over to the Father that he saves mankind. Only the Father's will deserves to be done to the very end, for it gives man the means to bloom fully in his vocation as a child of the Father. Only the Father's will can truly fill man's heart by giving a profound meaning to life. All that we do outside of this will disappear irretrievably. Praying is not asking God to bless our own intentions, however good they may be. Praying is asking God for a new way of looking at the world, at others, and at oneself, as well as the grace to live in conformity to the divine will.

An adorer testifies: "At the beginning, I thought that adoration meant loving God greatly. But the Lord made me understand that he desires above all that I let myself be loved in my miseries and my faults. For me this is so much more demanding. Letting Jesus look at me, hold me, lead me to God his Father—that is adoration in spirit and in truth!"

Eucharistic adoration does not consist so much in "loving greatly" but rather in "letting oneself be greatly loved" despite our lacks and infidelities. In other words, it is not our qualities that attract Jesus but our faults. Eucharistic grace can then act through its transformative power. Let us allow Christ to continue in us the work of healing and sanctification that he began two thousand years ago. He comes not to receive our merits and virtues but to save and raise what is broken in our heart.

Eucharistic adoration makes us pass from "I" to "thou". It is inappropriate to begin by asking Jesus graciously to hear our will. Rather let us ask him to enlighten us about his will and to give us the grace to accomplish it. Adoration decenters us from ourselves in order to center us on the person of Christ and on his holy will. Too often we pray like this: "Listen, Lord, for your servant speaks." Adoration drives us to say: "Speak, LORD, for your servant hears" (1 Sam 3:9).

> In life today, often noisy and dispersive, it is more important than ever to recover the capacity for inner silence and recollection. Eucharistic adoration permits this not only centered on the "I" but more so in the company of that "You" full of love who is Jesus Christ, "the God who is near to us."[1]

> Be faithful in abiding in God's presence without worrying about being unable to do anything. . . . Do not be at all reluctant to be in God's presence without doing anything, for since he desires nothing from you but silence and annihilation, you will always be doing much when you leave and abandon yourself unreservedly to his omnipotence. Be faithful to this, do not be discouraged by your distractions, let them pass, and abide humbly at the feet of Jesus.[2]

Many saints' words about the ingratitude that Jesus receives in the Blessed Sacrament can be surprising. For example, Blessed Dina Bélanger, a religious in Quebec beatified by John Paul II, wrote: "Oh! how harrowing are the plaints of Jesus! How he suffers, the silent Captive of our tabernacles, imprisoned day and night by love! So my greatest sorrow became that of the suffering of the Eucharistic Heart. How can one remain unmoved when it is Jesus who is abandoned and despised!"[3] What are we to make of this?

---

[1] Benedict XVI, Angelus, June 10, 2007 (2007).
[2] Saint Catherine de Bar, *Adorer et adhérer* (Paris: Éditions du Cerf, 1994), 97.
[3] Blessed Dina Bélanger, *Autobiographie* (Éditions Québec, 1995), 203.

It is true that since his Resurrection our Lord in the Host cannot suffer. But all the same, insult, contempt, hate, forgetfulness, indifference, and ingratitude reach and wound his Eucharistic Heart. Since his Resurrection, Christ enjoys a perfect beatitude. He is in no way a prisoner in tabernacles and not at all wounded by men's sins. However, when contemplative souls see our Lord suffering, even moaning to them about the sins and ingratitude of men, it is in no way an illusion. Jesus, in his sorrowful Passion, suffered from all the insults and all the ingratitude that were to be poured out upon him throughout the centuries, in his Sacrament of love. It is this suffering, and especially that proceeding from sins being committed at that moment, that he shares with his most faithful friends. So they have the impression that Jesus is suffering in the moment. They see, at that moment, Jesus such as he suffered in his agony, and they are called, then, to sympathize with his sufferings and to share them. It is thought that the angel who consoled our Lord in the garden on the Mount of Olives did so by showing him all the faithful souls who were to share in his sufferings until the end of the world. We can also say that our Lord suffers from men's offenses as the good God does (do we not say that sin gives sorrow to the good God), in the sense that he detests sin and that he acts toward it as if he were suffering from it. As Pope Pius XI explained in 1928, at Gethsemane, through "an angel who comforted him" (cf. Lk 22:43), Jesus, in his divine foreknowledge, foresaw our future efforts to console him and in his solitude that evening drew a real comfort from them.

∼

He Is the Good Shepherd Who
Leads Me to the Father

STAGE 33

"Abba, Father"
Adoration: Remedy for
Pride and Despair

Eucharistic adoration comes to heal man's heart. His heart is transformed into the heart of a child of God because the two great maladies of our time are pride and despair. Mankind's inordinate pride makes man believe that he can save himself all alone and that he can establish peace through science, technology, and the economy alone. And despair plunges our society into meaninglessness, into an interior decay. Pride consists in telling God that we have no need of him—no need of a Father. And despair does not know the Father; it makes us orphans. These two attitudes are sins against the virtue of hope. Saint Thomas Aquinas explains that the language of hope is the Our Father: "Abba, Father". To be healed from pride and despair we must say "Abba, Father". How can we live from the power of the Holy Spirit if this gift is not renewed in the Eucharist? Eucharistic adoration is a perpetual outpouring of the Holy Spirit to give us the heart of a child, to put us at the disposal of the Heart of God, to learn in those long hours spent before the Blessed Sacrament how to say "Abba, Father" with the right attitude: that is, in full charity, in the certitude that without him I can do nothing, and in acquiring the freedom of the children of God, which consists in being in perfect communion with the Father. Jesus came to do the will of the Father, to make the Father manifest.

This text takes up the principal themes and expressions of a lecture by Father Nicolas Buttet at Paray-le-Monial, July 17, 2007, on the theme: "Adoration for World Transformation".

Man's natural path consists in separating from Dad and Mom in order to follow his own path. Spiritually, the path is just the opposite. So long as I do not depend upon the Father, I am a kid! But the more I enter into the heart of the Trinity, the more I become an adult in my humanity—in my humanity's spiritual dimension.

In respect to humanity, adoration's first fundamental healing is to give back a filial heart. The consequences affect not only us but also ecology. Saint Paul says:

> Creation waits with eager longing for the revealing of the sons of God; for the creation was subjected to futility, not of its own will but by the will of him who subjected it in hope; because the creation itself will be set free from its bondage to decay and obtain the glorious liberty of the children of God. We know that the whole creation has been groaning with labor pains together until now; and not only the creation, but we ourselves, who have the first fruits of the Spirit, groan inwardly as we wait for adoption as sons, the redemption of our bodies. (Rom 8:19–23)

One of the ways of interpreting this text is the following: creation suffers, groaning while waiting for men to behave as children of God, as sons of that heavenly Father who has given us creation as something in gestation and not as a possession to destroy. Thus today's ecological crisis concerning everything that must be done in order to avoid the tragedies that might occur has a profoundly spiritual root that we see explicitly here. Creation moans and groans in ecological catastrophes, waiting for man to behave as a child of God.

An Orthodox patriarch said: "Either the world will be transfigured by worship, or it will be disfigured by consumption." Here we touch upon that mysterious communion of all beings. Man is at the summit of creation and participates in all material nature through his physical nature. When man is no longer united to God, there is, as it were, a seismic tremor that radiates throughout the universe by the very fact that man's heart is no longer united to God. The first break happened through this disunity of mankind and God. To be attached to the Eucharistic Heart frees man, giving him the extraordinary freedom of the children of God. This freedom consists in living in charity, but without all of those subordinations into which we can fall. Adoration introduces us into that freedom of the children of God with all the consequences this implies for our daily behavior.

Adoration is a duty of justice within the natural virtue of justice. We find it in the first gift of the Spirit, that of fear or adoration, which places us as creatures before the Creator in total adoration before him from whom all things come. This attitude of adoration is very important for our time. The world has lost its sense of adoration. It has lost its sense of kneeling. Man is great only on his knees, in adoration before God. A mankind that wants to remain standing, in its presumption, its pride, its self-satisfaction, that no longer knows how to kneel, has lost its sense of the essential. Going and kneeling before God interiorly, but also physically, is the fundamental attitude of the human heart. Eucharistic adoration comes to heal mankind from this secret wound rooted in original sin, which is the refusal to kneel before God, before him from whom all things come. On Christmas night 1886, Wagner wrote to Nietzsche about his searing spiritual experience. And Nietzsche responded: "What, ignoble man, you too have kneeled, you too have become a weakling, you too have prostrated yourself!" For the superman must not kneel. Mankind is caught in this myth of the superman and in his daily awareness of not being this superman. Adoration comes to break this structure of thought.

Adoration situates us in harmony. No power, no person, no thing, nothing is useless in creation; everything has its place in a spiritual symphony. Adoration is the revalorization of every human being, of everything that is in us. Adoration is a transfiguration of the human being. A power of anthropological transformation acts through it. Fallen man is raised back up to the full stature of the dignity of a child of God. Personal adoration is also a place where the universe is transformed because it transforms man's heart. This is how God refashions the world. Adoration is the place where God reconstructs man.

Psychologically, our gaze fixes its attention on the Heart of Christ —the eyes of the flesh, but also the eyes of hope and charity, fixed on the Real Presence. There is no emotional excrescence in adoration! Rather it is peaceful and sometimes dry and arid. But this roots us in a deep distinction between what is of the emotional order and what comes from the faith at our very depths. This comes and profoundly heals what is wounded in us. "The sun of righteousness shall rise, with healing in its wings" (Mal 4:2). Adoration reconstructs man in his whole being, in an extremely profound way, even physically: he is there. Our body, our psychology, and our spiritual soul, with the intellect and the will, are transformed through the mystery of Eucharistic adoration. This transformation of the human person will be the key to the transformation of all mankind. The unity of the person will come through adoration.

Adoration urges us to action. We cannot stop where we are. After having contemplated Christ, King of glory, King of mankind, in the Blessed Sacrament, we must give forth actions, we must act. This Kingship must shine forth everywhere. "Faith is not the opiate of the people", said the economist François Perrou. "There is not a night I can go to sleep saying that I loved enough today." I will by lacking in love each time, imploring God's grace to love more.

As Saint Peter Julian Eymard said so well:

Exposition is the form of worship our time needs. . . . It is necessary in order to save society. Society is killing itself, because it no longer has a center of gravity and charity. There is no more family life: everyone isolates himself, concentrates on himself, wants to suffice unto himself. Disintegration is imminent. But society will be born again, full of vigor, when all its members come and join together around our Emmanuel. Spiritual relationships will be reformed quite naturally, under a common truth: the ties of true and strong friendship will be renewed under the action of just such a love. . . . The great evil of the time is that we no longer go to Jesus Christ. We abandon the only foundation, the only law, the only saving grace. . . . Returning to the source of life, to Jesus, and not only to Jesus passing through Judea or to Jesus glorified in heaven, but also and above all to Jesus in the Eucharist. . . . Let us be quite clear, a century grows or declines in proportion to its worship of the divine Eucharist. This worship is the life and measure of its faith, its charity, and its virtue. May it come more and more, then, this Reign of the Eucharist."[1]

Your personal act of adoration assumes a cosmic and social dimension. It drives us toward action and gives rise to the transfiguration of the whole society. With the intellect's gaze, we would imagine at first

---

[1] Saint Peter Julian Eymard, "Le siècle de l'Eucharistie", *Le Très Saint Sacrement*, 1864.

sight that political and economic actions require great expertise, which is true. But with the gift of the intellect and of faith, we understand that if there is not this movement of adoration, this filial return of mankind to the Heart of God; if there is not this outpouring of the Holy Spirit, who brings together all of creation to the Father through mankind and who restores peace from the throne of mercy instituted by God on earth—his Blessed Sacrament—mankind cannot go forward. But if there is this movement, then we will see the most beautiful period of mankind shine forth before our eyes, the advent of the civilization of love, this kingdom of peace and justice that will radiate through mankind in that nuclear fission of the Eucharist. And then there will be a historic Hosanna, a historic Palm Sunday when God is acclaimed King of kings upon the little donkey of the little Host.

Spiritual Warfare

STAGE 34

"Be Still, and Know that I Am God!"
Sensible Graces and Dryness

God is our refuge and strength, a very present help in trouble. Therefore we will not fear though the earth should change, though the
mountains shake in the heart of the sea; though its waters roar and
foam, though the mountains tremble with its tumult. . . . The Lord
of hosts is with us; the God of Jacob is our refuge. Come, behold
the works of the Lord, how he has wrought desolations in the earth.
He makes wars cease to the end of the earth; he breaks the bow, and
shatters the spear, he burns the chariots with fire! *"Be still, and know
that I am God.* I am exalted among the nations, I am exalted in the
earth!" The Lord of hosts is with us; the God of Jacob is our refuge.
(Ps 46:1–3, 7–11)

Going into a chapel of adoration or a church to spend some time before the Blessed Sacrament is learning how to be still! It is responding
to the psalmist's invitation: "Be still, and know that I am God" (Ps
46:10). Jesus said: "Come away by yourselves to a lonely place, and
rest a while" (Mk 6:31). Faced with daily stress and our overloaded
lives, the need to be still becomes necessary. Physical strength can be
renewed during a period of vacation. Spiritual strength can be renewed
in a period of spiritual retreat or simply before the resurrected Christ
who awaits us in the Blessed Sacrament!

During the day, Saint Thérèse of Lisieux would stop frequently to
offer the world to God and to offer herself as a living host. Momentary
fatigue often got the better of her. She writes: "I should be desolate
for having slept (for seven years) during my hours of prayer and my
thanksgivings after Holy Communion; well, I am not desolate. . . . I remember that *little children* are as pleasing to their parents when they are

173

asleep as well as when they are wide awake; I remember, too, that when
they perform operations, doctors put their patients to sleep. Finally,
remember that 'The Lord knows our weakness, that he is mindful that
we are but dust and ashes.' "[1]

It is not what we do that makes a "holy hour", but what Jesus does:
he pours into us his Holy Spirit, which sanctifies us. "If any one thirst,
let him come to me and drink. He who believes in me, as the Scripture
has said, 'Out of his heart shall flow rivers of living water' " (Jn 7:37–
38). What counts above all for Jesus is our desire to love him. Instead
of keeping an hour in our day free for our personal occupations, we
choose to meet him in an hour of adoration.

Even if you think you cannot pray well because you are easily distracted, Jesus wants you to know that he understands this. It is natural. What he wants you to understand is supernatural: he loves you so
much that the simple fact of choosing to spend an hour with him in
prayer brings his Sacred Heart an indescribable joy!

And when we feel nothing or stop feeling anything? In adoration,
what is most important is not what we feel but him whom we meet
and what we give him! Love seeks, not its own interest, but the interest
of the beloved. One does not go worship for oneself or to feel something. We adore God for himself and because he deserves our adoration. Adoring is a "very sweet duty";[2] it is the first commandment:
"You shall worship the Lord your God and him only shall you serve"
(Mt 4:10).

One who states, "I no longer feel anything, so I'm going to stop
adoration", has in fact never begun to adore! Prayer is never a question
of feelings. For Jesus said, "true worshipers will worship the Father in
spirit and truth, for such the Father seeks to worship him" (Jn 4:23),
and not, "true worshipers will worship the Father in order to feel
something, for such the Father seeks to worship him"!

Blessed be the God and Father of our Lord Jesus Christ, the Father of
mercies and God of all comfort, who comforts us in all our afflictions,

---

[1] Saint Thérèse of Lisieux, *Story of a Soul: The Autobiography of St. Thérèse of Lisieux*,
trans. John Clark, O.C.D., 2nd ed. (Washington, D.C.: ICS Publications, Institute of
Carmelite Studies, 1976), 165.
[2] Paul VI, *Solemni Hac Liturgia* (1968), no. 26.

so that we may be able to comfort those who are in any affliction, with the comfort with which we ourselves are comforted by God. For as we share abundantly in Christ's sufferings, so through Christ we share abundantly in comfort too. (2 Cor 1:3–5)

During times of adoration, Jesus can give the soul, in a limited way, very sensible graces. He gives us the consolations appropriate to our situation and according to our needs. But during his prayer, the adorer ought never to seek these graces for themselves. Sensible graces are transitory. Graces that build up the interior life are lasting and fortify divine union. Too often adorers feel discouraged when adoration becomes arid, because of their excessive attraction to the sensible consolations that they have stopped receiving. The Lord purifies the adorer's faith. He prunes the soul according to these words: "Every branch that does bear fruit [my Father] prunes, that it may bear more fruit" (Jn 15:2). The Father always lavishes us with his graces. They become less sensible but act more profoundly in the soul and bear more abundant fruit. The soul then passes from a sensible attachment to God to an adoration of God in spirit and truth.

Content yourself, not with what you are, not with what you feel, but with what God is and what he will be forever. . . . The rest is not worth thinking about. Only worry about God. All the rest is nothing. So the soul knows one thing, which is that God is, and it is there she stops, no longer amused with watching or reflecting upon all that is happening inside of her or outside of her. Paying no attention to all that, she abides always in God.[3]

And distractions?

It is with the heart that we pray, and a sincere and persevering will to pray is a true prayer. Distractions that are entirely involuntary do not interrupt the bending of the will toward God. . . . Do not attack distractions directly: to protest against the distraction itself is to be distracted. . . . You would spend all your time warring against the flies making noise around you: let them drone in your ears, and accustom yourself to continuing your journey as if they were far from you. Take hold of the places in the Gospel that touch you most. Read

---

[3] Catherine de Bar, *Adorer et adhérer* (Paris: Éditions du Cerf, 1994), 81.

slowly, and when some word touches you, let this truth drip little by little into your heart.[4]

In the midst of distractions, we can also change our bodily position by, for example, getting back on our knees for a few minutes. We can also choose another way of praying, like meditating on the rosary, on the Gospel, or reading a passage from a devotional book.

Why do so many distractions monopolize us? Throughout the day, preoccupations, meetings, and worries so solicit the spirit that it makes sense that it needs time to calm down. This is why many distractions often assail the spirit during the first part of an hour's adoration. Afterward, the imagination is less of a disruption and the spirit is less active. It is often then that the heart is receptive to divine inspirations and that prayer of adoration becomes a real heart-to-heart. This also explains why nighttime adoration is much more conducive to recollection, because the day's activities solicit the spirit less.

To overcome dryness and spiritual droughts, committing to an hour of adoration per week is strongly recommended. Some people refuse to choose a specific hour, preferring to come "freely", according to their pleasure. A deceptive desire and a dangerous fidelity! Love drives us to commitment. Freedom is fully exercised when it is committed to fidelity in love. To overcome an affective adoration (adoring when one feels like it, going to see "one's own little Jesus") and move on to an adoration "in spirit and truth", an adoration in the Church and for the Church, it is necessary to pray faithfully and regularly! Adoration then becomes a service for mankind. We keep watch in the name of the Church for those most in need of it. Experience shows that commitment to a fixed hour allows us to persevere through dry periods and spiritual droughts.

～

[4] Fénelon, Archbishop of Cambrai, excerpt from the letter of May 31, 1707.

Spiritual Warfare

STAGE 35

Jacob's Struggle and Spiritual Advice

Jacob was left alone; and a man wrestled with him until the breaking of the day. When the man saw that he did not prevail against Jacob, he touched the hollow of his thigh; and Jacob's thigh was put out of joint as he wrestled with him. Then he said, "Let me go, for the day is breaking." But Jacob said, "I will not let you go, unless you bless me." And he said to him, "What is your name?" And he said, "Jacob." Then he said, "Your name shall no more be called Jacob, but Israel, for you have striven with God and with men, and have prevailed." Then Jacob asked him, "Tell me, I pray, your name." But he said, "Why is it that you ask my name?" And there he blessed him. So Jacob called the name of the place Peniel, saying, "For I have seen God face to face, and yet my life is preserved." (Gen 32:24-30)

Note from the Jerusalem Bible:

This enigmatic story . . . speaks of a physical struggle, a wrestling with God from which Jacob seems to emerge victor. Jacob recognises the supernatural character of his adversary and extorts a blessing from him. The text, however, avoids using the name of Yahweh and the unknown antagonist will not give his name. The author has made use of an old story as a means of explaining the name "Peniel" ("face of God") and the origin of the name "Israel". At the same time he gives the story a religious significance: the patriarch holds fast to God and forces from him a blessing: henceforth all who bear Israel's name will have a claim on God. It is not surprising that this dramatic scene later served as an image of the spiritual combat and of the value of persevering prayer (Saint Jerome, Origen).

Humble yourselves therefore under the mighty hand of God, that in due time he may exalt you. Cast all your anxieties on him, for

177

he cares about you. Be sober, be watchful. Your adversary the devil prowls around like a roaring lion, seeking some one to devour. Resist him, firm in your faith, knowing that the same experience of suffering is required of your brotherhood throughout the world. And after you have suffered a little while, the God of all grace, who has called you to his eternal glory in Christ, will himself restore, establish, and strengthen you. (1 Pet 5:6–10)

In this passage, the apostle Peter invites us to enter into the spiritual battle of prayer. It is a battle greater than we are, for which God remains our only help: "Put on the whole armor of God, that you may be able to stand against the wiles of the devil. For we are not contending against flesh and blood, but against the principalities, against the powers, against the world rulers of this present darkness, against the spiritual hosts of wickedness in the heavenly places" (Eph 6:11–12). The devil will do anything to keep us from praying. Activism will always be a temptation not to pray any more. Even works that are good in themselves can become pretexts to stop praying or to not pray at all. God himself must always come before works for God. In prayer, the Spirit comes to fight in us against the spirit of the world and to make us say: "Abba, Father". "For all who are led by the Spirit of God are sons of God. For you did not receive the spirit of slavery to fall back into fear, but you have received the spirit of sonship. When we cry, 'Abba, Father!' it is the Spirit himself bearing witness with our spirit that we are children of God" (Rom 8:14–16). This warfare is not simply against the demon; first of all it is against ourselves, against our sin. Praying is hard, not only for us, but for the "brotherhood throughout the world". Everyone who is baptized must participate in the same warfare, with the same temptations and the same difficulties. For each victory in faithfulness and perseverance, God rewards us by strengthening our communion with him. He will "restore, establish, and strengthen you" (1 Pet 5:10). Hence the importance of committing to a weekly hour of adoration in order to be supported by the community and persevere to the end!

Let us be "soldiers for peace"! Through the centuries, innumerable men have sacrificed their lives during wars. Today, so few are ready to make the least sacrifice to win peace. Evil wins in our world today because those against God are more active than those for God. This spiritual warfare between good and evil is taking place today. It is the greatest war in human history because the destiny of the Church and the world depends on it. It is a spiritual "red alert". Who will react against general indifference and become a courageous soldier for Christ, fighting for peace through prayer? Who will become a man of God, arming himself with the spiritual arms of prayer and self-renunciation? "For God did not give us a spirit of timidity but a spirit of power and love and self-control" (2 Tim 1:7). Who will respond to Christ's call launched in the middle of the night: "Simon, are you asleep? Could you not watch one hour?" (Mk 14:37).

Some Advice on How to Spend an Hour
with Jesus in the Blessed Sacrament

Is there a universal method for adoring the Blessed Sacrament? No, because adoration has us enter into a relationship of love. And in love, there can be no rules or laws. It is a heart that meets another heart in perfect freedom. "Man's humility is needed in order to respond to God's humility."[1] Time, silence, and patience are required. All the saints knew how to let the Holy Spirit lead them in this intimate relationship with Christ. Jesus awaits us in the sacrament of his Love. Praying an hour in the presence of Jesus is not hard, because Jesus is without doubt the easiest person to meet. We can help ourselves with a prayer book, passages of Scripture, or the rosary. Better yet, know how to enter into interior silence by speaking heart-to-heart with Jesus as with a friend. More than anything, the Lord desires our heart. He desires to speak with us, bless us, sanctify us, take hold of us, and lead us to his Father. It may happen that we are so tired and weak that we do not want to do anything but sit and rest to feel the sweet peace that comes from the simple fact of being in the presence of him who loves us most, Jesus in the Blessed Sacrament, who says: "Come to me, all who labor and are heavy laden, and I will give you rest" (Mt 11:28). "My peace I give to you" (Jn 14:27).

Adoring with Holy Scripture: "If you read the Gospel, bring it to the Eucharist, and from the Eucharist into yourself. You then have a

---

[1] Benedict XVI, Address to the World of Culture, Collège des Bernardins, Paris, September 12, 2008.

much greater power. The Gospel becomes clear, and you have before your eyes and in reality the continuation of what you are reading"[2] (cf. *end of Stage 14*).

Adoring with the rosary: when you pray the rosary in the presence of the Blessed Sacrament, you love Jesus with the heart of Mary. You offer Jesus Mary's perfect adoration. Jesus welcomes your hour of adoration as if it came from Mary herself. Mary receives you into her heart, and Jesus accepts your hour spent with him as if it came directly from the heart of his most blessed Mother. Mary's heart fills the deficiencies in our own heart. "The Rosary itself, when it is profoundly understood in the biblical and christocentric form . . . , will prove a particularly fitting introduction to Eucharistic contemplation, a contemplation carried out with Mary as our companion and guide."[3]

Mother Teresa wrote:

I do an hour of adoration every day in the presence of Jesus in the Blessed Sacrament. All my Missionary Sisters of Charity also do their hour of adoration. For us, thanks to this daily hour of adoration, our love for Jesus becomes more intimate, our love for each other more meaningful, and our love for the poor more compassionate. Our daily hour of adoration is our family prayer when we come together before the Blessed Sacrament exposed in the monstrance. For the first half hour, we recite the rosary, and for the second half hour we pray in silence. Through our adoration, the number of our vocations has doubled. In 1963, we did one hour of adoration together each week, but it was only in 1973, when we began doing our daily hour of adoration, that our community began to grow and prosper.[4]

The Holy Sacrifice of the Mass is the most sublime of prayers. In it, Jesus Christ offers himself to his Father, adores him, thanks him, asks his forgiveness, and implores him for the good of his Church, for sinful men. Jesus continues this majestic prayer through his state of victimhood in the Eucharist. Saint Peter Julian Eymard suggests dividing the hour of adoration into four periods, corresponding to the four ends of

[2] Saint Peter Julian Eymard, *Adorer en esprit et vérité* (Paris: Éditions F.-X. de Guibert, 2009), 186.

[3] John Paul II, Apostolic Letter *Mane Nobiscum Domine* (2004), no. 18.

[4] Blessed Mother Teresa, *Tu m'apportes l'amour: Écrits spirituels* (Paris: Éditions du Centurion, 1975).

the sacrifice of the Mass, namely: adoration, thanksgiving, reparation, and supplication. Here are a few of the saint's words:[5]

1. *Adoration:* If you begin with love, you will end with love. Offer Christ your person, your actions, your life. Adore the Father through the Eucharistic Heart of Jesus. He is God and man, your Savior and your brother at once. Adore the heavenly Father through his Son, the object of all his kindness, and your adoration will be worth Jesus' adoration: it will be his adoration.

2. *Thanksgiving:* Thanksgiving is the act of love that is sweetest to the soul and most pleasing to God; it is the perfect homage to his infinite goodness. The Eucharist itself is the perfect act of gratitude. Eucharist means *thanksgiving*: in it Jesus gives thanks to his Father for us. In it he is our own thanksgiving. Thank the Father, the Son, the Holy Spirit for giving us the gift of the Eucharist.

3. *Reparation:* for all the sins against his Eucharistic presence. What sadness for Jesus to remain ignored, abandoned, despised in so many tabernacles! How few Christians believe in his Real Presence, how many forget him, all this because he made himself so very small, so very humble in order to show us his love! Ask forgiveness, make the mercy of God descend upon the world for all crimes.

4. *Intercession, supplication:* Pray that his kingdom come, that men believe in his Eucharistic presence. Pray for the world's intentions, for your own intentions. And end your adoration with acts of love and adoration.

~

---

[5] Saint Peter-Julian Eymard, *Adorer en esprit et en vérité*, 28–32.

STAGE 36

The Trial in the Wilderness
Adoration in Battle,
Recollection, Contemplation

The Israelites wandered through the wilderness for forty years before arriving in the Promised Land. This symbolizes our faithful progress in faith until the day when we see God face to face. In the wilderness, the Israelites sometimes had the experience of desolation and sometimes were filled with divine favors. In fact, the word "wilderness" in Hebrew signifies the place of "desolation" where one abandons God or, conversely, the place of the "Word" where one seeks him with all one's heart. It is in the wilderness that God addressed his people at Sinai, there that he gave the tablets of the Law, there that he made a covenant with them, there that he chose them as his bride. It is there that he desired to bring back his unfaithful people to recover the abandoned Covenant: "Therefore, behold, I will allure her, and bring her into the wilderness, and speak tenderly to her. . . . And I will espouse you for ever; I will espouse you in righteousness and in justice, in steadfast love, and in mercy" (Hos 2:14, 19). The permanent presence of the Host in each church reveals God's unceasing faithfulness toward us. Contemplating the Host is choosing God anew; it is allowing oneself to be looked at, called, and espoused anew!

Each year, the Church offers periods of grace, like that of Lent, to renew our covenant with God—a covenant sealed in the Eucharist. When worldly cares have taken the upper hand, God can send us into the wilderness in order to recover the love we had at the beginning: "I know you are enduring patiently and bearing up for my name's sake, and you have not grown weary. But I have this against you, that you have abandoned the love you had at first. Remember then from what you have fallen, repent and do the works you did at first" (Rev 2:3-5).

When the Lord leads us into the wilderness, we feel the dryness, the drought. So it is the place of adoration: we adore; it is hard; we must dig, dig. This depends on us. But this difficult and tiring step requires a great deal of willpower, effort, perseverance. It is the time of *"adoration in battle"*[1] so valuable to the soul because God is strengthening its faith. Adoration in the wilderness requires a great deal of willingness! So we must beg the Holy Spirit to strengthen in us the "gift of fortitude" so as never to be discouraged. We must strengthen our will by digging ever deeper so as never to remain in places where there is no more water.

> You are in dryness, glorify the grace of God, without which you can do nothing; open your soul to heaven, then, as the flower opens its calix at the rising of the sun to receive the life-giving dew.[2] You are in a state of total powerlessness, the spirit is in darkness, the heart under the weight of its nothingness, the body suffering, so practice the adoration of the poor man. Leave your poverty and go abide in our Lord, or offer him your poverty so that he may enrich it. This is a masterpiece worthy of his glory. But you are in the state of temptation and sorrow; everything in you revolts; everything prompts you to stop adoring on the pretext that you are offending God, that you are dishonoring him more than you are serving him; do not listen to this specious temptation, this is adoration in battle, adoration faithful to Jesus against yourself. No, no, you are not displeasing him; you are giving joy to your Master at whom you are looking. He expects from us the homage of perseverance until the last minute of time that we are to devote to him.[3]

Faced with our efforts in adoration, the Holy Spirit always gives a little dew, a little love that makes us pass from adoration in battle against ourselves to a life-giving adoration or a *recollective adoration*. "The laborer deserves his wages" (Lk 10:7). The Spirit transforms everything according to the prophecy of Ezekiel: "I will give them one heart, and put a new spirit within them; I will take the stony heart out of their

[1] Saint Peter-Julian Eymard, *Adorer en esprit et en vérité* (Paris: Éditions F.-X. de Guibert, 2009), 23.
[2] The French word "calice" means both "calix" (also spelled "calyx": the part of a flower that surrounds the petals) and "chalice"; the word "rosée", meaning "dew", is a homonym with "rosé", the pinkish wine.—TRANS.
[3] Ibid.

flesh and give them a heart of flesh" (Ezek 11:19). This is what Jesus revealed to Saint Faustina:

> While I was at the church, to confess, I perceived these same rays (those represented on the divine mercy image) coming forth from the monstrance. They spread throughout the whole church. This lasted the whole length of the office. After benediction, they spread from the two sides, then came back to the monstrance. They looked clear and transparent like crystal. I prayed to Jesus that he might deign to light the fire of his love in all cold souls. Under these rays, their heart would warm, even if it was cold as ice, and it would be reduced to dust, even if it was as hard as rock.[4]

But the Holy Spirit does not want us to think of this grace as something owed to us. We must not stop digging; rather, we must continue to seek this love with our will, always deeper, relentlessly. Sometimes the Holy Spirit carries us in such a way that we can no longer dig. Then we must let him do so. This happens regularly to some souls that are advanced in the interior life. The Spirit leads us to a true intimacy with the Heart of Christ. God then gives *contemplative graces* of light, of presence. This is an anticipation of the beatific vision. This is the Spirit who wants us already to participate, despite the darkness of faith, in the face-to-face encounter that awaits us in heaven, with God, Mary, the saints, the angels. Through contemplation, love becomes so strong that the presence exceeds anything that we could see. This presence changes our way of looking at the world and at others. It pushes us to action. So we should let the Spirit lead us into the wilderness!

Here are a few reflections on the value of nighttime adoration:

Language of love: A father and mother must make many sacrifices to feed, shelter, and educate their children. Without sacrifice, there is no love. The spirit of sacrifice is the spirit of the Christian. Through love Jesus sacrificed everything for us and our salvation. Through love of him, will we agree to offer one hour at night each week with him, in adoration of the Blessed Sacrament, so that our parish might have perpetual Eucharistic adoration?

God abundantly blesses us: The holy Eucharist is the sacrament of God's infinite generosity toward men. By our generous response to this sacra-

---

[4] Saint Faustina, *Petit Journal*, 369.

ment of Love, God pours his infinite goodness on mankind. God will greatly bless you, your family, and the whole world for this precious gift of your time, because God never allows himself to be outdone in generosity. Whatever we may give to him, he gives us back tenfold or a hundredfold. Those who generously accept to make the effort of choosing one of the most difficult hours of the night bring down divine blessings upon earth, like rain falling from heaven. This is why John Paul II affirmed: "Let us be generous with our time in going to meet Him in adoration."[5]

Our act of faith will make the streets safer! Through his prophets Haggai and Zechariah, God declares that the dangers of the streets will disappear for his people when they seek the glory of the sanctuary. Those who agree to come visit Jesus in the middle of the night are those seeking the glory of his sanctuary. It is they who release God's power, thus bringing safety into the streets. In uniting ourselves to Jesus in the Blessed Sacrament, we unite ourselves to the all-powerfulness of the Resurrected One. When we go before Jesus in the Blessed Sacrament, we release his power and his graces for the whole world. This is why Jesus said: "If you had faith as a grain of mustard seed, you could say to this sycamine tree, 'Be rooted up, and be planted in the sea,' and it would obey you" (Lk 17:6). Those who agree to make the sacrifice of coming to Jesus in the middle of the night have this faith! They put their faith in the greatest power on earth. This explains why the rate of crime diminishes in the vicinity of a church where perpetual adoration has been instituted!

We make reparation for the world's great errors: Evil must be vanquished by good. The greatest evil must be vanquished by the greatest good. The extraordinary evil of our society must be vanquished by the extraordinary good of perpetual adoration of Jesus in the Blessed Sacrament. The sacrifice of spending an hour in the middle of the night each week will drive away evil from our land, turning the waterworks of merciful love upon mankind. This is why Pope John Paul II, in calling for "adoration never [to] cease", asks us to be "ready to make reparation for the great faults and crimes of the world".[6]

[5] John Paul II, Apostolic Letter *Dominicae Cenae: On the Mystery and Worship of the Eucharist* (1980), no 3.
[6] Ibid.

Spiritual Warfare

STAGE 37

The Power of Intercession
Moses Fights against the Amalekites
The Paralytic

Then came Amalek and fought with Israel at Rephidim. And Moses said to Joshua, "Choose for us men, and go out, fight with Amalek; tomorrow I will stand on the top of the hill with the rod of God in my hand." So Joshua did as Moses told him, and fought with Amalek; and Moses, Aaron, and Hur went up to the top of the hill. Whenever Moses held up his hand, Israel prevailed; and whenever he lowered his hand, Amalek prevailed. But Moses' hands grew weary; so they took a stone and put it under him, and he sat upon it, and Aaron and Hur held up his hands, one on one side, and the other on the other side; so his hands were steady until the going down of the sun. And Joshua mowed down Amalek and his people with the edge of the sword. (Ex 17:8–13)

Moses was the great intercessor between God and Israel. Yet in this passage, Moses could not sufficiently intercede on his own strength. He needed to ask for help from Hur, the commander of his army, and from his brother, Aaron. The two supported Moses' arms raised up toward God. Thus, Moses' intercession became unceasing. And God gave his people total victory against their enemies. It is the same with perpetual adoration. Parishioners arrange their schedules together, one after another, forming an uninterrupted chain of prayer and intercession in such a way that the heart of the parishioners is turned unceasingly toward God. And God also gives his people total victory by abundantly pouring forth his light, which drives away shadows, and his mercy, which warms hearts.

This is the power of the intercessory prayer of a Christian community that prays day and night at the feet of the Lord. The spiritual benefits of such a prayer are not primarily personal but above all communal. The more the earth comes into alignment with itself by perpetually adoring God, the more the kingdom of God descends upon earth with its peace, light, and Spirit.

Isaiah prophesied about the new Jerusalem that prefigures the Church:

You shall no more be termed Forsaken, and your land shall no more be termed Desolate; but you shall be called My delight is in her, and your land Married; for the LORD delights in you, and your land shall be married. For as a young man marries a virgin, so shall your sons marry you, and as the bridegroom rejoices over the bride, so shall your God rejoice over you. Upon your walls, O Jerusalem, I have set watchmen; all the day and all the night they shall never be silent. (Is 62:4–6)

When a parish organizes perpetual adoration, the "watchmen" are the adorers on the "walls" who are "never silent". In other words, through their unceasing prayer, they are held up between heaven and earth and bring down upon mankind the waterworks of divine mercy. The adorer enters into Christ's unceasing intercession of his Father at the tabernacle. The adorer is put on the fractures of mankind. His supplication embraces all situations where man has lost his dignity, his wholeness, his resemblance to the Father. Adoration evangelizes by pouring forth the graces of redemption through the Church on all situations where man no longer responds to his vocation as a child of God.

Thus, through Eucharistic adoration, we do a great service for mankind.

Through adoration, the Christian contributes to the radical transformation of the world. Every person who prays to the Lord brings the whole world along with him, raising the world to God. Thus those who remain before the Lord fulfill a great service.[1]

Isaiah also prophesies that the new Jerusalem will be the perfect bride of the divine Bridegroom. Perpetual adoration is the love song of the Church-Bride to her Bridegroom who gives himself in the Eucharist. "Come, Lord Jesus!" (Rev 22:20) for the eternal nuptials, first with

[1] John Paul II, letter to Bishop Houssiau for the 750th anniversary of Corpus Christi, May 28, 1996.

the soul, but one day with all of mankind. In giving the Lord the honor and glory that are due to his name through perpetual adoration, we proclaim Jesus King of love and mercy. We pray unceasingly that he take possession of his kingdom (Rev 11:17; 19:6), while waiting for him to realize his promise: "Behold, I make all things new" (Rev 21:5) because "according to his promise we wait for new heavens and a new earth in which righteousness dwells" (2 Pet 3:13).

Finally, through unceasing adoration, the light of the Resurrected One drives away the shadows from the world and makes present in our lives his victory on the Cross. As the Lord gave victory to his people by destroying the walls of Jericho after having encircled them seven times, likewise the Lord gives it to us to vanquish all our Jerichos, whether they be evil itself or our personal failings, when we perpetually adore him in the Blessed Sacrament. "By faith the walls of Jericho fell down after they had been encircled for seven days" (Heb 11:30). Since seven represents fullness, when the people of God remain day and night in faith before the Blessed Sacrament, the Lord works the miracles that the Church and mankind need.

> When he returned to Capernaum after some days, it was reported that he was at home. And many were gathered together, so that there was no longer room for them, not even about the door; and he was preaching the word to them. And they came, bringing to him a paralytic carried by four men. And when they could not get near him because of the crowd, they removed the roof above him; and when they had made an opening, they let down the pallet on which the paralytic lay. And when Jesus saw their faith, he said to the paralytic, "Child, your sins are forgiven." (Mk 2:1–5)

Jesus is teaching in Peter's house at Capernaum. The masses crowd around him to hear him. The paralytic's four friends are not discouraged by the apparent impossibility of presenting the sick man to Jesus. They give evidence of daring, perseverance, determination. Seeing their faith, Jesus says: Your sins are forgiven. Nothing is said about the faith of the paralytic. Maybe he asked to be presented to Jesus, maybe not. What is certain is that Jesus lets himself be moved by the faith of the four men. It is their persevering faith that pushes Jesus to forgive sins. It is not said, "when Jesus saw his faith", but "when Jesus saw their faith".

In the same way, when we are at the foot of the Blessed Sacrament, we can present to Jesus those close to us, our friends, the members of our family, or simply the whole world. Then Jesus likewise says: "Your sins are forgiven." Through intercessory prayer, Jesus gives the graces to return to God the Father to those for whom we intercede. Through our faith in adoration, we touch the Heart of Jesus, which touches the Heart of God. In return, God touches all the hearts of mankind.

Here are some words by Saint Maximilian Kolbe, a Polish priest who died at Auschwitz by freely taking the place of a man condemned to death: "Prayer is a poorly known means, and yet the most effective, for establishing peace in souls, for giving them happiness, since it serves to bring them closer to the love of God."[2] "The most important activity, namely, prayer, is in the midst of development. To the practices we had before has been added perpetual adoration of the Most Blessed Sacrament. At first two brothers taking turns, then four, and now six brothers take half-hour turns all day long; and thus a torrent of prayer flows uninterruptedly throughout the whole day, the greatest power of the universe, capable of transforming us and changing the face of the world."[3] "The value of each member of Niepokalanów depends only and exclusively on his prayer life, on his interior life, on our personal coming closer to the Immaculate and, through her, to the Heart of Jesus."[4]

∽

---

[2] SK (Sketches for a Book) 903.
[3] SK 895.
[4] SK 925.

STAGE 38

"A Prophet Is without Honor in His Own Country" Welcoming the Savior

He went away from there and came to his own country; and his disciples followed him. And on the sabbath he began to teach in the synagogue; and many who heard him were astonished, saying, "Where did this man get all this? What is the wisdom given to him? What mighty works are wrought by his hands! Is not this the carpenter, the son of Mary and brother of James and Joses and Judas and Simon, and are not his sisters here with us?" And they took offense at him. And Jesus said to them, "A prophet is not without honor, except in his own country, and among his own kin, and in his own house." And he could not do mighty work there, except that he laid his hands upon a few sick people and healed them. And he marveled because of their unbelief. (Mk 6:1–6)

Jesus comes to Nazareth, his hometown. He comes to announce the Good News of the kingdom of God. He hopes to work the miracles he has accomplished elsewhere in his own home. But because of the unbelief of the inhabitants, "he could not do mighty work there." What pathos to see Jesus sorrowfully retain the graces coming from the Father in his Heart because of their unbelief. Yes, faith is the key that opens the Heart of Jesus and sets free his power, his healing love, his divine life, and the glory of his Resurrection. Without man's response, God can do nothing in the soul. God infinitely respects human freedom. But his greatest desire is to find open hearts that await everything from him.

"A prophet is not without honor, except in his own country." Too often what so sadly happened at Nazareth continues in the Church.

Jesus is present today among his own, his country, in the heart of each church. In the tabernacle, Christ is present in person with his body, blood, soul, and divinity. He is there, his hands filled with spiritual treasures that he wishes to pour forth abundantly upon his children. Unfortunately, our churches are so often closed, deserted. Today in the tabernacle, as yesterday at Nazareth, Jesus is ignored, misunderstood, and cannot "do mighty work" because of our unbelief!

Along these lines, Saint Peter Julian Eymard implored: "Do not leave hosts sterile!"[1] We should of course understand that there is no sterility possible in the Eucharist, because it is the Sacrament of divine fruitfulness that gives us divine life and makes us supportive of one another: "I am the vine, you are the branches. He who abides in me, and I in him, he it is that bears much fruit, for apart from me you can do nothing" (Jn 15:5). All the same, if we do not have faith, Jesus cannot grant his graces and renew his mighty works in our hearts. Let us pray that our Christian communities never experience this tragic episode from Nazareth. May all our pastoral activities find their source and center in the tabernacle, "the living heart of each of our churches".[2]

> In many places, *adoration of the Blessed Sacrament* is also an important daily practice and becomes an inexhaustible source of holiness. . . . Unfortunately, alongside these lights, *there are also shadows.* In some places the practice of Eucharistic adoration has been almost completely abandoned.[3]

By recognizing him today under the appearances of bread, Jesus calls us blessed, as he said to Thomas: "You have believed because you have seen me. Blessed are those who have not seen and yet believe" (Jn 20:29). Blessed the soul that knows how to find Jesus in the Eucharist and all things in Jesus!

Blessed Dina Bélanger of Quebec wrote: "If souls understood what a treasure they possessed in the divine Eucharist, it would be necessary to protect tabernacles with impregnable walls; for, in the delirium of a holy and devouring hunger, they would go themselves to be nourished

[1] Saint Peter Julian Eymard, *Adorer en esprit et en vérité* (Paris: Éditions F.-X. de Guibert, 2009), 52.
[2] Paul VI, Apostolic Letter *Solemni Hac Liturgia* (1968), no. 26.
[3] John Paul II, Encyclical Letter *Ecclesia de Eucharistia* (2003), no. 10.

by the Manna of the Seraphim. Churches, at night as during the day, would overflow with adorers consumed by love for the noble prisoner."[4]

> When he drew near and saw the city he wept over it, saying, "Would that even today you knew the things that make for peace! But now they are hidden from your eyes. For the days shall come upon you, when your enemies will cast up a bank about you and surround you, and hem you in on every side, and dash you to the ground, you and your children within you, and they will not leave one stone upon another in you; because you did not know the time of your visitation." (Lk 19:41-44)

Here, Jesus weeps over Jerusalem. Just as the inhabitants of Nazareth had not understood Jesus' divine origin and mission, so too Jerusalem does not recognize the Lord and the peace that he comes bearing from his Father. The act of faith made in order to recognize Jesus two thousand years ago is the same act that must be made today in order to recognize him in the Eucharist. His mission is to bear peace, "for he is our peace" (Eph 2:14). Jesus said to Saint Faustina, "Mankind will not find Peace so long as it does not turn with confidence to my Mercy."[5] "The throne of Mercy is the Tabernacle."[6] Thus, there cannot be true peace in hearts, in families, and in the world without turning entirely to the tabernacle, to the Eucharist.

Here is the circumstance in which Mother Mechtilde was inspired to found the institute of Perpetual Adoration. Finding herself at the home of Madame de Boves, she:

> saw there a painting representing a pagan ceremony, where priests and priestesses worshipped an idol, holding a flame in their hands, and vestal virgins looked after the sacred fire. Gripped by a profound emotion in the presence of this canvas, the venerable Mother could not keep herself from saying to the marchioness: "Madame, the idolaters will one day be our damnation and that of Christians who have so little respect for the Most Blessed Sacrament in churches. What we do not do for our God that these pagans did for their false gods! Why, in his house where he continually dwells, should he not be

[4] Blessed Dina Bélanger, *Autobiographie*, edited by the Sisters of Jesus and Mary in Canada.
[5] Saint Faustina, *Petit Journal*, 300.
[6] Ibid., 1484.

continually adored? Why should not the sentinels of Israel watch day and night, never growing tired, around the throne of the Solomon of the New Law?"[7]

The mission of the adorer's prayer is eminently apostolic. Although it seems that nothing is happening, everything is happening before the Blessed Sacrament. John Paul II reminded us:

In the Holy Eucharist—this is also the meaning of perpetual adoration—we enter into the movement of love from which all interior progress and all apostolic fruitfulness flows: "I, when I am lifted up from the earth, will draw all men to myself" (Jn 12:32).[8]

By exposing him and uniting ourselves to his prayer and apostolate through our adoration, we make our Lord work for the conversion of souls. This is the special privilege of our calling to expose our Lord and put him in the solemn exercise of his role as mediator. *Indeed, it is only because we are at his feet that he is on his throne.* The Church would not allow him to perpetuate his presence day and night if he were not to find adorers following one after another in order to serve him day and night: to make himself manifest in his exposition, we are necessary for him; we release his power.[9]

Now, we must quickly get to work, saving souls through the divine Eucharist and awakening France and Europe, numbed in its sleep of indifference because it does not know God's gift, Jesus the Eucharistic Emmanuel. It is the flame of love that we must carry into tepid souls that think themselves pious and are not, because they have not established their center and life in Jesus in the Holy Tabernacle; and every devotion that does not have a tent on Calvary and one around the tabernacle is not a solid piety and will never amount to much. We distance ourselves too much from the Holy Eucharist; we do not preach often enough about this mystery of love par excellence; so souls suffer, they become entirely sensual and material in their piety, inordinately attaching themselves to creatures, because they do not know how to find their consolation and strength in our Lord.[10]

---

[7] Catherine de Bar, *Mère Mechtilde du Saint-Sacrement* (Publication Bénédictine PAX, 1922), 82.

[8] John Paul II, Message to the Faithful Gathered in the Basilica of the Sacred Heart of Montmartre, Paris, June 1, 1980, no. 4.

[9] Saint Peter Julian Eymard, *Œuvres Complètes*, PR 99, 4.

[10] Ibid., CO 325, 1.

TRANSITION

- In Stages 1–15 (Part I), we deepened our understanding of how to adore the Son who *comes to us, who calls us to him*.

- In Stages 16–28, we clarified what the *signs of the Covenant* are, in order to rediscover what the Eucharist is and how to approach our Lord in faith so as to be truly nourished by him.

- In Stages 29–38 (Part II), in confidence and faithfulness we let *the Son lead us to the Father* through his love, despite inevitable spiritual droughts.

- In the last stages, we evoke *life in the Spirit* (Part III): we adore the Father, through the Son present in the Eucharist, who gives us the Spirit and sends us forth on a mission in the Church following Mary.

~

III. THE SPIRIT

Animated by the Spirit,
Engaging in the Church's Mission

In the School of Mary,
Eucharistic and Missionary Woman

STAGE 39

The Mass and the Annunciation

During his last meal with his disciples, Jesus instituted the Eucharist. Nothing in the Gospel indicates the presence of his mother, Mary. Should we imagine that Mary nonetheless took part in the Last Supper among a bigger circle of guests? Or should we think that Jesus did not invite his mother to this meal that he had so very "earnestly desired to eat . . . before [suffering]" (Lk 22:15)? We cannot know the answer. What is important, however, is to remember that Mary had already received within herself what the apostles received during the first Eucharist and what we receive at each Mass. Mary received the Word Incarnate in her womb, not the evening of Holy Thursday, but long before, when the angel Gabriel visited her (Lk 1:26–38). Yes, the Annunciation is the first and most beautiful Mass in history![1] Let us enroll in the school of Mary, the Eucharistic woman, who shows us how to live intensely the different stages of the Mass. At each Communion, the Word, which took flesh in Mary's womb, descends into our hearts and sends us forth on a mission.

> The piety of the Christian people has always very rightly sensed a profound link between devotion to the Blessed Virgin and worship of the Eucharist: . . . Mary guides the faithful to the Eucharist."[2]

In the very first place, the angel greets Mary with these words: "Hail, full of grace, the Lord is with you!" (Lk 1:28). Likewise, the priest begins Mass with this beautiful *greeting*: "The grace of our Lord Jesus Christ, and the love of God, and the communion of the Holy Spirit be

---

[1] This stage is inspired by the book *L'Eucharistie à l'école de Marie* (Paris: Mame-Edifa, 2000), chap. 1, by Father Guillaume de Menthière.

[2] John Paul II, Encyclical Letter *Redemptoris Mater* (1987), no. 44.

with you all" (2 Cor 13:14). How much more appropriate this greeting is than a simple "good morning"! At the beginning of Mass, it is Jesus himself who greets the community gathered in his name through the voice of the priest. Jesus solemnly greets his Church, his own Bride.

The angel's greeting prompts a profound turmoil within Mary. "Hail (Chaíre)" belongs to the language of reverence. Saint Alphonsus Liguori wrote: "Her profound humility did not permit [such a] thought. Those praises had no other effect than to cause her great fear."[3] At each Mass, Jesus' greeting through the priest should trouble us even more! If the Virgin Mary considers herself unworthy of the angel's praise, how much more should we, the sinful faithful, be troubled at this moment! Thus the Church-Bride cries forth: "Lord, have mercy" (Mt 15:22). This is the *penitential rite*. We ask for the aid of the Lord's grace, because we are unworthy of the mysteries in which we are about to participate. Then we receive forgiveness for our venial sins and the charity that is our best defense against evil and temptations. In the joy of knowing that we are forgiven, we sing the *Gloria*, the song of the angels in wonder before the goodness of God our Father.

Next comes the *liturgy of the Word*. The angel Gabriel is the messenger of the Good News. Mary listens devoutly to the Word before consenting to it with all her being. She is the daughter of Zion, the throne of Wisdom. Mary is familiar with the first commandment: "Hear, O Israel" (Deut 6:4). The Christian, likewise, must set about to listen to the Word proclaimed at the ambo. "The mind of the wise man will ponder the words of the wise, and an attentive ear is the wise man's desire" (Sir 3:29). Solomon asks for "a heart that knows how to listen". Saint Augustine says that Mary conceived Jesus in faith before conceiving him in her flesh. When the biblical texts are proclaimed, it is God himself who addresses his people. Let us not waste "the crumbs of the Word of God" (Origen), but rather listen to the voice of the Lord!

Mary then questions the angel in order better to understand how the Word is going to be fulfilled in her: "How can this be, since I have no husband?" (Lk 1:34). This is the time of the *homily*, which has the goal of making the Word of God current in daily life. The homily

---

[3] Saint Alphonsus Liguori, discourse 4, "On the Annunciation of Mary", in *The Glories of Mary*, trans. P. J. Kenedy (London: Catholic Way Pub., 2013), 244.

aims to put us in dialogue with the Word of God who is beginning to become incarnate in our hearts.

Next comes the great *epikleses*. To Mary's "How?" the angel answers: "The Holy Spirit will come upon you, and the power of the Most High will overshadow you" (Lk 1:35). When we ask ourselves how the bread and wine become the Body and Blood of Christ during the Consecration (transubstantiation), we can find the answer in the prayer that the priest addresses to the Father *in persona Christi*: "Make holy, therefore, these gifts, we pray, by sending down your Spirit upon them." For the Creed asserts: "By the Holy Spirit [he] was incarnate of the Virgin Mary." And at Mass, through the same Spirit, he takes flesh in the Eucharist. "In the Anglo-Saxon world, 'Abracadabra' is said 'Hocus Pocus', a contraction of the formula 'Hoc est enim corpus meum.' The Anglo-Saxon Reformers wanted to mock the Mass, which they took for so much magic. The priest is not a magician. The Consecration is only possible through the Holy Spirit who comes over the gifts."[4]

Mary will receive the Holy Spirit a second time, at Pentecost, among the disciples gathered together in the Upper Room, when the Spirit descends upon the Church being born. The Mass also contains *two epikleses*. The first over the offerings, and the second over the faithful to make of them an ecclesial community, animated by the same Spirit, and not a juxtaposition of individuals: "Humbly we pray, that, partaking of the Body and Blood of Christ, we may be gathered into one by the Holy Spirit."

Finally Mary's response comes forth: "I am the handmaid of the Lord" (Lk 1:38). This is Mary's *Fiat* (*Amen*) whereby she espouses the divine will of salvation with all her heart. This *Fiat* echoes the *Fiat* in Genesis: "*Fiat lux*: Let there be light." Cardinal de Bérulle said that Mary's *Fiat* was more powerful than God's *Fiat* at the creation, "because if the latter made the world, the former made the Author of the world".[5]

Immediately after Mary's *Fiat*, the Word of God became incarnate in her. This is true *communion!* Our *Amen* ("I firmly believe", in Hebrew)

---

[4] Guillaume de Menthière, *L'Eucharistie à l'école de Marie*, 33.
[5] Cardinal de Bérulle, "Discours sur l'état et les grandeurs de Jésus", 1623.

at communion echoes Mary's *Fiat* ("Let it be so", in Latin). Just after our "Amen" to the priest who is holding up the Host, Jesus descends into our heart to become incarnate in us.

> As a result, there is a profound analogy between the *Fiat* which Mary said in reply to the angel, and the *Amen* which every believer says when receiving the body of the Lord. Mary was asked to believe that the One whom she conceived "through the Holy Spirit" was "the Son of God" (Lk 1:30–35). In continuity with the Virgin's faith, in the Eucharistic mystery we are asked to believe that the same Jesus Christ, Son of God and Son of Mary, becomes present in his full humanity and divinity under the signs of bread and wine.[6]

Then the angel leaves her. Why remain, since Mary has the Lord in her? The Virgin, the first tabernacle of the Most High, is driven by the Spirit to set about serving her cousin: this is the Visitation. The Mass concludes with a *sending forth*, a new departure, a setting in motion: "Ite, missa est." Our Mass ends when we begin to serve our neighbor.

A small reminder: the Annunciation is certainly the most beautiful of Masses. We, however, do not receive Jesus with the same faith and love as Mary, and each Mass does not produce the same fruit in us! Let us recall two points:

The gift received by Mary and by each communicant is identical, even if the mode is different. We truly receive the eternal Son of the Father who became incarnate in Mary, the living Jesus! God cannot give more than this tiny Host.

> The sacraments act *ex opere operato* (literally: "by the very fact of the action's being performed"), i.e., by virtue of the saving work of Christ, accomplished once for all. It follows that "the sacrament is not wrought by the righteousness of either the celebrant or the recipient, but by the power of God."[7] From the moment that a sacrament is celebrated in accordance with the intention of the Church, the power of Christ and his Spirit acts in and through it, independently of the personal holiness of the minister. Nevertheless, the fruits of the sacraments also depend on the disposition of the one who receives them.[8]

[6] John Paul II, Encyclical Letter *Ecclesia de Eucharistia* (2003), no. 55.
[7] Saint Thomas Aquinas, *Summa Theologiae* III, 68, 8.
[8] CCC 1128.

That is to say, by our interior preparation, our state of grace, and our faith in the Eucharist. For this reason, it is unfortunately possible to receive Communion every day without its carrying the desired fruit, namely, a greater charity. However, every Communion should change our heart, renewing our hope and strengthening our charity.

Here is the story of Saint Imelda, nicknamed the Flower of the Eucharist. She is the patroness of first communicants: It was the practice to give First Communion to children only at the age of fourteen. Imelda, consumed by the ardor of her desires, begged to be at last admitted to the holy Table. But it was thought an exception should not be made for the young novice. The day of Ascension 1333, Imelda reached her twelfth year. Again she beseeched her confessor to allow her to receive Holy Communion, but he remained unyielding. The child went to the chapel in tears in order to hear Mass there. The Lord Jesus, so weak in the face of love, could no longer resist the wishes of this angelic soul. At the moment of Communion, a Host escaped from the ciborium, elevated itself in the air, crossed the choir grille, and came to rest above Imelda's head. As soon as the sisters noticed the Host, they alerted the priest to the marvel. As he approached with the paten, the motionless Host came to place itself upon it. No longer in doubt as to the Lord's will, the trembling priest gave Communion to Imelda, who seemed an angel rather than a mortal creature. The sisters, seized with inexpressible amazement, remained long in contemplation of this child, prostrate in adoration, entirely illuminated with a supernatural joy. Finally sensing a vague disquiet, they called to Imelda, prayed her stand, then ordered her to stand. The child, always so prompt to obey, appeared not even to hear them. Going to raise her up, the sisters perceived with astonishment that Imelda was dead: dead from joy and love at the hour of her First Communion.

∽

In the School of Mary,
Eucharistic and Missionary Woman

STAGE 40

The Magnificat
Mary, Ark of the New Covenant
Humility and Joy

"My soul magnifies the Lord,
and my spirit rejoices in God my Savior,
for he has regarded the low estate of his handmaiden.
For behold, henceforth all generations will call me blessed;
for he who is mighty has done great things for me,
and holy is his name.
And his mercy is on those who fear him
from generation to generation.
He has shown strength with his arm,
he has scattered the proud in the imagination of their hearts,
he has put down the mighty from their thrones,
and exalted those of low degree;
he has filled the hungry with good things,
and the rich he has sent empty away.
He has helped his servant Israel,
in remembrance of his mercy,
as he spoke to our fathers,
to Abraham and to his posterity for ever." (Lk 1:46–55)

Mary leads her children to Jesus. She helps them know him better in order to love him better. God took flesh in the Virgin Mary and became man. He remains among us in the Eucharist. Everything God does, he does through his Son, present in the Eucharist. There, Jesus is present in his body. There, he reveals the Father's tenderness. Thence he acts and rules the world. Thence he comes to dwell in our hearts and renew divine charity in us. In other words, in order to understand God and his work in our lives, we must approach the tabernacle, our heaven on earth. We must adore! The tabernacle is the footstool of his heavenly throne (cf. Is 66:1). Since Jesus is hidden there under the appearances of bread, Mary, in her Magnificat, helps us to lift the Eucharistic veil in order to find the Lord, in order to understand how he acts in our lives, and in order to respond to his infinite and personal love. Mary "exalts the Lord". To exalt is to proclaim the great things, the wonders. What is hidden in the Host is proclaimed by Mary in her hymn. "Nothing is covered that will not be revealed, or hidden that will not be known" (Mt 10:26).

Mary begins by magnifying the Lord. The joy of her praise immediately irradiates her spirit! This exultation comes from an outpouring of the Holy Spirit springing forth from the incarnate Word in her. A great joy that does not come from the world and that the world does not know always accompanies the presence of the Spirit. Likewise, an outpouring of the Holy Spirit at once sweet, discreet, effective, and ever-new springs forth unceasingly from the Eucharistic Heart of Jesus upon those who approach in faith: " 'If any one thirst, let him come to me and drink. He who believes in me, as the Scripture has said, "Out of his heart shall flow rivers of living water." ' Now this he said about the Spirit" (Jn 7:37–39).

In promising his disciples the Holy Spirit, Jesus says: "These things I have spoken to you, that my joy may be in you, and that your joy may be full" (Jn 15:11). This joy should be the joy of him who knows Jesus in the Eucharist. It is also the joy of him who has just received his sweet Savior in his heart. This joy extends after Communion, during thanksgiving. How precious it is to spend a few minutes after Mass in the silence of thanksgiving for Communion! But how sad it is to see most Christians lose themselves in useless talking as soon as Mass is over, without taking the time to welcome their Master worthily. He descends into their heart and awaits a heart-to-heart from them. Insofar as possible, we should spend ten to fifteen minutes in thanksgiving after each Eucharist. That wholly divine joy felt during thanksgiving will make "our spirit exult".

Only our Lord Jesus Christ can adore God perfectly in spirit and truth, and we can only do so through union with him. The time when we are most united with him is after Holy Communion. Then he takes our whole substance into him. Oh! If only it were possible to see the wonders taking place in a person receiving Communion! The person is then entirely transformed into Jesus Christ. Jesus Christ in that person adores God, and that person adores God through Jesus Christ, and this adoration can go on as long as desired.[1]

"He has regarded the low estate of his handmaiden [and] all generations will call me blessed." Her low estate, her humility, this is one of Mary's great virtues. By humbling herself, Mary enters into God's plan. The eternal Word nearly obliterates itself by taking flesh in Mary. In Mary is fulfilled the revelation of God's humility. The Magnificat reveals this mystery. Humility is the sign of true power. God's power is in no way power as the world understands it. It is spiritual strength, the power of Love, which consists in freely bowing before what is least of all. That is the power of God; it is an infinite power of self-abasement, a power of which not even the greatest man or angel is capable. The Incarnation is eternal humility. That is why Jesus comes as a slave. His birth reveals what God's power is—the power of being the servant of the least among us. All other forms of power do not allow for a true relationship of love with God.

In contemplating the Host, which is so fragile, so vulnerable, so often despised and ignored, we might ask why God does not defend himself? In fact, his self-abasement tells us more about his love and who God is than a crushing, justice-exacting power. "*The nature of love is to humble oneself*", said Saint Thérèse of Lisieux. Mary directs us into this movement of self-abasement and humility in order that we might discover the self-abasement and humility of God that is made present in the Eucharist.

"He who is mighty has done great things for me, and holy is his name." Here below are the last stanzas of a poem by Saint Teresa Benedicta of the Cross (Edith Stein) that lists a few of the wonders accomplished in the Eucharist, wonders worked in Mary when the Word became incarnate in her:

---

[1] Catherine de Bar, *Adorer et adhérer* (Paris: Éditions du Cerf, 1994), 59.

You come to me as early morning's meal each daybreak.
Your flesh and blood become food and drink for me
And something wonderful happens.

Your body mysteriously permeates mine
And your soul unites with mine:
I am no longer what once I was.

You come and go, but the seed
That you sowed for future glory, remains behind
Buried in this body of dust.

A luster of heaven remains in the soul,
A deep glow remains in the eyes,
A soaring in the tone of voice.

There remains the bond that binds heart to heart,
The stream of life that springs from yours
And animates each limb.

How wonderful are your gracious wonders!
All we can do is be amazed and stammer and fall silent.
Because intellect and words fail.[2]

"And his mercy [love] is . . . from generation to generation", because in the Eucharist Christ is permanently present to his Church. The Eucharist fulfills his promise: "I will not leave you desolate; I will come to you" (Jn 14:18); "I am with you always, to the close of the age" (Mt 28:20). The Eucharist supports the Church. It keeps the Church in existence and at work in her heavenly mission. "Those who fear him" are those who seek him, who desire him and want to respond to his love, because the "fear of the LORD is the beginning of knowledge" (Prov 1:7). "Fear" in the Bible is what we call "religion" or "piety toward God". It is the principle and the crowning of wisdom. It allows us to enter into a filial relationship with the Father.

"He has shown strength with his arm, he has scattered the proud in the imagination of their hearts, he has put down the mighty from

---

[2] "I Will Remain with You", a poem written for the feast of Corpus Christi 1938, the day when Sister Marie (Ernst) took her vows, from *The Collected Works*, vol. 4, *The Hidden Life*, trans. Waltraut Stein (Washington, D.C.: ICS Publications, Institute of Carmelite Studies, 2014), p. 135.

their thrones, and exalted those of low degree; he has filled the hungry with good things, and the rich he has sent empty away." The proud do not seek simple things and cannot imagine that the Most High, in his infinite mercy, comes in so small a Host to fill them with his Spirit of truth and light. The mighty are put down from their thrones, that is, from their convictions, from what gives them security. Jesus praises his Father for having "hidden these things from the wise and understanding and revealed them to infants" (Mt 11:25). The hungry are those who look to God for everything and find everything in the Eucharist. The rich seek their salvation in this world, but will find nothing eternal in it. "Happy is the soul that knows how to find Jesus in the Eucharist and in the Eucharist all things!"[3]

"He has helped his servant Israel, in remembrance of his mercy, as he spoke to our fathers, to Abraham and to his posterity for ever." The Eucharistic presence is revealed to the little ones, to the humble. God will never take it away from them, as he has spoken in promise. The Eucharist is really the memorial ("memory") of the Lord's Passion. All his love is concentrated in it. In the Eucharist God recapitulates, integrates, and assumes all his promises. The Eucharist contains not only all God's graces, but the Author of grace! What gift could exceed it?

Mary is the Ark of the New Covenant, the Theotokos, the Mother of God. In other words, Mary receives the One who unites heaven and earth. She carries him who carries everything. She gives to the world the One who gives life "abundantly" (Jn 10:10)! Thus Mary is the model of perfect receptivity and total offering. She gives back completely him whom she received from God: Jesus Christ. She helps us to become in turn the Ark of the Covenant, a monstrance, and a grain of wheat: the Ark of the Covenant by welcoming Jesus Christ as our Lord and our God, a monstrance by letting Jesus act in us and shine forth from us, and a grain of wheat by generously giving our life so that the world might encounter true witnesses of the Father's tenderness.

---

[3] Saint Peter Julian Eymard, *Adorer en esprit et vérité* (Paris: Éditions F.-X. de Guibert, 2009), 26.

In the School of Mary,
Eucharistic and Missionary Woman

STAGE 41

Jacob's Ladder and the Angels
Our Lady of Fatima

[Jacob] dreamed that there was a ladder set up on the earth, and the top of it reached to heaven; and behold, the angels of God were ascending and descending on it! And behold, the LORD stood above it and said, "I am the LORD, the God of Abraham your father and the God of Isaac; the land on which you lie I will give to you and to your descendants; and your descendants shall be like the dust of the earth, and you shall spread abroad to the west and to the east and to the north and to the south; and by you and your descendants shall all the families of the earth bless themselves. Behold, I am with you and will keep you wherever you go, and will bring you back to this land; for I will not leave you until I have done that of which I have spoken to you. (Gen 28:12–15)

Several Church Fathers saw Jacob's ladder as an image of the Providence God exercises on earth through the ministry of angels. For others, the ladder prefigured the Incarnation of the Word, the bridge thrown between heaven and earth. The Incarnation of the Word is continued and prolonged in the Sacrament of the Eucharist, our heaven on earth, as Paul VI affirmed:

The unique and indivisible existence of the Lord glorious in heaven is not multiplied, but is rendered present by the sacrament in the many places on earth where Mass is celebrated. And this existence remains present, after the sacrifice, in the Blessed Sacrament which is, in the tabernacle, the living heart of each of our churches. And it is our very sweet duty to honor and adore in the blessed Host which our eyes

209

see, the Incarnate Word whom they cannot see, and who, without leaving heaven, is made present before us.[1]

Rising up into heaven on the day of the Ascension, Jesus Christ goes to take possession of his glory and to prepare a place for us there. With Jesus Christ, redeemed humanity comes home to heaven: we know that heaven is not closed to us any more, and we live in expectation of the day when its gates will open before us. This hope supports and encourages us. If need be, it is enough to make us lead a Christian life, and we would suffer all the sorrows of life so as not to lose it. However, in order to maintain and increase the effectiveness of our hope for heaven, our Lord has created the beautiful heaven of the Eucharist. For the Eucharist is a beautiful heaven, the beginning of heaven. Is it not Jesus in glory coming from heaven to "earth" —and bringing heaven with him? Wherever our Lord is, is that not heaven? His state in the Eucharist, while veiled to our senses, is glorious, triumphant, blessed; there is no more of the misery of life, and when we receive Communion, we receive heaven, since we receive Jesus, who comprises all the happiness and all the glory of paradise. What glory for a subject to receive his king! Let us glory for ourselves, too: we receive the King of heaven! Jesus comes into us so that we do not forget our true homeland, so that we do not die from desire and fatigue in thinking on it. He comes and remains bodily in our hearts so long as the Sacrament remains; then, when the species are destroyed, he goes back up to heaven but remains in us in the forms of his grace and his loving presence. Why does he not remain longer? Because the condition of his bodily presence is the completeness of the Holy Species: coming into us, Jesus brings the fruits and flowers of paradise. What are they? I do not know; we do not see them, but we smell their aroma. He brings us his glorified merits, his sword victorious over Satan; he brings us his weapons, so that we might make use of them; his merits, so that we might make our own merits fruitful by addition to his. The Eucharist is the ladder, not of Jacob but of Jesus, which continually rises to heaven and descends from it for us. This ladder moves unceasingly toward us.[2]

---

[1] Paul VI, *Solemni Hac Liturgia* (1968), no. 26.

[2] Saint Peter Julian Eymard, *Adorer en esprit et en vérité* (Paris: Éditions F.-X. de Guibert, 2009), 262.

"I am the living bread which came down from heaven" (Jn 6:51). When Jesus comes down, so do the angels. It is impossible for the Eucharist to be anywhere without being surrounded and adored by God's angels. Saint John Chrysostom tells the story of a saint whom God granted the grace to see what happened at Mass: "During the Holy Sacrifice, he saw a multitude of angels descending all at once into the sanctuary in human form, dressed in brilliant robes. They surrounded the altar, standing with great respect and their heads deeply bowed, as is done at court in the presence of a great king."[3] Saint Claude de la Colombière wrote:

> It is in our churches, in this tabernacle, that the living body of the Savior rests. He was but nine months in the womb of Mary, three hours on the Cross, three days in the tomb. Yet he is always in our churches. This is why they do not empty of angels, archangels, and seraphim unceasingly adoring him. They adore him with signs of respect, with prostrations that, if we could perceive them, would strangely confound us. Our churches, if we might speak in such a way, are like an annex of paradise; there the Creator is adored, there the resurrected Savior finds a body and a soul, thereto the heavenly spirits journey, and there they delight in the same happiness savored beyond the firmament.[4]

Our guardian angel's joy is being able to adore the Lord present in the Eucharist with us. He adores the eternal Word that he sees; we adore the incarnate Word that our eyes cannot see but whom our faith discerns. "How many people say: I would like to see his face, his features, his beauty. . . . But in the Eucharist, it is he himself that you see, he himself that you touch, he himself that you eat. Think of that and adore, for the same is in the heavens adored by the angels!"[5]

In 1916, at Fatima in Portugal, the archangel Michael appeared to three children: Francisco, Lúcia, and Jacinta. The angel presented a Host above a chalice to them. A few drops of blood spilled into the chalice from the Host. He gave them the Eucharist, saying: "Take and drink the Body and the Blood of Jesus, horribly offended by ungrateful men. Make reparations for their crimes, and console your God."

[3] Saint John Chrysostom, *On the Priesthood*, VI.
[4] Saint Claude de la Colombière, *Réflexions chrétiennes*, 13, *De la messe*, 357.
[5] Saint John Chrysostom, *Homily on Saint Matthew* 84, 4.

A few days later, the Virgin Mary appeared to the children. Mary showed them that many souls are eternally lost in hell because no one prays or does penance for them. "With all your might, offer a sacrifice to God as an act of reparation for the sins committed against him and an act of supplication for the conversion of sinners. In this way you will bring peace upon your homeland." The sacrifice of spending an hour with Jesus in the middle of the night obtains the graces these souls need in order to turn toward divine mercy and return to God. The Fatima prayer of reparation brings us into the prayer and intercession of Jesus-the-Host to the Father: "My God, I believe, I adore, I hope, and I love You! I beg pardon for all those who do not believe, do not adore, do not hope, and do not love You!"

Our Lady of Fatima's "peace plan" calls for prayer, penance, and sacrifice. Mary affirms that if we respond to her requests, Russia will be converted, her Immaculate Heart will triumph, and a true peace will spread across the earth. The angel, elevating the sacred Host, taught this prayer of adoration: "Most Holy Trinity, Father, Son, and Holy Ghost, I offer You the most precious Body, Blood, Soul, and Divinity of Jesus Christ, present in all the tabernacles of the world, in reparation for the sacrileges, outrages, and indifference by which He Himself is offended. And through the infinite merits of His most Sacred Heart and the Immaculate Heart of Mary, I beg of you the conversion of poor sinners." Perpetual adoration fulfills Our Lady of Fatima's requests: prayer, penance, and sacrifice.

After having transmitted a number of messages about the importance of praying the rosary and on the last things, Mary invited them to a final apparition. A heavy rain was falling on Fatima, a sign of the tears that flow down our faces due to man's inhumanity to man. Mud had covered everything, as corruption covers our world. Then, suddenly, a miracle: the sun began to turn, with rays of all colors warming the earth. The rain stopped, the mud disappeared, and everything became radiant as though nothing had been soaked or muddy a few seconds before. Seventy thousand people witnessed this prodigious event, reported on by the press. This extraordinary happening foretells the glorious manifestation of Jesus, the conquering Lamb. When he returns in his glory, he will no longer remain hidden in the tabernacle, but all shall see him with their eyes. The colored rays evoke the richness of the Eucharistic graces we receive even now, in expectation of this prophecy:

> I saw a new heaven and a new earth; for the first heaven and the first earth had passed away. . . . "Behold, the dwelling of God is with men. . . . He will wipe away every tear from their eyes, and death shall be no more, neither shall there be mourning nor crying nor pain any more, for the former things have passed away." (Rev 21:1, 3–4)

> And the city has no need of sun or moon to shine upon it, for the glory of God is its light, and its lamp is the Lamb. (Rev 21:23)

~

The Living Water that
Flows from the Pierced Heart

STAGE 42

Our Lady of Lourdes

On February 11, 1858, our Lady was sent by God to Lourdes, to a young woman named Bernadette. In his divine mercy, God our Father unceasingly calls his people to return to him with all their heart. After sending prophets in the Old Covenant, God sent his only Son, Jesus, our Way, our Truth, and our Life. He promised to remain with us until the end of time. To that end he dwells day and night in all the tabernacles of the world. Mary was sent by God to Lourdes to lead us to Jesus and help us live the Gospel in its entirety. We go to the Father through the Son, for Jesus said: "No one comes to the Father, but by me" (Jn 14:6). In our day Mary continues her mission of leading us to her Jesus, present in the Eucharist. She says anew: "Do whatever he tells you" (Jn 2:5).

At Lourdes, Mary calls, first of all, for conversion. She asks us to do penance so as to be able to prepare a path for Jesus in our life.

In those days the grotto of Massabielle, like the manger at Bethlehem, was a dirty, hidden, damp, and cold place. It was a shelter for pigs; a place known for prostitution. And yet it was in this place that the Virgin Mary appeared, showing herself as the *Immaculate Conception*. Dressed in white as a sign of purity, she reminds us how God loves us and what he desires for each one of us. Make note of the contrast between the damp and dark grotto where sinners meet and the resplendent presence of the *Immaculate Conception*. Mary reminds us of the Gospel: our God, infinitely pure, descends into the heart of our poverty, for "the Son of man came to seek and to save the lost" (Lk 19:10).

Massabielle means "old rock". This reminds us that God comes to us, despite our resistance, our hardness of heart. In the Holy Eucharist,

Jesus comes to visit our heart of stone. He purifies and transforms it with the tenderness of his love according to the promise: "I will sprinkle clean water upon you, and you shall be clean from all your uncleannesses, and from all your idols I will cleanse you. A new heart I will give you, and a new spirit I will put within you; and I will take out of your flesh the heart of stone and give you a heart of flesh" (Ezek 36:25–26).

During the third apparition, Bernadette offered a piece of paper and a pencil to the "Lady" so that she might write her name. Smiling, our Lady responded that her message did not need to be written down, because it concerned a relationship of love. Bernadette was invited to open the depths of her heart to our Lady's message of love. It is just the same with Jesus in the Eucharist: he desires to establish in our hearts an authentic relationship of love. Bernadette felt respected and loved by our Lady. Mary invited her to the grotto every fifteen days. To the eyes of the world, Bernadette was contemptible. Before the Virgin, she rediscovered her true dignity. Likewise Jesus invites us with such delicacy to come to him in the Eucharist as often as possible. By discovering how much we are loved personally, we rediscover our most fundamental identity: I am a child of the Father!

From the eighth to the twelfth apparition, Bernadette responded to the Virgin's surprising invitations. She moved on her knees toward the deepest point of the grotto. She embraced the disgusting and dirty earth. She ate its bitter herbs. She scratched the ground three times and tried to drink the muddy water. She took the mud into her hands and smeared it over her face. All these actions have a biblical foundation. What our Lady asked of her goes back to the Incarnation, the Passion, and the death of her Son Jesus Christ.

Bernadette moves on her knees to the deepest point of the grotto: Through the Incarnation, the eternal Word abases itself by assuming human nature, like someone descending into a vertiginous abyss.

Bernadette kisses the earth: This act of humility evokes the divine mercy that unceasingly pursues God's unfaithful people. This love is still abasing itself today in the Eucharist in order to seek our love.

Bernadette eats bitter herbs: This gesture recalls the hasty departure of the Israelites breaking free from slavery in Egypt: "They shall eat the flesh that night, roasted; with unleavened bread and bitter herbs they shall eat it" (Ex 12:8). In ancient texts, the Jews wanted to show that God had taken upon himself all the bitterness of the sins of the world. They killed a lamb, filled it with bitter herbs, and made the following prayer: "Behold the Lamb of God who takes away and upon himself all the bitterness of all the sins of the world." Today, at each Mass, the priest elevates the sacred Host and declares: "Behold the Lamb of God who takes away the sins of the world."

Bernadette smears her face with mud: Isaiah prophesied about the Messiah that he would be "acquainted with grief" (Is 53:3). "He was wounded for our transgressions, he was bruised for our iniquities; upon him was the chastisement that made us whole, and with his stripes we are healed" (Is 53:5). "His appearance was so marred, beyond human semblance, and his form beyond that of the sons of men" (Is 52:14). "He was oppressed, and he was afflicted, yet he opened not his mouth; like a lamb that is led to the slaughter" (Is 53:7). In the grotto, the mud soils Bernadette's face, to the point that the crowd takes her for a fool.

The spring was obstructed by the grass and the mud. Bernadette scratches the ground and discovers this spring. This immense treasure must be shown to all. She drinks from it and washes herself with the muddy water that is becoming clear. This reveals the mystery of the Heart of Jesus: "One of the soldiers pierced his side with a spear, and at once there came out blood and water" (Jn 19:34). The Heart of Jesus, beating with love in the Eucharist, is an inexhaustible spring of living water. If we cannot go to Lourdes, we can draw from the spring flowing from the pierced Heart of Jesus at every moment. At each Mass, during each period of adoration, we are quenched at this spring of "water welling up to eternal life" (Jn 4:14). The grass and mud represent our failings in faith and charity, which distance us from the Eucharist: "If any one thirst, let him come to me and drink" (Jn 7:37). "Come, buy wine and milk without money and without price" (Is 55:1).

During the thirteenth apparition, our Lady said to Bernadette: "Go tell the priests that a chapel is to be built here and that people are to come here in procession." Mary's mission has always been to give Jesus to the world and to bring the world to Jesus. Mary does so today for

Jesus present in the Eucharist. At Lourdes, there are numerous daily Masses and prolonged Eucharistic adoration. Eucharistic processions with the blessing of the sick also occur frequently. For that matter, it is then that the major miracles and healings of Lourdes are worked! Mary describes Jesus in the Eucharist as a fountain overflowing with spiritual riches spilling over upon those who come into its presence. Scripture says that he made himself poor through love of us, divesting himself of glory and majesty, in order to enrich us with his grace and array us with his glory (cf. 2 Cor 8:9; Phil 2:8) each time we go to him in the Blessed Sacrament.

At the sixteenth apparition, Mary presented herself as the *Immaculate Conception*, thus confirming the proclamation of the dogma of the *Immaculate Conception*, solemnly declared four years earlier by Pius IX: Mary, "from the first moment of her conception, by a singular grace and privilege of almighty God and by virtue of the merits of Jesus Christ, Savior of the human race, preserved immune from all stain of original sin."[1] The Immaculate Conception anticipates what the world is called to become when God recreates it. Through a unique privilege, Mary was conceived immaculate and could thus adhere fully to the divine will through her *Fiat*. Likewise, the *Immaculate Conception* wishes to take us by the hand so that we might pronounce our *Fiat* to the divine will. This gives the true meaning to our pilgrimage on earth. Mary first welcomed the eternal Word into her heart before conceiving it bodily in her virgin womb. Mary is our mother according to the order of grace. She supports and gives life to our faith so that we might benefit abundantly from all the spiritual favors with which the Eucharist seeks to enrich us.

At Lourdes, Mary invites a great many volunteers to come together for the help of sick and suffering members of her Son's Mystical Body, those who mysteriously participate in the Lord's Passion. She invites the ill to approach Jesus in the Blessed Sacrament, this living and life-giving food which strengthens the body and heals the soul. Jesus Christ redeemed the world through his suffering, his death, and his Resurrection. He remains among us as our traveling companion in this land of exile. Since the Eucharist is the gift of God for the life of the world,

[1] Pius IX, *Ineffabilis Deus*, December 8, 1854, as quoted in CCC 491.

in return we must become bread "broken" for the life of others, by being engaged fully in the service of others.

Just before instituting the Eucharist, Jesus washed the feet of his apostles. "If I then, your Lord and Teacher, have washed your feet, you also ought to wash one another's feet" (Jn 13:14). At Lourdes, Mary invites her children to wash in baths. This is possible thanks to the generosity of many volunteers who conform their actions to Jesus' words. Yet the true purification takes place when Jesus sheds his precious blood upon our soul in the sacrament of reconciliation, or penance. This is what Mary repeats so often at Lourdes: "*Penance, be converted!*" This sacrament allows us to receive, worthily and with confidence, the Eucharist that nourishes our life as a child of God.

In January 1858, Bernadette was returning from Bartrès to prepare for her First Communion. Since she had not been able to go to catechism, Mary prepared Bernadette for the reception of her Son. On June 3, the Feast of Corpus Christi, Bernadette received Mary's Son in the Eucharist. By doing so, Mary's promise began to be realized: "I do not promise to make you happy in this life, but in the other." The Eucharist is a foretaste of heaven. When one of Bernadette's friends asked her the day after her First Communion: "What made you more happy: your First Communion or the apparitions?" Bernadette immediately responded: "Those are two things that go together but cannot be compared. I was happy in both."

With Mary's apparitions and the discovery of the spring, the grotto of Massabielle, known as a pig's shelter, famous for being dirty and dark, became a haven of light, healing, and life. Unlike the prodigal son, who had to content himself with eating the pods that the swine ate, let us not dwell in the shadows of sin. Let us be converted! Let us respond to Mary's call by returning with all our heart to our Father. He gives us his Son in the Eucharist, spring of light and life. With his Son we receive the whole of heaven into our soul. Let us claim our inheritance—nothing other than Jesus Christ himself.

The Living Water that
Flows from the Pierced Heart

STAGE 43

The Water Gushing from Christ's Side

In a vision the prophet Ezekiel was led to the door of the temple in Jerusalem. To the east of Jerusalem there is the Dead Sea, the lake whose salt content prevents the appearance of any form of life. Nothing can grow or live in this water or the area surrounding it.

And behold, water was issuing from below the threshold of the temple toward the east (for the temple faced east); and the water was flowing down from below the right side of the threshold of the temple, south of the altar. . . . Going on eastward with a line in his hand, the man measured a thousand cubits, and then led me through the water; and it was ankle-deep. Again he measured a thousand, and led me through the water; and it was knee-deep. Again he measured a thousand, and led me through the water; and it was up to the loins. Again he measured a thousand, and it was a river that I could not pass through, for the water had risen; it was deep enough to swim in, a river that could not be passed through.

And he said to me, "Son of man, have you seen this?" Then he led me back along the bank of the river. As I went back, I saw upon the bank of the river very many trees on the one side and on the other. And he said to me, "This water flows toward the eastern region and goes down into the Arabah; and when it enters the stagnant waters of the sea, the water will become fresh. And wherever the river goes every living creature which swarms will live, and there will be very many fish; for this water goes there, that the waters of the sea may become fresh; so everything will live where the river goes. . . . And on the banks, on both sides of the river, there will grow all kinds of trees for food. Their leaves will not wither nor their fruit fail, but they will bear fresh fruit every month, because the water for them flows from the sanctuary. Their fruit will be for food, and their leaves for healing" (Ezek 47:1, 3–9, 12).

In the vision, a mysterious spring flows under the altar, from the right side of the temple. This becomes a stream of water, then a small river, and finally an unfordable river that flows into the Dead Sea. Thus the living water flowing down from the temple purifies the oily saline water of the lake. Life, nonexistent in the Dead Sea, appears with all manner of animals, aquatic plants, and trees on the banks of the lake.

This prophetic vision of Ezekiel will be realized in Jesus. First, let us discover the symbolism of the Dead Sea, the temple with abundant water flowing from its right side, and the purification of the salty water giving rise to a profusion of life. The Dead Sea evokes the world that has separated itself from God. The salt represents sin, which poisons everything and destroys divine life in hearts, because "the wages of sin is death" (Rom 6:23). Jesus' humanity (his body) is the new temple, the sanctuary, from which gushes the fullness of divine life: "[Jesus] spoke of the temple of his body" (Jn 2:21). "For in him the whole fullness of deity dwells bodily" (Col 2:9). The living water flowing forth from Jesus' humanity represents the Spirit, which gives life: " 'If any one thirst, let him come to me and drink. He who believes in me, as the Scripture has said, "Out of his heart shall flow rivers of living water." ' Now this he said about the Spirit, which those who believed in him were to receive" (Jn 7:37–39). The "right side" of the temple and the "breast" of the incarnate Word refer to the Heart of Christ, pierced on the Cross: "One of the soldiers pierced his side with a spear, and at once there came out blood and water" (Jn 19:34). So the right side of the temple from which gushes the impassable river that purifies the Dead Sea evokes the pierced side of Christ from which gush water and blood, that is, the living water of baptism that purifies sin and the blood of the Eucharist that strengthens the divine life received at baptism. Also, through confession, Jesus spreads his precious blood upon the soul in order to give back to it the innocence and purity received at baptism. The prophet Zechariah likewise announced the living water that flows forth from the pierced Heart and washes away every stain: "When they look on him whom they have pierced . . . on that day there shall be a fountain opened for the house of David and the inhabitants of Jerusalem to cleanse them from sin and uncleanness" (Zech 12:10; 13:1).

By dying on the Cross, it is as though Christ's humanity were torn in two. So sin as well as death are destroyed. The resurrection of the flesh, then, is anticipated by these mysterious words: "The curtain of the temple was torn in two, from top to bottom; and the earth shook, and the rocks were split; the tombs also were opened, and many bodies of the saints who had fallen asleep were raised" (Mt 27:51-52).

The pierced Heart of Jesus beats today in the Blessed Sacrament of the altar. The Eucharist makes the whole work of redemption present and effective in our lives. When the Eucharist is celebrated or adored, Jesus abundantly spreads the living water from his Heart, healing sick hearts and giving life to the world. The vision of the Apocalypse takes up Ezekiel's vision, where the Lamb represents Jesus' humanity in the Eucharist:

> [The angel] showed me the river of the water of life, bright as crystal, flowing from the throne of God and of the Lamb through the middle of the street of the city; also, on either side of the river, the tree of life with its twelve kinds of fruit, yielding its fruit each month; and the leaves of the tree were for the healing of the nations. . . . The throne of God and of the Lamb shall be in it, and his servants shall worship him. (Rev 22:1-3)

> The Spirit and the Bride say, "Come." And let him who hears say, "Come." And let him who is thirsty come, let him who desires take the water of life without price. (Rev 22:17)

The Bride indicates the Church in general and each soul in particular. The Bridegroom is the Lamb, Jesus present in the Eucharist. The Holy Spirit comes to the aid of the Bride so that she might be worthy of the Bridegroom. The Spirit is represented by the water of life that flows from the throne of the Lamb, preparing and purifying the Bride for the eternal nuptials with the Bridegroom.

Finally, going back to the beginning of Genesis, let us recall that in the Eucharist man regains the tree of life of which his disobedience deprived him.

> Out of the ground the LORD God made to grow every tree that is pleasant to the sight and good for food, the tree of life also in the midst of the garden, and the tree of the knowledge of good and evil. A river flowed out of Eden to water the garden, and there it divided and became four rivers. (Gen 2:9-10)

The Easter liturgy acclaims: "O happy fault which gained for us so great a Redeemer." Our Redeemer gives himself in the Eucharist and communicates all the fruits of the Resurrection there. "Their fruit will be for food, and their leaves for healing" (Ezek 47:12). The Eucharist is a "medicine" for immortality. It is the resurrected body of Christ which comes to place in our mortal body a seed of immortality and heals the soul from sin and the injuries of life. The Eucharist also nourishes the divine life. The many "fruits" evoke the richness of Eucharistic grace. This grace contains all the benefits needed for advancing toward sanctity.

Here is an extract from a poem by Edith Stein that she wrote before being deported to the Auschwitz extermination camp; it is entitled, "God's Dwelling-place among Men"!

> You say: it is finished, and you bowed your head in silence. It was finished, your path as a man on earth. From the beginning your throne of glory was prepared for you at the right side of the Father, and you ascended thereto. But you did not separate yourself from the earth. You were united to it for all time. From the moment you descended from the heights of the heavens unto the final annihilation. You truly love your own, O good Shepherd, as no other human heart has ever loved, and you did not wish to leave your children orphans. You built yourself a tent in their midst. You take pleasure in dwelling there. And you will be there unto the end of time. Your blood spilt generously for your own must serve them as an elixir of life.

> You offer it with the coming of every morning. Every morning the sound of the bells calls across all the streets in invitation to the nuptial meal. Men, tight-lipped and busy, hasten down the ways. The sound reaches their ears but not their heart. Only a small remnant of faithful sheep hears the voice of the Shepherd. With a peaceful joy, they follow the call inviting them to the holy tent, to the table which you spread. Their eyes never have their fill of the sublime spectacle that is renewed there day after day, the meaning and end of all the world's course.

> While outside rage the storms and battles terrible, for broken is the seal of the abyss, unleashing monsters of the deep who fight mightily for the reign of the great dragon, here meanwhile is peace, the throne of the Lamb upon the earth, the holy court that leads to heaven, and

no created spirit could conceive the marvels that your presence full of grace prepares for eternity in the hearts become your temples by their consecration. It is here, hidden from the eyes of the world, that you accomplish the work that renews the face of the earth. Concealed from the sight of men in your peaceful tent, you hold the world in your hand; you have set the measure and the term of its tumults. . . . My Lord and my God, hidden under the species of bread, when will you manifest yourself in glory visible? In the pains of childbirth the world groans. In expectation the Bride perseveres. Come quickly!

The Living Water that
Flows from the Pierced Heart

STAGE 44

The Mass and the Disciples at Emmaus

Two [disciples] were going to a village named Emmaus, about seven miles from Jerusalem, and talking with each other about all these things that had happened. While they were talking and discussing together, Jesus himself drew near and went with them. But their eyes were kept from recognizing him. And he said to them, "What is this conversation which you are holding with each other as you walk?" And they stood still, looking sad. Then one of them, named Cleopas, answered him, "Are you the only visitor to Jerusalem who does not know the things that have happened there in these days?" And he said to them, "What things?" And they said to him, "Concerning Jesus of Nazareth, who was a prophet mighty in deed and word before God and all the people, and how our chief priests and rulers delivered him up to be condemned to death, and crucified him. But we had hoped that he was the one to redeem Israel. Yes, and besides all this, it is now the third day since this happened. Moreover, some women of our company amazed us. They were at the tomb early in the morning and did not find his body; and they came back saying that they had even seen a vision of angels, who said that he was alive. Some of those who were with us went to the tomb, and found it just as the women had said; but him they did not see." And he said to them, "O foolish men, and slow of heart to believe all that the prophets have spoken! Was it not necessary that the Christ should suffer these things and enter into his glory?" And beginning with Moses and all the prophets, he interpreted to them in all the Scriptures the things concerning himself.

So they drew near to the village to which they were going. He appeared to be going further, but they constrained him, saying, "Stay with us, for it is toward evening and the day is now far spent." So he went in to stay with them. When he was at table with them, he took the bread and blessed and broke it, and gave it to them. And their eyes were opened and they recognized him; and he vanished out of their sight. They said to each other, "Did not our hearts burn within us while he talked to us on the road, while he opened to us the Scriptures?" And they rose that same hour and returned to Jerusalem; and they found the Eleven gathered together and those who were with them, who said, "The Lord has risen indeed, and has appeared to Simon!" Then they told what had happened on the road, and how he was known to them in the breaking of the bread. (Lk 24:13–35)

As with the passage on the Annunciation, the twenty-fourth chapter of Saint Luke contains the different stages of the Eucharistic liturgy. Let us try to distinguish the major parts. The disciples are on the road, recalling that life is a long pilgrimage, a passage, a Passover. In each Eucharist we are given what they are about to experience on the road to Emmaus with the resurrected Christ. Each Mass is a Passover, a passage where Christ comes to visit us, to teach us, to feed us, and to send us forth to announce the Good News.

The text begins with the disciples' sorrow. Defeated, their faces "look sad". They have lost their hope. With Jesus' death, sin seems to have triumphed. At the beginning of each Mass, through the sober *penitential liturgy*, we invoke divine mercy for our sins, saying: "Lord, have mercy; Christ, have mercy; Lord, have mercy."

Following the penitential liturgy comes the *liturgy of the Word*. This includes the biblical readings followed by the homily. In the passage about the Emmaus pilgrims, Jesus says: " 'O foolish men, and slow of heart to believe all that the prophets have spoken!' And beginning with Moses and all the prophets, he interpreted to them in all the Scriptures the things concerning himself."

Listening to the Word with religious devotion must increase the heart's desire for the Lord to come again. As the disciples little by little approach Emmaus, the darkness of night sets in. "Stay with us, for it is toward evening and the day is now far spent." Christ's light, however, sweetly illumines their hearts. Likewise, each day of ours may be compared to an empty and hopeless shell if Christ does not dwell inside of it. Jesus is about to bring his disciples into his luminous Day. It is

Easter Day, the day of the Resurrection, the day when God manifests himself through his light that chases away the shadows of the heart and gives profound meaning to existence.

In our analogy, we come now to the *offertory*. This is not an intermission between the liturgy of the Word and the liturgy of the Eucharist! Rather it is the moment for expressing to Jesus our desire to receive him more fully. The Word we have heard is going to become incarnate in our hearts through the coming of his glorious Body, hidden though it may be under the appearances of bread. This food, which is Jesus, the Truth in person, enlightens our hearts.

Note that Jesus reminds us: "Was it not necessary that the Christ should suffer these things and enter into his glory?" In other words, Jesus had to suffer the sorrows of the Cross in order to give himself in the Eucharist. As wheat is ground to become bread, so Jesus was beaten, his heart ground by sorrow and pierced, to become the living bread come down from heaven, God's gift for the life of the world. The crucifixion is the price Jesus endured to come each day in the Eucharist, to nourish our heart and illumine us with his sweet presence in the tabernacle.

"[Jesus] went in to stay with them." He blessed the bread, broke it, and gave it to them. Through the *Eucharistic liturgy* (or the "breaking of the bread"), Jesus descends into the most intimate reaches of the heart. He alone can eternally fill it. Through *Communion*, Jesus takes nothing away but gives everything. Saint Augustine said: "You have made us for yourself, O Lord, and our hearts are restless until they rest in you."[1] After Communion the soul's capacity to receive God is enlarged.

Then, the disciples' eyes open, and they recognize Jesus. What is happening? Before the breaking of the bread, the disciples see Jesus with their eyes of flesh but do not recognize him. In receiving the Eucharist, they recognize him with the eyes of the heart, but he disappears from their eyes of flesh. At each Eucharist, we too are invited to recognize, not with our eyes of flesh but with faith or the eyes of the heart, the presence of the Resurrected One under the appearances of bread. The interior light that the Eucharist provides unveils all the meaning of the Word sowed in the hearts of the disciples: "Did not our hearts

---

[1] Saint Augustine, *Confessions* I, I, I.

burn within us while he talked to us on the road." The liturgies of the Word and of the Eucharist are intrinsically linked. The liturgy of the Eucharist makes real and fulfills what the liturgy of the Word announces. Mary first conceived through her faith in hearing the Word of God before conceiving in her flesh through the power of the Holy Spirit. This same Word wants to become incarnate in us. To do so, the Word extends its incarnation in the Eucharist and comes to dwell in the hearts of men, giving them life and putting them in the heart of the Holy Trinity: "From the heights of the Trinity, the incarnate Word descends to man in the Eucharist so that through Communion man might rise up to his final end, the adorable Trinity."[2]

Filled with joy, the two disciples can no longer stay where they are! They leave immediately to announce the Good News. Strengthened by their new conviction, they announce with zeal: "It is really true. Christ is truly resurrected!" It is the time of *sending forth*. Mass ends only when we boldly bear witness to our faith.

After the Annunciation, Mary, carrying the incarnate Word within her, goes with great haste to serve her cousin Elizabeth. The Emmaus pilgrims, after having received the resurrected Word in the breaking of the bread, hasten to announce their faith. These are the two integral parts of the mission of those who have just received Communion: serving our neighbor and announcing the Good News. "For the love of Christ urges us on" (2 Cor 5:14).

> God alone knows what happens in the hearts of those who adore him in spirit and in truth, expressing their love by keeping vigil by the Eucharist all night long. As the hours pass, the adorer is transformed by what he adores; he takes part in the Passover of the Lord, in his death and his Resurrection. Thus is born the Eucharistic man, a man full of wonder, a man of contemplation, indwelt by interior peace and joy. Thus is born the Marian man, in faith carrying within him his Lord, man visited by God radiant with his gifts: love, joy, peace, patience, goodness, kindness, faith, sweetness, and self-mastery. (Cardinal Godfried Danneels)

> I will give them a heart to know that I am the LORD; and they shall be my people, and I will be their God, for they shall return to me with their whole heart. (Jer 24:7)

[2] Bernadot, *De l'Eucharistie à la Trinité* (Paris: Éditions du Cerf, 1920), 15.

The Sorrowful Hearts of Jesus and Mary
Our Lady of the Blessed Sacrament

The greatest sorrow ever felt was that of Mary at the sight of Jesus crucified. When we think of her full of tears at the foot of the Cross, we understand that the greatest joy is that of Mary at the sight of Jesus glorified. For no one more greatly desires to see Jesus loved and adored than his mother Mary, who, at the foot of the Cross, saw him rejected in that way. Christ's Cross is the image of a Heart broken for having loved so much without being loved in return. The sorrow of that Heart is the sorrow of being despised and rejected.

"We have no king" (Jn 19:15), the people cried. And they knelt in a cruel and perverse worship. When we think of this utmost humiliation, could there be a better time than now at the dawn of this new millennium to sound the clarion and begin perpetual adoration? When we think of the way man dethroned him with such cowardice, what better place than our parish to proclaim him King, giving him the honor due to his Name?

The prophet Simeon saw in the child Jesus a sign that is contradicted: "Behold, this child is set for the fall and rising of many in Israel, and for a sign that is spoken against" (Lk 2:34). Jesus will be the stone that is rejected, ignored, despised by men. This will provoke the sorrowful compassion of Mary's heart because her Immaculate Heart beats in unison with the sacred Heart of Jesus. "And a sword will pierce through your own soul also" (Lk 2:35).

After having been crowned with thorns, whipped, and disfigured, he became the object of the people's opprobrium and did not even appear human any more. Likewise, here in the Blessed Sacrament, "he ha[s] no form or comeliness that we should look at him, and no beauty that

228

we should desire him" (Is 53:2); he is crowned with indifference, contempt, and so often ignored, as though he were not there, as though he did not have a Heart burning with love for us. Yet beyond the humble species of the sacred Host, it is really Jesus in person, awaiting us and repeating his eternal call: "Could you not watch with me one hour?" (Mt 26:40).

Instituted at the Last Supper, the Eucharist flows from the Lord's Passion. He spread his arms upon the Cross to give himself in the Holy Eucharist and to fill us with his divine life. There, he uttered a cry that can be heard in the deepest recess of each heart: "I thirst, and with so great a thirst, to be loved that this thirst consumes me."[1] For our good he remained alone in agony upon the Cross. In return, each hour of adoration requites his love, bearing him an ineffable consolation for keeping him company as a friend.

This is why, just as two thousand years ago man totally abandoned him, now his heavenly Father draws all men to him in perpetual adoration. In this way we give him the praise he deserves, the glory due to his Name, the honor worthy of a king. Through our adoration, we gratefully say: "Worthy is the Lamb who was slain, to receive . . . honor and glory and blessing" in unceasing worship for all he has done for our salvation (Rev 5:12; cf. Rev 7:15; 5:9).

Thus in place of the sign above his head where his condemnation was written—since he was not in fact accepted as king—we become a luminous sign for the world of his kingship and presence: "O King of the ages! Who shall not fear and glorify your name, O Lord? For you alone are holy. All nations shall come and worship you" (Rev 15:3–4). In place of the dark hour when man abandoned him, we are witnesses resplendent in the true Light that expels the shadows: the Lord on the throne "is Lord of lords and King of kings" (Rev 17:14).

When we proclaim Jesus King by giving him the glory due to his Name through perpetual adoration, then he takes possession of his kingdom and establishes his reign of love in our hearts. The prophecy is accomplished: God "will wipe away every tear from their eyes" (Rev 21:4) because Mary's tears will have ceased to flow.

---

[1] Letter 133, *Vie et œuvres de sainte Marguerite-Marie Alacoque*, 2 vols., ed. R. P. Croiset (Paris: Éditions Saint-Paul, 1990), 2:487.

If man's hatred for Jesus made Mary's tears flow in unceasing streams, then man's uninterrupted love for Jesus in perpetual adoration will be the cause of her eternal happiness. If man's hatred for Jesus pierced Mary's heart, then unceasing love for Jesus in the Blessed Sacrament will console her broken heart and change her sorrow into ineffable joy. And with Mary all creation shall cease from crying and lamentation, rejoicing with her in "a new heaven and a new earth" (Rev 21:1) recreated by Jesus when, in his unspeakable joy at being loved by men, he fulfills his promise: "Behold, I make all things new" (Rev 21:5).

God's love for man created the world. Man's love for the Son of God in the Blessed Sacrament will recreate the world and bring down upon the earth a new and more glorious paradise. Today, Mary leads her children to recognize her Son in the Eucharist and to requite his love. Thus the triumph of Mary's Immaculate Heart will be the advent of the reign of her Son's Heart in the Eucharist, when this Heart is loved and recognized by all and adored unceasingly in all the tabernacles of the world.

Our Lady of the Blessed Sacrament

Here are Mary's words to Juan Diego in Mexico 1531:

> Know and understand, smallest of my sons! I am the ever-virgin, holy Mary, Mother of the true God; the life-giving Creator of all people; the Lord of what is near and what is far, heaven and earth. I deeply desire that a chapel be built to me here where I can show, praise and testify to him forever. Here I will give people all my love, compassion, help, comfort and salvation. For I am truly your compassionate Mother: your Mother and the Mother to all who dwell in this land and to all other nations and peoples who love me and call and entreat me. I am the Mother of all who seek me and place their trust in me.[2]

On the tilma where the Virgin imprinted her image, Mary stands upright before the sun. She prepares the hearts of her children to receive Jesus, the spiritual sun of souls and the light of the world. Just as the sun

---

[2] In Paul Badde, *María of Guadalupe: Shaper of History, Shaper of Hearts*, trans. Carol Cowgill (San Francisco: Ignatius Press, 2009), 27–28.

is the source of all warmth and all light, the Eucharist, the resurrected body of Jesus, is the source of all divine life and all spiritual light. On the tilma Mary also wears a black belt, like pregnant Aztec women. Welcoming Mary means receiving Jesus, because Mary gives Jesus to the world and especially to those who pray to her.

Mary, giving the Eucharist to the world and drawing the world to the Eucharist, is Our Lady of the Most Blessed Sacrament! "Jesus is the flower that blooms from the root of Jesse: if you want to pluck this blessed flower, bend the branch that bears it through your prayers, and do not seek Jesus the Eucharist but in the virginal womb of Mary."[3]

We invoke Mary under the title "Our Lady of the Most Blessed Sacrament" because Mary is the Mother of the Savior, who lives in the Eucharist; Mary is the sovereign dispenser of this Sacrament and of the graces that it holds; Mary, by being the first to observe the duties of the Eucharistic life, teaches us to hear Mass well, to receive Communion well, and to visit the Most Blessed Sacrament often and piously. Adore our Lord in the company of the Blessed Virgin. I do not say: Remain in her. No, Jesus is there before you that you might address him directly, but do so with Mary. . . . In this way you will discover the very perfect union of these two hearts, that of Jesus and that of Mary, lost in a single love and a single life.[4]

Here is a poem by Blessed Dina Bélanger of Québec: "Lend Me Your Heart":

From your pure heart, Mary, peerless Virgin,
I have come to draw the most perfect love,
To delight the Eucharistic Heart, oh! lend me your ardors
Ever more.

In your blessed soul, O mystical oven,
I have come to draw the love that adores,
To pay homage to the Eucharistic Heart, Virgin of love,
Oh! Lend me your heart.

[3] Saint Bonaventure.
[4] Saint Peter Julian Eymard, *Adorer en esprit et en vérité* (Paris: Éditions F.-X. de Guibert, 2009), 292.

Our Lady, O seraphic canyon,
I have come to draw the love that restores,
To console the Eucharistic Heart, O mother of love,
Oh! Lend me your heart.

Alongside you, angelic Sovereign,
I have come to draw the love that mirrors,
To imitate the Eucharistic Heart, O Queen of love,
Oh! Lend me your heart![4]

∼

---

[4] Saint Peter Julian Eymard, *Œuvres Complètes*, PR 99, 4.

"All Things New"

Mary Gives Birth to a People of Adorers

Let us go through a few passages from the last book of the Bible. "Apocalypse" does not mean "catastrophe" but, rather, "unveiling". It is not a book about chastisements, punishments, and divine wrath; rather, it is about a mystery kept secret from the eyes of the world that is gradually going to unveil itself. In our context, the Eucharist is the hidden presence of God in the midst of the world. This hidden presence is called to be unveiled, made manifest, and known to all, "for nothing is covered that will not be revealed, or hidden that will not be known" (Mt 10:26). Moreover, the words that reappear most in the book are "adoration/worship" and "lamb". As each Mass recalls, it is in the sacred Host that we find the Lamb of God, dead for the sins of the world, but living for our salvation.

The book presents a great battle. On one side, there are the different beasts or idols seeking their own adoration. They represent everything in our lives that wants to distance us from God. On the other side: the Lamb upon the throne adored by the companions of the Lamb. When the Eucharist is celebrated worthily, when it is received into a heart prepared for it, and when it is adored unceasingly, the Lamb reigns upon his throne, as Saint Eymard remind us: "We make our Lord work for the conversion of souls by exposing him and uniting ourselves through our adoration to his prayer and his apostolate. . . . In fact, it is only because we are at his feet that he is upon his throne."[1]

Behold, he is coming with the clouds, and every eye will see him, every one who pierced him; and all tribes of the earth will wail on account of him. Even so. Amen. "I am the Alpha and the Omega,"

[1] Saint Peter Julian Eymard, *Œuvres Complètes*, PR 99, 4.

says the Lord God, who is and who was and who is to come, the Almighty. (Rev 1:7–8)

Jesus returns upon the clouds, in the same way he left us on the day of his Ascension (cf. Acts 1:9). In the Old Testament, clouds evoke the hidden presence of God in the midst of his people. These same clouds, in our context, evoke the permanent but hidden presence of Christ among his people. "He is *(today in the Eucharist)*, he was *(because the Eucharist makes present Christ's death and Resurrection)*, and he is to come *(every day, to the extent that we seek him in faith, knowing that one day he will make himself manifest to all)*."

Chapter 4 places us before the glorious throne of God in heaven. There, God is adored without end by all living creatures: "Day and night they never cease to sing, 'Holy, holy, holy' " (Rev 4:8). We unite ourselves to the heavenly liturgy during the *Sanctus* of each Mass. Before the throne, the crystalline sea (Rev 4:6) evokes the reign of God over all things. This sea also represents all the graces that descend from the divine throne.

Chapter 5 presents the adoration due to the immolated Lamb. He receives the adoration of all the creatures of the universe, because he spilled his blood to ransom the world: "Worthy is the Lamb who was slain, to receive power and wealth and wisdom and might and honor and glory and blessing!" (Rev 5:12). Here we are in the heart of a great liturgy uniting heaven and earth. It is a Eucharistic liturgy where Jesus, the Lamb of God, is adored upon the earth by the baptized as he is in heaven by the angels and saints. In other words, each Mass is a participation in the great heavenly liturgy. Through the Eucharist, we are united to the adoration addressed to God by the angels, the saints in heaven, and even our own faithful departed. "Jesus will have two thrones, one of glory in heaven, another of sweetness and goodness in the Blessed Sacrament; two courts: the celestial and triumphant court and the court of the redeemed here below."[2]

After this I looked, and behold, a great multitude which no man could number, from every nation, from all tribes and peoples and tongues, standing before the throne and before the Lamb, clothed in white

---

[2] Saint Peter Julian Eymard, *Adorer en esprit et en vérité* (Paris: Éditions F.-X. de Guibert, 2009), 53.

robes, with palm branches in their hands, and crying out with a loud voice, "Salvation belongs to our God who sits upon the throne, and to the Lamb!" And all the angels stood round the throne and round the elders and the four living creatures, and they fell on their faces before the throne and worshiped God. . . . "Who are these, clothed in white robes[?] . . . These are they who have come out of the great tribulation; they have washed their robes and made them white in the blood of the Lamb. Therefore are they before the throne of God, and serve him day and night within his temple; and he who sits upon the throne will shelter them with his presence. . . . For the Lamb in the midst of the throne will be their shepherd, and he will guide them to springs of living water; and God will wipe away every tear from their eyes." (Rev 7:9–11, 13–15, 17)

A multitude stands before the Lamb, recalling those who celebrate and adore the Eucharist. Their robes are white, because they are purified by the blood of the Lamb in confession and the Eucharist. Each time that the sacred Host is elevated in faith, the Lamb spills his precious blood upon those who come to him. The palm branches held in hand belong to the martyrs. In the Bible, the "martyr" is the "witness" who spills his blood through fidelity to his faith in Jesus Christ. They have come out of "the great tribulation". These persons represent those who suffer humiliations, calumnies, or persecutions for their faith in general, but also for their faith in the Eucharist in particular. How many grandparents are scolded by their children when they go to Mass to celebrate Christmas, Easter, or another Christian feast? How much does it cost today to go adore the Lamb upon his throne each week in the middle of the night? We should note that they stay "day and night within his temple" (Rev 7:15). The Body of Christ in the Eucharist is the new temple of God on earth. "He . . . will shelter them with his presence"—or: "He will spread his tent over them" (Rev 7:15); he "dwelt [literally, 'pitched his tent'] among us" (Jn 1:14). In the tabernacle, the living heart of our parishes, Jesus is the "true Shepherd" of his people. During Mass or in a chapel of adoration open "day and night", he gathers his children and "guide[s] them to springs of living water" (Rev 7:17; cf. Jn 7:37). From his pierced Heart beating in the Blessed Sacrament gushes a spring of living water, fountain of all comfort and all consolations. This prophecy is accomplished even now in the Eucharist.

And a great sign appeared in heaven, a woman clothed with the sun, with the moon under her feet, and on her head a crown of twelve stars; she was with child and she cried out in her pangs of birth, in anguish for delivery. And another sign appeared in heaven; behold, a great red dragon, with seven heads and ten horns, and seven diadems upon his heads. His tail swept down a third of the stars of heaven, and cast them to the earth. And the dragon stood before the woman who was about to bear a child, that he might devour her child when she brought it forth; she brought forth a male child, one who is to rule all the nations with a rod of iron, but her child was caught up to God and to his throne, and the woman fled into the wilderness, where she has a place prepared by God, in which to be nourished for one thousand two hundred and sixty days.

Now war arose in heaven, Michael and his angels fighting against the dragon; and the dragon and his angels fought, but they were defeated and there was no longer any place for them in heaven. And the great dragon was thrown down, that ancient serpent, who is called the Devil and Satan, the deceiver of the whole world—he was thrown down to the earth, and his angels were thrown down with him. And I heard a loud voice in heaven, saying, "Now the salvation and the power and the kingdom of our God and the authority of his Christ have come, for the accuser of our brethren has been thrown down, who accuses them day and night before our God. And they have conquered him by the blood of the Lamb and by the word of their testimony, for they loved not their lives even unto death" (Rev 12:1–11).

The Woman, in Christian tradition, is Mary. She gave birth in joy to the Savior of the world. She gives birth now to the Church, this people of adorers. Mary "is our mother in the order of grace".[3] Though Mary did not suffer in bringing Jesus into the world, on the other hand, Mary "cries out in her pangs of birth, in anguish for delivery" of the Church. Wounded by the consequences of original sin, by their own personal sins and infidelities against God, the children of Mary are tested in their souls and bodies, thus making Mary, Mother of Compassion, suffer. The passage above feeds the hope of the children of Mary. They are protected by God and by Mary herself. Vanquished in the great battle with Saint Michael, Satan is cast down to earth with his demons. In his plan, God wants men to participate in Christ's victory over the

[3] Second Vatican Council, *Lumen Gentium* (1964), no. 61.

devil. "They have conquered him by the blood of the Lamb and by the word of their testimony": each time the Eucharist is celebrated and adored, the precious blood of the Lamb is spread upon the children of Mary. This blood protects them against the snares of the devil and strengthens them in faith, hope, and charity. The bold witness of the children of Mary to the Good News, Christ, personally present in all the tabernacles of the world, also builds up the kingdom of Jesus on earth, overturning that of the devil. Thus living faith in the Eucharist, accompanied with brave testimony about the Eucharist, "fount and apex of the whole Christian life",[4] makes the children of Mary victorious over the devil and his traps.

> Then I saw heaven opened, and behold, a white horse! He who sat upon it is called Faithful and True, and in righteousness he judges and makes war. His eyes are like a flame of fire, and on his head are many diadems; and he has a name inscribed which no one knows but himself. He is clothed in a robe dipped in blood, and the name by which he is called is The Word of God. And the armies of heaven, wearing fine linen, white and pure, followed him on white horses. From his mouth issues a sharp sword. . . . On his robe and on his thigh he has a name inscribed, King of kings and Lord of lords. (Rev 19:11–16)

Cardinal Daniélou writes: "This white horse is the little Host. It is the Host that must traverse the earth bearing Christ to the adoration of peoples before he comes in his glory."[5] The armies of heaven following the horse are the angels that surround the Host unceasingly. The robe dipped in blood recalls that Jesus makes present in the Host his Passion and his victory over death.

⌒

---

[4] Ibid., no. 11.
[5] Jean Cardinal Daniélou, *Le mystère du salut des nations* (Paris: Éditions du Seuil, 1946), 104.

"All Things New"

STAGE 47

The Lamb Shall Be Its Lamp

It shall come to pass in the latter days that the mountain of the house of the LORD shall be established as the highest of the mountains, and shall be raised above the hills; and all the nations shall flow to it, and many peoples shall come, and say: "Come, let us go up to the mountain of the LORD, to the house of the God of Jacob; that he may teach us his ways and that we may walk in his paths." For out of Zion shall go forth the law, and the word of the LORD from Jerusalem. He shall judge between the nations, and shall decide for many peoples; and they shall beat their swords into ploughshares, and their spears into pruning hooks; nation shall not lift up sword against nation, neither shall they learn war any more. O house of Jacob, come, let us walk in the light of the LORD. (Is 2:2-5)

The Eucharist accomplishes this prophecy of Isaiah. People of all nations gather each week to celebrate the victory of the Resurrected One. The mountain of the house of the Lord evokes the tabernacles of the whole world. The Church never ceases to send out this invitation: "Come, let us go up to the mountain of the LORD", inviting her children to meet Christ, who awaits us in the Eucharist. This mountain is higher than the others, because the Eucharist received in faith raises the soul in love, transforming it through divine charity. Saint John Chrysostom said:

> Who, then, must be purer than he who participates in this sacrifice? Which ray of sunlight must not give way in splendor to the hand that distributes this flesh, to the mouth filled with this spiritual fire, to the tongue stained red by this dread blood? Think upon the honor bestowed on you, at which table you are seated. He upon whom the angels gaze only in trembling, or, rather, upon whom they dare not gaze for the brilliance that emanates from him, the very same serves

238

us as food, mixes with us, and makes up with us but one single flesh and one single body.

When you see the Lord immolated and stretched out, and the priest bowed over the sacrifice in prayer, and all the people stained red by this so precious blood, do you think yourself still among men on earth? Are you not rather transported into the heavens, having laid down every carnal thought, there to contemplate what is happening with a bared soul and purified spirit? O miracle, O divine love for man![1]

They shall beat their swords into ploughshares, and their spears into pruning hooks; nation shall not lift up sword against nation, neither shall they learn war any more. (Is 2:4)

No longer producing arms for war, but working only to make the earth fruitful, constructing a just and fraternal world—how greatly desired is this vision of peace! In Hebrew, the word *shalom* means "peace". Its opposite in Hebrew is not the word "war" but, in fact, "emptiness". For the emptiness in man's heart is the source of all covetousness, jealousy, and rivalry. On the other hand, Jesus "is our peace" (Eph 2:14). Through the Eucharist, Jesus gives his most holy Heart, which alone can fulfill man's heart. First, the peace of Christ comes to fill man's heart. Then, through our burning faith in his power, Christ spreads his peace through our cities:

A few centuries earlier, a Eucharistic miracle saved Saint Clare and her convent from the Saracens. Frederick II had engaged a group of Saracens to lead a fight against the papacy. This group came to Assisi and attacked the convent of San Damiano where Saint Clare and her sisters were enclosed. Clare rose from her sick bed. It was a Friday in September 1241, close to three in the afternoon. She had the ciborium with the Blessed Sacrament brought out and prayed to God to protect her sisters, as she could not protect them herself. She heard a sweet voice like that of a child come from the ciborium: "I will keep you safe always." She then walked to where the wall had been broken by the aggressors and presented the ciborium through the opening. The Saracens fell down, blinded by the rays emanating from the ciborium, and left Assisi in panic.[2]

---

[1] Saint John Chrysostom, *De sacerdotio*, bk. III, no. 4; PG 48:642.
[2] Madeleine Havard de la Montagne, *Sainte Claire d'Assise: Sa vie et ses miracles* (Paris: Perrin et Cie, Libraires-Éditeurs, 1917), 79.

Here are two passages from chapter 21 of Revelation. The Father alone has set the time of the glorious return of his Son and the new creation that will accompany him. Nevertheless, this new creation is already present in us through baptism. We await its full manifestation at the end of time, and the Eucharist is its pledge. The apostle Peter explains that our behavior and prayers hasten the glorious coming of Christ:

> What sort of persons ought you to be in lives of holiness and godliness, waiting for and hastening the coming of the day of God, because of which the heavens will be kindled and dissolved, and the elements will melt with fire! But according to his promise we wait for new heavens and a new earth in which righteousness dwells. (2 Pet 3:11–12)

> Then I saw a new heaven and a new earth; for the first heaven and the first earth had passed away, and the sea was no more. And I saw the holy city, new Jerusalem, coming down out of heaven from God, prepared as a bride adorned for her husband; and I heard a great voice from the throne saying, "Behold, the dwelling of God is with men. He will dwell with them, and they shall be his people, and God himself will be with them; he will wipe away every tear from their eyes, and death shall be no more, neither shall there be mourning nor crying nor pain any more, for the former things have passed away." And he who sat upon the throne said, "Behold, I make all things new." Also he said, "Write this, for these words are trustworthy and true." And he said to me, "It is done! I am the Alpha and the Omega, the beginning and the end. To the thirsty I will give water without price from the fountain of the water of life." (Rev 21:1–6)

Behold the new Jerusalem coming down out of heaven. She fulfills the eternal nuptials between Christ and his Church. These nuptials begin here below through the sacraments. Through faith, baptism represents the exchange of vows between the spouses. The Eucharist is the consummation of the nuptials through divine charity. Confession cleans the wedding gown when it is soiled by breaches of faith, hope, and charity. The Bridegroom dwells in the tabernacle. He awaits his reign upon his throne, that is, in the hearts of the baptized who form the Church, his true Bride. "He will wipe away every tear from their eyes", because in the Eucharist, Christ consoles his children and unceasingly renews in them his ardent charity. He also makes present his victory over eternal death. From this throne, he dispenses "without price from the fountain of the water of life": this is his living and life-giving Spirit.

The rest of the chapter describes the glorious heavenly Jerusalem still to come, though she is anticipated today in the Eucharist. As the final prophets of the Old Testament prophesied, the temple of stone has disappeared. But the Lamb is the true temple. He illuminates men through the light emanating from his resurrected body. This glorious body is present in the Eucharist, from which it pours forth all the light and glory of his Resurrection. Saint Gertrude wrote: "As many times as a man looks with desire and reverence upon the Host that contains the Body and Blood of Christ sacramentally, that many times he increases his future merits. For in the eternal possession of God, he shall taste new and special delicacies in recompense for each look of love he has directed to Jesus in the Blessed Sacrament."[3]

> And I saw no temple in the city, for its temple is the Lord God the Almighty and the Lamb. And the city has no need of sun or moon to shine upon it, for the glory of God is its light, and its lamp is the Lamb. By its light shall the nations walk; and the kings of the earth shall bring their glory into it, and its gates shall never be shut by day —and there shall be no night there; they shall bring into it the glory and the honor of the nations. But nothing unclean shall enter it, nor any one who practices abomination or falsehood, but only those who are written in the Lamb's book of life. (Rev 21:22–27)

When the Lamb lets his light be seen, all creation will be astounded. "The city has no need of sun or moon to shine upon it, for the glory of God is its light, and its lamp is the Lamb." The light of the Lamb will be such that the other lights of the world will lose their brilliance. "There shall be no night there" because of the light springing from the throne of the Lamb. Then this will be the greatest joy of the Lamb's companions! A chapel of perpetual adoration—behold the victory of the Lamb who already illuminates the world day and night. These oases of peace draw so many adorers who offer their lives, like precious treasures, in silent hours of prayer. Despite fatigue and overscheduled days, they take the time to adore their King and their Lord. Thus they hasten

---

[3] Saint Gertrude, *Héraut de l'Amour divin* IV, 25, 8.

the coming of his kingdom in their lives and our world. By changing their hearts, these hours of adoration change the world.

> Closeness to Christ in the silence of contemplation does not distance us from our contemporaries but, just the opposite, makes us attentive and open to the joys and distresses of men, stretching the heart to the dimensions of the world. It puts us in solidarity with our brothers in mankind, particularly with the least among us, who are especially beloved by the Lord. Through adoration, the Christian contributes mysteriously to the radical transformation of the world and the germination of the Gospel. Every person who prays to the Lord brings the whole world along with him, raising the world to God.[4]

~

---

[4] John Paul II, letter to Bishop Houssiau for the 750th anniversary of Corpus Christi, May 28, 1996.

The Five Graces of Adoration and Mission

The Transfiguration and Mission

Recalling the homily with which he solemnly inaugurated his pontificate, Benedict XVI proclaimed:

"There is nothing more beautiful than to be surprised by the Gospel, by the encounter with Christ. There is nothing more beautiful than to know him and to speak to others of our friendship with him." These words are all the more significant if we think of the mystery of the Eucharist. The love that we celebrate in the sacrament is not something we can keep to ourselves. By its very nature it demands to be shared with all. What the world needs is God's love; it needs to encounter Christ and to believe in him. The Eucharist is thus the source and summit not only of the Church's life, but also of her mission: "An authentically eucharistic Church is a missionary Church." We too must be able to tell our brothers and sisters with conviction: "That which we have seen and heard we proclaim also to you, so that you may have fellowship with us" (1 Jn 1:3). Truly, nothing is more beautiful than to know Christ and to make him known to others. The institution of the Eucharist, for that matter, anticipates the very heart of Jesus' mission: he is the one sent by the Father for the redemption of the world (cf. Jn 3:16–17; Rom 8:32). At the Last Supper, Jesus entrusts to his disciples the sacrament which makes present his self-sacrifice for the salvation of us all, in obedience to the Father's will. We cannot approach the eucharistic table without being drawn into the mission which, beginning in the very heart of God, is meant to reach all people. Missionary outreach is thus an essential part of the eucharistic form of the Christian life.[1]

Before sending out his disciples on their mission, Jesus called them to him:

[1] Benedict XVI, Apostolic Exhortation *Sacramentum Caritatis* (2007), no. 84.

[Jesus] went up on the mountain, and called to him those whom he desired; and they came to him. And he appointed twelve, to be with him, and to be sent out to preach. (Mk 3:13–14)

Adoration is *being with*. Evangelization is *being sent toward*. Before going toward others in the name of Jesus, we must first come to him. Before evangelizing, we must let ourselves be evangelized. We must let ourselves be touched by his healing love that comes from the Eucharist. "It is pleasant to spend time with him, to lie close to his breast like the Beloved Disciple (cf. Jn 13:25) and to feel the infinite love present in his heart."[2] John Paul II asked Christians to know and passionately love the Eucharist in order to become true witnesses of his love: "To evangelize the world there is need of apostles who are 'experts' in the celebration, adoration and contemplation of the Eucharist."[3]

As the Second Vatican Council puts it, living the Eucharist naturally pushes us to give our lives to others:

The Most Blessed Eucharist contains the entire spiritual boon of the Church, that is, Christ himself, our Pasch and Living Bread, by the action of the Holy Spirit through his very flesh vital and vitalizing, giving life to men who are thus invited and encouraged to offer themselves, their labors and all created things, together with him. In this light, the Eucharist shows itself as the source and the apex of the whole work of preaching the Gospel.[4]

And after six days Jesus took with him Peter and James and John his brother, and led them up a high mountain apart. And he was transfigured before them, and his face shone like the sun, and his garments became white as light. And behold, there appeared to them Moses and Elijah, talking with him. And Peter said to Jesus, "Lord, it is well that we are here; if you wish, I will make three booths here, one for you and one for Moses and one for Elijah." He was still speaking, when behold, a bright cloud overshadowed them, and a voice from the cloud said, "This is my beloved Son, with whom I am well pleased; listen to him." When the disciples heard this, they fell on their faces, and were filled with awe. But Jesus came and touched them, saying, "Rise, and have no fear." And when they lifted up their eyes, they saw

[2] John Paul II, Encyclical Letter *Ecclesia de Eucharistia* (2003), no. 25.

[3] John Paul II, Message for World Mission Sunday, "Eucharist and Mission" (2004), no. 3.

[4] Second Vatican Council, *Presbyterorum Ordinis* (1965), no. 5.

no one but Jesus only. And as they were coming down the mountain, Jesus commanded them: "Tell no one the vision, until the Son of man is raised from the dead." (Mt 17:1–9)

Jesus finishes by evoking his imminent Passion. Let us compare the texts of the Passion and of the Transfiguration:

Transfiguration		Passion
Mount Tabor with Peter, John, James	→	Gethsemane with Peter, John, James
Face gloriously transfigured	→	Crowned with thorns, suffering and disfigured face
Surrounded by a luminous cloud	→	Darkness over the land for three hours
Elijah is present	→	Jesus calls to Elijah
Moses is present	→	He is condemned in Moses' name
God speaks (This is my beloved Son, with whom I am well pleased; listen to him)	→	God is silent (My God, why have you abandoned me)
Shining robes	→	Bloody, torn tunic
Peter remains	→	Peter flees
Recognized as "Rabbi"	→	Treated with derision . . .

The Transfiguration occurs exactly one week after Peter's profession of faith. Since his profession coincides with Yom Kippur, we can deduce that the Transfiguration takes place during the Festival of Booths. For the Festival of Booths the Jewish people would construct cabins both in memory of the divine protection in the wilderness and to prefigure the *sukkot* (tents) in which the just were to live in future centuries. Here, thanks to the manifestation of Jesus' glory, Peter understands that the Messianic times have arrived: he wants to pitch three tents. In fact the Festival of Booths is accomplished in Jesus' presence. Saint John writes: "The Word became flesh and dwelt among us and we have beheld his glory." "To dwell" is literally "to camp, to pitch one's tent". This new tent is the humanity of Christ. This tent is pitched today, wherever his body is found in the Eucharist.

Let us reread this text in light of Exodus 34: on Mount Sinai, Moses prays. Jesus, too, is in the middle of praying when he is transfigured and shines like the sun on Mount Tabor. Moses receives the tables of the Covenant: at the moment that the "glory" of the Lord manifests itself on Mount Sinai, God calls to Moses from the cloud. This is the *shekinah*, the presence of God in the midst of his people. This presence is then manifested in the "tent of meeting" in the wilderness. At the Transfiguration, the same cloud covers them all. Today this "divine presence" or "glory" is communicated through the holy humanity of Jesus, the new tent where God resides. From this new "tent of meeting"—that is, the Eucharist—the *shekinah* covers the other tents: us and our neighbor, the new place of the divine presence. In other words, the Eucharist creates new links of charity between people.

> All the sons of Israel saw Moses, behold, the skin of his face shone, and they were afraid to come near him. But Moses called to them . . . and he gave them in commandment all that the LORD had spoken with him in Mount Sinai. And when Moses had finished speaking with them, he put a veil on his face; but whenever Moses went in before the LORD to speak with him, he took the veil off, until he came out; and when he came out, and told the sons of Israel what he was commanded, the sons of Israel saw the face of Moses, that the skin of Moses' face shone. (Ex 34:30–34)

His face shone, but from an exterior light. Whereas Jesus shines on his own from inside: he is himself the light, born of the light. He makes visible his union and intimacy with the Father. Through our baptism, we become children of God. We are dressed in the white robe and the light of Christ who shines in us.

Here are a few conclusions:

—The true Festival of Booths has come in Jesus: he lives among us in the Eucharist. Jesus himself is also the living Torah, the complete Word of God: "This is my beloved Son, with whom I am well pleased; listen to him." This Word, which took flesh in Jesus, remains among us in the Blessed Sacrament.

—Jesus reveals the "power" of the kingdom of God in his person. Today, the Eucharist contains the whole power of the Resurrection spilling forth upon those who come into its presence. The glorious body of Christ in the Host transfigures the soul that contemplates it, just as for Moses in the "tent of meeting": "We all, with unveiled face, beholding the glory of the Lord, are being changed into his likeness from one degree of glory to another; for this comes from the Lord who is the Spirit" (2 Cor 3:18). Jesus said the same thing to Saint Faustina: "When a soul approaches me in confidence, I fill it with so many graces that it cannot contain them all and so casts them upon other souls."[5]

—Peter wants to "pitch three tents" in order to remain in the at once sweet and glorious presence of Jesus. After having experienced this love, Christ will ask him to witness to what he has seen:

The wonder we experience at the gift God has made to us in Christ gives new impulse to our lives and commits us to becoming witnesses of his love. We become witnesses when, through our actions, words and way of being, Another makes himself present. Witness could be described as the means by which the truth of God's love comes to men and women in history, inviting them to accept freely this radical newness. Through witness, God lays himself open, one might say, to the risk of human freedom. Jesus himself is the faithful and true witness (cf. Rev 1:5; 3:14), the one who came to testify to the truth (cf. Jn 18:37). Here I would like to reflect on a notion dear to the early Christians, which also speaks eloquently to us today: namely, witness even to the offering of one's own life, to the point of martyrdom. Throughout the history of the Church, this has always been seen as the culmination of the new spiritual worship: "Offer your bodies" (Rom 12:1). One thinks, for example, of the account of the martyrdom of Saint Polycarp of Smyrna, a disciple of Saint John: the entire drama is described as a liturgy, with the martyr himself becoming Eucharist. We might also recall the eucharistic imagery with which Saint Ignatius of Antioch describes his own imminent martyrdom: he sees himself as "God's wheat" and desires to become in martyrdom "Christ's pure bread". The Christian who offers his life in martyrdom enters into full communion with the Pasch of Jesus Christ and thus becomes Eucharist with him. Today too, the Church does not lack martyrs who offer the supreme witness to God's love. Even if the test of martyrdom is not asked of us, we know that worship pleasing to God demands that we should be inwardly prepared for it. Such worship culminates in the joyful and convincing testimony of a consistent Christian life, wherever the Lord calls us to be his witnesses.[6]

[5] Saint Faustina, *Petit Journal*, 1073.
[6] Benedict XVI, Apostolic Exhortation *Sacramentum Caritatis* (2007), no. 85.

The Five Graces of Adoration and Mission

STAGE 49

"Abide in My Love"

Before sending his disciples on their mission, the resurrected Christ "showed them his hands and his feet" (Lk 24:40) with his five glorified wounds, fonts of grace for humanity. For "he has borne our griefs and carried our sorrows . . . with his stripes we are healed" (Is 53:4-5). A particular grace flows from each of Christ's glorious wounds, and we receive them by coming to spend time in his Eucharistic presence. These are the five Eucharistic fruits: transformation, reparation, sanctification, salvation, and restoration. Let us begin with the grace of transformation, rereading a passage from John 15.

> "I am the vine, you are the branches. He who abides in me, and I in him, he it is that bears much fruit, for apart from me you can do nothing. . . . If you abide in me, and my words abide in you, ask whatever you will, and it shall be done for you. By this my Father is glorified, that you bear much fruit, and so prove to be my disciples. As the Father has loved me, so have I loved you; abide in my love. . . . These things I have spoken to you, that my joy may be in you, and that your joy may be full. This is my commandment, that you love one another as I have loved you. Greater love has no man than this, that a man lay down his life for his friends. You are my friends if you do what I command you. No longer do I call you servants, for the servant does not know what his master is doing; but I have called you friends, for all that I have heard from my Father I have made known to you. You did not choose me, but I chose you and appointed you that you should go and bear fruit and that your fruit should abide; so that whatever you ask the Father in my name, he may give it to you. This I command you, to love one another." (Jn 15:5, 7-9, 11-17)

Jesus is the true vine. He comes to recreate his life in us so that we might bear many fruits. All the same, we must not confuse effectiveness

248

and fruitfulness. Effectiveness comes from personal talents and natural abilities. Men often make use of it, not to build up the kingdom of God, but to build up their own "kingdom". Fruitfulness, on the other hand, depends directly on our communion with Christ. This communion is strengthened by the Eucharist, sacrament of communion with God, creating a new communion with others in Christ. Blessed Charles de Foucauld is a luminous example of Eucharistic fruitfulness that sometimes appears as ineffectiveness to the eyes of the world. To adore is to enter into the poverty of Jesus in the sacred Host. Jesus was born poor; he lived simply; he died without anything. He still shows an immense poverty in making himself present under the very fragile species of bread and wine. To "remain in his love", we must not fear dryness, periods of spiritual drought, which strengthen the soul by purifying it interiorly. For Charles, the best spent hour of our life is the hour we loved Jesus most. Let us enter the school of Charles de Foucauld, spiritual master on the path of Eucharistic poverty: "Adoration of the Blessed Sacrament is repose, refreshment, joy."[1] "Adoring the sacred Host ought to be the center of every man's life."[2] "From his tabernacle Jesus will shine forth upon these lands and draw adorers to him. . . . Does my presence here do some good? If it does not, the presence of the Blessed Sacrament certainly does a lot: Jesus cannot be in a place without shining forth."

Charles writes to his cousin Madame de Bondy:

You tell me that I will be happy, happy with a true happiness, happy to the last day . . . that as all-wretched as I am, I am a palm tree planted beside living waters, the living waters of the divine will, of divine love, of grace . . . and that I will bring forth fruit in my time. I feel without fruit: I have been converted for eleven years now; what have I done? What were the works of the saints and what are mine? I see my hands empty of goodness. You deign to console me. You deign to console me: "You will bring forth fruit in your time", you tell me. What is this time? Everyone's time is the hour of judgment: You promise me that if I persist in goodwill and battle, however poor I see myself, I will have fruits in this last hour. . . . And you add: you will be a beautiful tree with eternal green leaves, and all your works

---

[1] Blessed Charles de Foucauld, letter to Madame de Bondy, January 19, 1903.
[2] Blessed Charles de Foucauld, letter to Suzanne Perret, December 15, 1904.

will come to a prosperous end, all of them will bring forth their fruit for eternity. My God, how good you are, how divinely consoling you are.

John Paul II spoke of this mysterious fruitfulness that pours forth from adoration: "In the Holy Eucharist—and this is the meaning of perpetual adoration—we enter into the movement of love from which springs all interior progress and all apostolic fruitfulness: 'I, when I am lifted up from the earth, will draw all men to myself' (Jn 12:32)."[3] Yet Charles de Foucauld would die murdered in front of his hermitage, alone, without a community, without having converted anyone. Where, then, are we to find the fruitfulness of such a life? Jesus asked Charles to go all the way in offering his person and dying like the grain of wheat if it wants to bear fruit (cf. Jn 12:24–25). Madame de Bondy was right, because after Charles' death, it was not one community but numerous religious families that found their foundation, example, and inspiration in the witness of the Blessed. So the fruitfulness of Charles' life was far beyond his expectations! We, too, must enter into Eucharistic poverty. Our adoration will bear all its fruit in its time, according to God's plan, but it will always be more beautiful and noble than we hoped for!

We must not forget that Jesus did not save the world through his great speeches or prodigious healings. Rather, by spreading his arms upon the Cross—cut through with a feeling of failure and rejected by all—he opened the locks of divine mercy to mankind. Likewise, when we remain silent before the Blessed Sacrament, it seems that nothing is happening and that we are wasting our time. Yet it is then that everything changes! We transform the world, because we are united to Jesus, who saves the world and brings us into his redemption! The Eucharist makes present Christ's sacrifice. Thus we become, with Mary at the foot of the Cross, co-redeemers. "Through adoration the Christian contributes mysteriously to the radical transformation of the world and the germination of the Gospel."[4]

"Sacred Heart of Jesus, thank you for this first tabernacle in the land of the Tuareg. Sacred Heart of Jesus, shine forth from the heart

[3] John Paul II, Homily at Sacré-Cœur de Montmartre, June 1, 1980.
[4] John Paul II, letter to Bishop Houssiau for the 750th anniversary of Corpus Christi, May 28, 1996.

of this tabernacle upon this people who adores you without knowing you. Enlighten, lead, save these souls that love you."[5] Thus the time we spend exposing our soul to the "divine radiation" of the Host is of more use for the world than all works done outside of Jesus. The more we are overworked, the more we must reinforce prayer and strew our days with adoration.

Here is the witness of Father Pierron, pastor of the parish of Vichy, after having instituted perpetual adoration:

> The parish of Saint Louis-Saint Blaise is experiencing graces of charity drawn from Eucharistic adoration: ties are being forged or strengthened, the parishioners are more attentive to one another, there is greater solidarity. Jesus, in his Blessed Sacrament, is shattering the heart of the parish and opening it little by little to missionary work since we are on the way to welcoming the grace of parish groups for evangelization. God says: 'A new heart I will give you, and a new spirit I will put within you; and I will take out of your flesh the heart of stone and give you a heart of flesh' (Ezek 36:26). . . . Due to this chain of uninterrupted prayer, all the parish groups are united in prayer. In the exercise of my ministry, I know that at each moment, a parishioner is praying for the parish and its pastor. I am touched by the fidelity of my parishioners to their commitment to prayer; it is so beautiful.

Father Bertrand Lorentz, a pastor in Sanary, writes:

> It has already been five years since our parish in Sanary began living from perpetual adoration. What a magnificent gift for a parish! It is the greatest gift there is because Jesus is loved in the Blessed Sacrament. Hour after hour, the young and old of the parish come to the source of love and leave filled with strength, joy, and peace. Adoration in our parish has allowed us to develop this great current of prayer and to bestow perseverance in faithfulness to many. Moreover, how can we think of evangelizing without beginning by getting on our knees? Adoration and evangelization are two words that go hand in hand.

Finally, Don Macchioni, author of a work about parish groups for evangelization, which were put in place at San Estorgio in Milan by Don Pigi Perini, explains:

[5] Blessed Charles de Foucauld, Diary, July 8, 1903.

The community that does not know to make this choice [of adoration] in faith will never see lasting fruits, whether of spiritual growth or an increase in the number of its members; it disposes its initiatives, however praiseworthy they may be, to failure. We can never repeat enough that this pastoral choice must precede and nourish all the others. Praise and adoration form an extraordinary barrier against the temptations that a growing community faces. Whoever has spent his hour of adoration in the service of the community and in praying with love for the brothers he is evangelizing will leave revived, having obtained Jesus' own way of seeing the circumstances around him. Furthermore, his interior wounds will be healed little by little, because he will have experienced the love of God and will continue to experience it.[6]

[6] Don Giuseppe Macchioni, *Évangéliser en paroisse* (Nouan-le-Fuzelier: Éditions des Béatitudes, 2009), 76.

The Five Graces of Adoration and Mission

STAGE 50

Vocations
(Graces for Reparation and Salvation)

How lovely is your dwelling place, O LORD of hosts! My soul longs, yes, faints for the courts of the LORD; my heart and flesh sing for joy to the living God. Even the sparrow finds a home, and the swallow a nest for herself, where she may lay her young, at your altars, O LORD of hosts, my King and my God. Blessed are those who dwell in your house, ever singing your praise! Blessed are the men whose strength is in you, in whose heart are the highways to Zion. As they go through the valley of Baca they make it a place of springs; the early rain also covers it with pools. They go from strength to strength; the God of gods will be seen in Zion. O LORD God of hosts, hear my prayer; give ear, O God of Jacob! Behold our shield, O God; look upon the face of your anointed! For a day in your courts is better than a thousand elsewhere. I would rather be a doorkeeper in the house of my God than dwell in the tents of wickedness. For the LORD God is a sun and shield; he bestows favor and honor. No good thing does the LORD withhold from those who walk uprightly. O LORD of hosts, blessed is the man who trusts in you! (Ps 84)

Reparation consists in returning "love for love" to Jesus. The Eucharist is the gift of the Sacred Heart of Jesus which loves "to the end" (Jn 13:1). Jesus manifests his Heart to men because, seeing them so poor in love, he wants to enrich them with the treasures of the Heart of God. Jesus "burns with the desire to be loved". His Heart is "an inexhaustible spring",[1] "a burning furnace".[2] On the one hand, he is ablaze with love for men. On the other, he is offended by their ingratitude.

---

[1] *Vie et œuvres de sainte Marguerite-Marie Alacoque*, 2 vols. (Paris: Éditions Saint-Paul, 1990), 2:335.

[2] Saint Margaret Mary, *Autobiographie*, nos. 55 and 56.

This double consideration must move us, on the one hand, to requite the love of the Heart of Jesus and, on the other hand, to offer him compensation for the offenses made against him. To make reparation, or to console the Heart of Jesus, is loving Jesus with all one's heart on behalf of those who reject or ignore him (cf. *Stage 41 on Fatima*). Jesus presents his Heart to Saint Margaret Mary, now as a *sun of divine love,* now surrounded by a *crown of thorns:*

> Jesus Christ showed himself to me, all dazzling in glory with his five wounds shining like five suns, and from this sacred humanity came forth flames from all parts, but above all from his adorable breast— which had opened itself—he revealed to me his all-loving and all-lovable Heart, which was the living source of these flames.[3]

> This divine Heart was presented to me surrounded by a crown of thorns, which signified the piercings that our sins have given him, and a cross above signified that, from the first instants of his Incarnation, from the formation of his Sacred Heart, the Cross was rooted there from the beginning, from among all the bitter things that were to humiliate him: poverty, pain, the contempt that the sacred humanity was to suffer throughout his whole life and in his sacred Passion.[4]

Jesus is true God and true man in one Divine Person. He loves with the Heart of God, that is to say, with immeasurable divine charity. He also loves with a human Heart, a Heart of flesh, a vulnerable Heart, that we call the Sacred Heart. The Gospel records that this Heart passionately loved each person it met two thousand years ago in Palestine. Requital of his love gave this Heart an indescribable joy, but hate or indifference broke it. At Paray-le-Monial, Jesus reminds us that this same Heart of flesh beats today in the Blessed Sacrament—for us who did not live beside him two thousand years ago. In the Blessed Sacrament he loves us with the same love and the same affection that he showed to his intimates in the Gospel. In the Blessed Sacrament, our indifference to his love tears apart his Heart. Thus the love or ingratitude of men toward the Blessed Sacrament is none other than love or ingratitude toward his Heart of flesh. Along these lines, Jesus reveals to Margaret Mary that his Heart is more offended by his friends today—by us, ourselves, who, knowing him in the Blessed Sacrament, love him so little—than by his enemies who, at Golgotha, put him on a Cross.

---

[3] *Vie et œuvres de sainte Marguerite-Marie Alacoque,* 2:335.
[4] Letter of Saint Margaret Mary to Father Croiset, November 3, 1689.

They crowned him with thorns. Today, we crown him with indifference and contempt through the way we treat him in the Sacrament of his Love. This is the origin of the crown of thorns upon his Heart in its traditional representation! On the other hand, our adoration and gratitude crown his heart with joy and consolations. We love him for others, in the name of others. This is reparation!

"Behold this Heart which so loved men that it held nothing back, exhausting itself, consuming itself in order to show them its love. And in exchange, I receive from the many only ingratitude, through their irreverence and sacrilege, through their coldness and the contempt they have for me *in this Sacrament of love*."[5] Margaret Mary will spend all her time passionately loving "the Heart of my lovable Jesus in the Most Blessed Sacrament, apart from which there is neither pleasure nor joy nor consolation in life",[6] in reparation for those who do not know him, who ignore him, or who despise him.

John Paul II recalls the goal of the [Second Vatican] Council and how to make reparation for the sins and the crimes of the world:

> The encouragement and the deepening of eucharistic worship are proofs of that authentic renewal which the council set itself as an aim and of which they are the central point. . . . The Church and the world have a great need of eucharistic worship. Jesus waits for us in this sacrament of love. Let us be generous with our time in going to meet Him in adoration and in contemplation that is full of faith and ready to make reparation for the great faults and crimes of the world. May our adoration never cease![7]

In the Blessed Sacrament, he could not be more loving! And yet, he is not loved. His love is not appreciated. He is not even known, not even by a great many of those who are his own. He has some good apostolic servants, a few pious adorers in his service. But how few spouses he has! How few friends even! who visit him out of affection! who converse from the heart, who are devoted purely to him![8]

[5] Saint Margaret Mary, *Autobiographie*, no. 92.

[6] Letter 138 of May 16, 1690, to the Reverend Father Croiset, in Bishop Gauthey, *Vie et œuvres de Marguerite-Marie Alacoque*, vol. 2: *Œuvres*, 3rd ed. (Paris: Éditions J. de Gigord, 1915), p. 608.

[7] John Paul II, Apostolic Letter *Dominicae Cenae* (1980), no. 3.

[8] Saint Peter Julian Eymard, *Œuvres complètes*, NR 44, 133.

On the subject of abortion, Mother Teresa of Calcutta said: "If people spent an hour each week in Eucharistic adoration, abortion would end." For perpetual Eucharistic adoration is a little corner of heaven on earth. Here below Jesus is adored without interruption, as in heaven where the saints and the angels unceasingly adore him. The divine life abundantly spills into hearts, thus protecting every human life from its conception to its natural end.

Beyond reparation, the Eucharist is the font of *salvation*. Recall these words of Jesus in his Eucharistic discourse:

> For this is the will of my Father, that every one who sees the Son and believes in him should have eternal life; and I will raise him up at the last day. (Jn 6:40)

John Paul II wrote:

> Every commitment to holiness, every activity aimed at carrying out the Church's mission, every work of pastoral planning, must draw the strength it needs from the Eucharistic mystery and in turn be directed to that mystery as its culmination. In the Eucharist we have Jesus, we have his redemptive sacrifice, we have his resurrection, we have the gift of the Holy Spirit, we have adoration, obedience and love of the Father. Were we to disregard the Eucharist, how could we overcome our own deficiency?[9]

Here are a few testimonies by pastors about the graces of salvation that flow from chapels of Eucharistic adoration.

Father Charles Fanelli, pastor of Saint John Mary Vianney Parish, reports that perpetual Eucharistic adoration in his parish is the direct cause of a constant entrance of newly converted persons into the catechumenate as well as of a clear spiritual growth in the life of the parishioners. His Excellency Ruben T. Profugo, bishop of Lucena in the Philippines, attests: "In my diocese, attendance at Mass has visibly grown not only on Sundays but also during the week. Many have returned to the sacraments thanks to perpetual Eucharistic adoration. There is a very strong link between adoration and the Mass. The weekly hour of adoration prepares parishioners to experience Sunday Mass or to give thanks for that which was just experienced."

[9] John Paul II, Encyclical Letter *Ecclesia de Eucharistia* (2003), no. 60.

It is not only that Penance leads to the Eucharist, but that the Eucharist also leads to Penance.[10]

Many priests who have set up perpetual adoration in their parish can testify to growth in requests for the sacrament of reconciliation as one of its consequences. The growth is not only quantitative but also qualitative. One cannot remain before the Blessed Sacrament without the light of Christ profoundly illuminating one's soul and enlightening one's conscience.

Vocations:

> In their encounter with the Eucharist, some men discover that they are called to become ministers of the Altar, other people, that they are called to contemplate the beauty and depth of this mystery, others that they are called to pour out again its impelling force of love on the poor and weak, and others again that they are called to grasp its transforming power in the realities and gestures of everyday life. Each believer finds in the Eucharist not only the interpretative key of his or her own existence, but the courage to actualize it, indeed to build up, in the diversity of charisms and vocations, the one Body of Christ in history.[11]

If we put ourselves at the service of the Gospel and live from the Eucharist, we mature in love for God and neighbor, thus contributing to the building up of the Church as communion. Eucharistic love motivates and provides the foundation for the vocational activity of the whole Church. Mother Teresa of Calcutta attests: "It was not until 1973, the year we began daily Eucharistic adoration, that our community began to grow and flourish."[12] His Excellency John Magee, bishop of Cloyne in Ireland, recounts that priestly vocations in his diocese tripled from the time he instituted perpetual Eucharistic adoration.

The Congregation for Clergy encourages the practice of perpetual adoration in parishes in order to awaken vocations. The urgency [of responding to a vocation] becomes clear from

[10] John Paul II, Apostolic Letter *Dominicae Cenae* (1980), no. 7.

[11] John Paul II, Message of the Holy Father for the 37th World Day of Prayer for Vocations, May 14, 2000, no. 2.

[12] Mother Teresa, *Tu m'apportes l'amour: Écrits spirituels* (Paris: Éditions du Centurion, 1975).

a movement of prayer, placing twenty-four-hour continuous Eucharistic adoration at the center, so that a prayer of adoration, thanksgiving, praise, petition, and reparation will be raised to God, incessantly and from every corner of the earth, with the primary intention of awakening a sufficient number of holy vocations to the priestly state and, at the same time, spiritually uniting with a certain spiritual maternity —at the level of the Mystical Body—all those who have already been called to the ministerial priesthood and are ontologically conformed to the one High and Eternal priest.[13]

A parish that adores the Blessed Sacrament day and night obtains the grace of "spiritual maternity". It "gives birth" for the Church to holy vocations to the priesthood and religious life.

A young Vietnamese priest who was practicing his ministry in a small parish in Singapore recounts:

Celebrating Mass for one of the Sundays of Lent, I was struck by the great number of catechumens: eighty young people between 18 and 35. At the end of Mass, a young priest showed me around his parish, and I noticed next to the church a small air-conditioned room filled with flowers. The Blessed Sacrament is exposed there day and night, as in the basilica of Sacré-Cœur on Montmartre, and there are always fifteen or so people. The pastor told me that the number of catechumens was linked to this adoration. For when he questioned these young people who were seeking baptism from him, they all answered that for months they had come at night to pray before the Blessed Sacrament, not really knowing what they were doing, but having been attracted by its Presence. Yes, adoration attracts, because every man has in himself this desire to see God. But the tragedy of our society is that man no longer hungers. We are sated beings, and the desire for the vision of God is smothered.[14]

$\sim$

---

[13] "Eucharistic Adoration for the Sanctification of Priests and Spiritual Maternity", Letter of Cardinal Hummes, Prefect of the Congregation for Clergy, December 8, 2007.

[14] Bishop Patrick Chauvet, *Il est là! L'adoration eucharistique* (Saint-Maur: Éditions Parole et Silence, 2008), 121–22.

The Five Graces of Adoration and Mission

The Reign of the Eucharist in the Soul

Every baptized person is called to sainthood. There are many paths for arriving there. Some have a Eucharistic vocation! They have a special attraction to the Eucharist and want to make the Eucharist the center of their spirituality and their life. Saint Peter Julian Eymard, upon founding his community of adorers, explained: "In the Sacrament, Jesus offers us the model of all the virtues. There is nothing more beautiful than the Eucharist! But only pious souls that receive Communion, and reflect, can comprehend this beauty. The others understand nothing at all. There are few who think about the virtues, the life, and the state of our Lord in the Blessed Sacrament. We treat him like a statue; we think he is there only to forgive us and receive our prayers. That is not true. Our Lord lives and acts: look upon him, study him, imitate him."[1] Knowing the love of Christ, being filled with his fullness: this is the reign of God in man. To enter fully into the Eucharistic vocation, the Blessed Sacrament must become our *model*, our *life*, and our *end:*

- *Our model:* in meditating on the Holy Scriptures, we contemplate the great virtues that animated the earthly life of Jesus. He is the Way to imitate. For us today, in his sacramental state, he continues the practice of all the exalted virtues of the Gospel. In the Blessed Sacrament, Jesus is the model for our offering, our humility, our sweetness, our patience, our poverty, and all the virtues that we must imitate to become holy. "If you read the Gospel, bring it to the Eucharist and from the Eucharist into yourself."[2] For example, if we had only the memory of the examples of the Savior during his earthly life, for twenty centuries now humility would be only

[1] Saint Peter Julian Eymard, *Adorer en esprit et en vérité* (Paris: Éditions F.-X. de Guibert, 2009), 185.
[2] Ibid., 186.

259

a name. We might reasonably say: "Lord, I have not seen you humiliated." But Jesus Christ is there to answer our excuses and insufficiencies. It is from the tabernacle, underneath the veil of the Host, that these words escape: "Come to me, . . . for I am gentle and lowly in heart" (Mt 11:28).

To this end, let us learn from Saint Thérèse of Lisieux, who knew how to enroll in the school of the Heart of Jesus in the Eucharist, a school of sweetness, humility, and burning charity. Meditating on the abasement of Jesus in the lowly Host, she sought every occasion for abasing herself in return. Contemplating the way Jesus gives himself defenselessly, she learned to give herself without reservation to the Lord and her sisters. Since Jesus hides in the tiny Host, Thérèse wanted to hide herself in order better to resemble her Lord. Here are a few of her notes, which highlight this:

> Living on Love is living on your life,
> Glorious King, delight of the elect.
> You live for me, hidden in a host,
> I want to hide myself for you, O Jesus![3]

> O my Lovable King,
> The sweet Sun of my life;
> Is your Divine Host,
> little like me? . . .[4]

O my Beloved, how gentle and humble of heart you seem under the veil of the white Host! To teach me humility you cannot humble yourself further. Therefore, to respond to your love, I desire that my sisters always put me in the lowest place and I want to convince myself that this place is indeed mine. . . . O Jesus, gentle and humble of heart, make my heart like yours![5]

---

[3] PN 17, 3rd stanza, *The Poetry of Saint Thérèse de Lisieux*, trans. Donald Kinney, O.C.D. (Washington, D.C.: ICS Publications, Institute of Carmelite Studies, 1996), 90.

[4] Ibid., PN 52, stanzas 11 and 12, May 1897, p. 207.

[5] Prayer 20, "Prayer for Acquiring Humility", July 16, 1897, in *The Prayers of Saint Thérèse of Lisieux*, trans. Sr. Aletheia Kane (Washington, D.C.: ICS Publications, Institute of Carmelite Studies, 1997), 116.

• *Our life:* In the Eucharist, Jesus is not simply our model for imitation, like a great actor showing his talent and extraordinary abilities and demanding us to do likewise! Here Jesus lavishes us with the graces necessary to put into practice the virtues he unveils in the Blessed Sacrament. Through the Eucharist, he comes to live his own life in us. He makes us participants in his divine life. Let us allow Jesus to live and act in us! It is only thus that we might put into practice the following commandment: "Love one another as I have loved you" (Jn 15:12). In order to love "as" Jesus loved, there is no other way but to let Jesus act in us.

Saint Peter Julian Eymard reminds us that the Eucharist is not just a grace from God; rather, it contains the author of grace himself:

Here our Lord carries his love unto its final consummation. Our vocation is holy because it gives us the most powerful means of sanctification by putting us in an immediate relationship, in a living relationship with Jesus Christ, who is not only a grace, but the very author of grace in his most holy Sacrament. Our vocation renders great glory to the heavenly Father, because it presents him with Jesus his Son in the Blessed Sacrament. Further, in the Eucharist, Jesus is in a more perfect state than during his mortal life: he is glorious, immortal, and it is this state of glory and royalty that he immolates unceasingly to the glory of his Father.[6]

• *Our end:* the Church today is in urgent need of apostles who, following the spirituality of Saint Peter Julian Eymard, commit themselves to "serve the divine Person of our God and King Jesus Christ, truly, really, and substantially present in the Sacrament of his Love; and, consequently, like good and faithful servants of this great King, to take care to consecrate to his greater glory all their gifts and virtues, their studies and works, without keeping anything for their own selves."[7]

"I came to cast fire upon the earth; and would that it were already kindled!" (Lk 12:49). This fire is the Eucharist. The arsonists of this

---

[6] Saint Peter Julian Eymard, Retreat at Rome, August 7–15, 1867 (Éditions M. Pisani, May 1957 [General House of the S.S.S.]), 42.

[7] *Premières Constitutions des Pères du Saint-Sacrement*, Décret, la Divine Eucharistie; series 1: La présence réelle, 15th ed. (Paris: Éditions Desclée de Brouwer), 5.

Eucharistic fire are all those who love Jesus in the Sacrament of his Love, because true love desires the reign and glory of the beloved. Let us light the fire of Eucharistic love to the four corners of the earth! Saint Peter Julian Eymard said, "Remember that, when a spark of the Eucharist has been placed in a soul, a divine seed of life and of all the virtues has been cast into the heart, which suffices unto itself."[8] "My great ambition is to be the knight of Jesus' pure Love and live for his greater glory in the Most Blessed Sacrament."[9]

In order to direct all things to Jesus in the Blessed Sacrament, the Most Blessed Sacrament must dominate all our external life like a habit. He who has made the sweet habit of thinking often of our Lord in the Blessed Sacrament loves talking to him and turning spirits and hearts toward the Eucharist. His witness brings to light love for the Real Presence. While he goes about the different affairs of his day, the memory of Jesus the Host pursues him, serving to transfigure all his actions. Meals are like a symbol of Holy Communion to him. Above all, bread and wine—those foods chosen to become the Eucharistic species—inspire pious respect in him. His steps, his visits, recall to him the words of the Gospel: "Go out to the highways and hedges, and compel people to come in, that my house may be filled" (Lk 14:23). Friendly relations evoke the memory of those encounters, a thousand times sweeter and more intimate, with the eternal friend of the tabernacle whose unction seems to spread to the most indifferent conversations. When traveling, the mere view of a distant bell tower signals the presence of Jesus to him and interests him more than the most lavish works of man. This view touches him more than all the splendors of nature! If we truly loved Jesus, he alone would enchant us more than all the rest of the world. Nothing would distract us from him. Everything in our life in this world would become an occasion to love him or make him loved. That is the Eucharistic vocation!

In a more general sense, John Paul II situates the mystery of the Eucharist at the heart of the new evangelization. He presents the three dimensions of the Eucharistic vocation (model, life, and end) differently, but the sense is the same: our evangelization begins *from* the Eucharist,

---

[8] Saint Peter Julian Eymard, *Œuvres complètes*, CO 325, 1.
[9] Ibid., CO 995,1.

it works *through* Eucharistic grace, and it achieves everything *for* the Eucharist:

> Ask Jesus Christ with me . . . that the entire Church may leave this Eucharistic congress strengthened for the new evangelization that the entire world needs: new also through the explicit and profound reference to the Eucharist as center and root of the Christian life, as seed and requirement of brotherhood, justice, and service to all men, beginning with those most in need in body and in spirit. Evangelization *for* the Eucharist, *in* the Eucharist, and *through* the Eucharist: these are three inseparable aspects of the way the Church lives out the mystery of Christ and fulfills her mission to communicate him to all men.[10]

As a deer longs for flowing streams, so longs my soul for you, O God. My soul thirsts for God, for the living God. When shall I come and behold the face of God?" (Ps 42:2–3)

---

[10] John Paul II, International Eucharistic Congress at Seville, 1993, *L'Osservatore Romano*, weekly edition in French, June 2, 1993.

The Five Graces of Adoration and Mission

The Samaritan Woman
(Grace of Restoration)

[Jesus] came to a city of Samaria, called Sychar, near the field that Jacob gave to his son Joseph. Jacob's well was there, and so Jesus, wearied as he was with his journey, sat down beside the well. It was about the sixth hour. There came a woman of Samaria to draw water. Jesus said to her, "Give me a drink." . . . Jesus answered her, "If you knew the gift of God, and who it is that is saying to you, 'Give me a drink,' you would have asked him and he would have given you living water." The woman said to him, "Sir, you have nothing to draw with, and the well is deep; where do you get that living water?" . . . Jesus said to her, "Every one who drinks of this water will thirst again, but whoever drinks of the water that I shall give him will never thirst; the water that I shall give him will become in him a spring of water welling up to eternal life." The woman said to him, "Sir, give me this water, that I may not thirst, nor come here to draw." . . .

"Our fathers worshiped on this mountain; and you say that in Jerusalem is the place where men ought to worship." Jesus said to her, "Woman, believe me, the hour is coming when neither on this mountain nor in Jerusalem will you worship the Father. You worship what you do not know; we worship what we know, for salvation is from the Jews. But the hour is coming, and now is, when the true worshipers will worship the Father in spirit and truth, for such the Father seeks to worship him. God is spirit, and those who worship him must worship in spirit and truth."

The woman said to him, "I know that the Messiah is coming (he who is called Christ); when he comes, he will show us all things." Jesus said to her, "I who speak to you am he." . . . So the woman left her water jar, and went away into the city, and said to the people, "Come,

see a man who told me all that I ever did. Can this be the Christ?"
They went out of the city and were coming to him. . . . Many Samaritans from that city believed in him because of the woman's testimony,
"He told me all that I ever did." So when the Samaritans came to him,
they asked him to stay with them; and he stayed there two days. And
many more believed because of his word. They said to the woman,
"It is no longer because of your words that we believe, for we have
heard for ourselves, and we know that this is indeed the Savior of the
world." (Jn 4:5–7, 10–11, 13–15, 20–26, 28–30, 39–42)

The Samaritan woman meets Jesus, who is tired from walking and
from the heat. He promises her living water that must be drawn from
his Heart. Jesus is going to help this woman to speak the truth about
herself. By revealing to her the number of husbands she has had, he
internally frees her, redirecting her life to him, who alone can fully
satisfy the human heart. Through this encounter, Jesus will make a
witness of her. She will attract all the inhabitants of the city to him!
Benedict XVI emphasizes that from the Eucharist Jesus still acts in the
same way for each of us:

> In the sacrament of the Eucharist, Jesus shows us in particular the
> *truth about the love* which is the very essence of God. It is this evangel-
> ical truth which challenges each of us and our whole being. For this
> reason, the Church, which finds in the Eucharist the very center of
> her life, is constantly concerned to proclaim to all, *opportune importune*
> (cf. 2 Tim 4:2), that God is love. Precisely because Christ has become
> for us the food of truth, the Church turns to every man and woman,
> inviting them freely to accept God's gift.[1]

The gift of God from which the living water flows is none other than
the Eucharist, food of truth and charity, which makes us true witnesses.
The conversion of the inhabitants of Sychar comes in two successive
steps. First, the Samaritan woman announces to them what Jesus has
done for her. Her witness arouses the surprise of the inhabitants, who
come to see Jesus out of curiosity. This personal encounter with Jesus
commits them to a more profound conversion: "They asked him to
stay with them" (Jn 4:40). Then they too become witnesses of the
Christ: "We have heard for ourselves, and we know that this is indeed

---

[1] Benedict XVI, Post-synodal Apostolic Exhortation *Sacramentum Caritatis* (2007),
no. 2.

the Savior of the world" (Jn 4:42). In the same way, our witness must lead our neighbors to meet Jesus personally in the Sacrament of his love. There, touched by this love, they in turn will become witnesses of the love of God.

> Go therefore and make disciples of all nations, baptizing them in the name of the Father and of the Son and of the Holy Spirit, teaching them to observe all that I have commanded you; and behold, I am with you always, to the close of the age. (Mt 28:19–20)

> What you have heard from me before many witnesses entrust to faithful men who will be able to teach others also. (2 Tim 2:2)

In the Old Testament, it was only possible to adore God at Jerusalem, in the temple, the place of his presence. Today, this temple is the most holy humanity of Christ, present in the Eucharist. Certainly it is possible to adore God everywhere, but nothing equals adoration of God in the Eucharist during or after Mass. In this Sacrament, Jesus adores the Father. By adoring the Eucharist, we enter into Christ's adoration of his Father. We offer the Father the perfect adoration of the Son. And Mary invites us there! She sustains our faith; she forms our heart. This adoration of the Father, through the Eucharistic body of the Son, leads us to the "spring of water welling up to eternal life" (Jn 4:14). The Spirit abundantly pours forth his gifts, making us brave witnesses, servants of truth, and apostles of charity. This is how we enter into the mission of the Church, by worshipping the Father in spirit and in truth, because "God is spirit, and those who worship him must worship in spirit and truth" (Jn 4:24).

Here are three final testimonies about the grace of restoration in parish life flowing from Eucharistic adoration, source of truth and peace that opposes every kind of lie and every form of violence against man. For "according to his promise we wait for new heavens and a new earth in which righteousness dwells" (2 Pet 3:13).

His Excellency Ruben T. Profugo, bishop of Lucena in the Philippines, attests: "Eucharistic adoration has protected my diocese from the violence that threatened to tear it apart. Priests just as much as lay people attribute to perpetual Eucharistic adoration not only protection from communism, but also the establishment of peace and order."

Likewise, Father James Swenson, pastor of Saint Bridget Parish in Las Vegas, explains: "We had prostitution in front of our church; drugs were sold there. When we began perpetual Eucharistic adoration, all that ended. When our Lord in the Blessed Sacrament was exposed upon the altar, crime noticeably diminished in the area. I am convinced of it."

His Excellency Josefino S. Ramirez, vicar-general of the Archdiocese of Manila in the Philippines, concludes: "Perpetual Eucharistic adoration is our Lady's peace plan. I am absolutely convinced that it is through this adoration that peace will come to our country and our world. When we do on earth what is done in heaven, namely, adore God perpetually, then we will see 'the new heavens and the new earth'. The only name, the only power, and the only love that will bring eternal peace to the face of the earth are the Name, the Power, and the Love of Jesus in the Blessed Sacrament."

This is the grace of restoration: our time in adoration kindles the fire of which Jesus spoke when he said: "I came to cast fire upon the earth" (Lk 12:49) to recreate "a new heaven and a new earth" (Rev 21:1) where God will be "everything to every one" (1 Cor 15:28). And all will be one in the Heart of Jesus. Indeed, through his Incarnation, the Son of God united himself to every man in such a way that, "by the power which enables him to subject all things to himself" (Phil 3:21), the "world is destined to be assumed in the Eucharist",[2] where everything and everyone will be made perfect in the fire of divine love!

∼

---

[2] John Paul II, Apostolic Letter *Lumen orientale* (1995), no. 11.